8/09

Rock Climbing

Outdoor Adventures

W9-BWJ-098

Wilderness Education Association

Editors

Timothy W. Kidd, PhD
John Brown University

Jennifer Hazelrigs, MEd
University of Arkansas

HUMAN KINETICS

Library of Congress Cataloging-in-Publication Data

Rock climbing / Wilderness Education Association ; Timothy W. Kidd,
Jennifer Hazelrigs, editors.
     p. cm. -- (Outdoor adventures)
     Includes bibliographical references.
     ISBN-13: 978-0-7360-6802-4 (soft cover)
     ISBN-10: 0-7360-6802-3 (soft cover)
  1. Rock climbing. I. Kidd, Timothy W. II. Hazelrigs, Jennifer. III.
Wilderness Education Asssociation (U.S.)
     GV200.2.R66   2009
     796.522'3--dc22
                                                    2009018665

ISBN-10: 0-7360-6802-3 (print)   ISBN-10: 0-7360-8642-0 (Adobe PDF)
ISBN-13: 978-0-7360-6802-4 (print)   ISBN-13: 978-0-7360-8642-4 (Adobe PDF)

This publication is written and published to provide accurate and authoritative information relevant to the subject matter presented. It is published and sold with the understanding that the author and publisher are not engaged in rendering legal, medical, or other professional services by reason of their authorship or publication of this work. If medical or other expert assistance is required, the services of a competent professional person should be sought.

The Web addresses cited in this text were current as of February 1, 2009 unless otherwise noted.

Acquisitions Editor: Gayle Kassing, PhD; **Developmental Editor:** Melissa Feld; **Assistant Editor:** Rachel Brito; **Copyeditor:** Patrick Connolly; **Proofreader:** Joanna Hatzopoulos; **Permission Manager:** Dalene Reeder; **Graphic Designer:** Nancy Rasmus; **Graphic Artist:** Yvonne Griffith; **Cover Designer:** Keith Blomberg; **Photographer (cover):** Jimmy Chin/National Geographic/Getty Images; **Photographer (interior):** Shullphoto, unless otherwise noted. See photo credits on pages 309-310. **Photo Asset Manager:** Laura Fitch; **Visual Production Assistant:** Joyce Brumfield; **Photo Production Manager:** Jason Allen; **Art Manager:** Kelly Hendren; **Associate Art Manager:** Alan L. Wilborn; **Illustrator:** Tim Brummett; **Printer:** United Graphics

Printed in the United States of America   10 9 8 7 6 5 4 3 2 1

The paper in this book is certified under a sustainable forestry program.

Human Kinetics
Web site: www.HumanKinetics.com

United States: Human Kinetics
P.O. Box 5076
Champaign, IL 61825-5076
800-747-4457
e-mail: humank@hkusa.com

Canada: Human Kinetics
475 Devonshire Road Unit 100
Windsor, ON N8Y 2L5
800-465-7301 (in Canada only)
e-mail: info@hkcanada.com

Europe: Human Kinetics
107 Bradford Road, Stanningley
Leeds LS28 6AT, United Kingdom
+44 (0) 113 255 5665
e-mail: hk@hkeurope.com

Australia: Human Kinetics
57A Price Avenue
Lower Mitcham, South Australia 5062
08 8372 0999
e-mail: info@hkaustralia.com

New Zealand: Human Kinetics
Division of Sports Distributors NZ Ltd.
P.O. Box 300 226 Albany
North Shore City, Auckland
0064 9 448 1207
e-mail: info@humankinetics.co.nz

Contents in Brief

Contents

Preface

Welcome to *Rock Climbing*. We hope you find this resource beneficial for your immediate interests in climbing and as a reference tool as you progress as a climber. This book is designed for the climber who wants to learn the foundational concepts of top-rope climbing, traditional climbing, sport climbing, bouldering, and climbing indoors. This text also serves as a supplemental resource for a secondary physical education curriculum or an introductory rock climbing class at the collegiate level.

Rock Climbing, along with *Hiking and Backpacking*, are part of the Outdoor Adventure series and have been written in cooperation with the Wilderness Education Association (WEA). WEA was founded in 1977 and serves as a nonprofit organization to promote the professionalism of outdoor leadership through the establishment of national standards, curriculum design, implementation, advocacy, and research-driven initiatives. WEA has over 40 affiliates, including both university and wilderness programs that offer WEA-sanctioned courses. WEA also fosters strategic alliances with federal land management agencies, conservation groups, and outdoor enthusiasts to support and sustain the wildlands of the world.

Rock Climbing is composed of two parts. Part I, Preparing for a Rock Climbing Adventure, contains five rich chapters. Chapter 1 presents an overview and history of climbing, areas to climb, introduction to Leave No Trace principles, and safety concerns related to climbing. Chapter 2 is loaded with fitness-related topics, including sample exercises, nutrition, injury prevention, stretching, and training plans. Chapter 3 contains information on the various structures, educational classes, and recreational opportunities in an indoor climbing environment. Chapter 4 presents types of climbing, information on selecting areas to climb, and the nuts and bolts of planning for a safe climbing trip. Chapter 5 provides important information about the appropriate equipment for the various types of climbing you have chosen to pursue.

Part II is On the Rock. Chapter 6 presents knots, knots, and more knots with detailed instructions and photos on the correct ways to tie them and on their applications in various climbing situations. Chapter 7 provides information on equipment related to belaying, various belay techniques and the associated applications, and common communication terms. Chapter 8 presents the concepts of natural and artificial anchor systems and explains how to set them. Chapter 9 contains information on proper climbing technique on varying terrain and tips on becoming more graceful on the rock. Chapter 10 contains information on descending safely and efficiently after you have topped out. Chapter 11 is an introduction to the fundamentals of lead climbing, including both sport and trad climbing and the importance of ongoing training from a professionally trained guide or recognized organization. In all 11 chapters you'll find chapter-opening quotes, highlighted tips, colorful images to illustrate key concepts, summaries to recap important information, and success checks to help you retain the content of each chapter.

We hope you enjoy *Rock Climbing* and that you find it informative as you explore the sport of rock climbing. We emphasize that rock climbing is a technical sport and no text can replace training received from professional instructors. This book provides you with a foundational knowledge of rock climbing so that you can develop your skills under the guidance of a professional instructor. So be safe, know your limitations, obtain training from an instructor, have fun, and pull hard.

Warning: Extreme risks exist in climbing, and serious injury or death can result. Although climbing is an enjoyable sport and the potential of injury or death can be minimized, the sport demands formal and competent training from a professional. Whether you are top-rope climbing, traditional climbing, sport climbing, bouldering, or climbing indoors, the sport requires a continuous skill base, repetition of sound practices, and numerous field experiences. Safety is the most important concern in any outdoor endeavor, particularly in climbing. This book is to be used as a reference tool only. It is not to replace or substitute professional training and field experiences. As the reader, you assume full responsibility of your own climbing safety, and you assume the risks associated with climbing. Be responsible: Get training, stay current on products and techniques, and know your limitations.

Preparing for a Rock Climbing Adventure

CHAPTER 1

Going Rock Climbing

When the pursuit of natural harmony is a shared journey, great heights can be attained.

Lynn Hill

Millions of people around the world are experiencing the exhilaration, enjoyment, and personal satisfaction of rock climbing every year. While elite climbers are able to climb seemingly impossible routes, newcomers to climbing are discovering that they can have fun climbing at any ability. This is one of the reasons the sport of rock climbing is exploding in popularity. Over 10 million people in the United States participate in rock climbing on some level (Outdoor Industry Association, 2005). Indoor climbing walls, a fairly recent innovation in the world of rock climbing, have made rock climbing much more accessible. Today, there are nearly 700 indoor climbing gyms in the United States alone. College campuses, local fitness gyms, and summer camps are just some of the places indoor climbing walls can be found. When you consider the "fun" factor of climbing and the increased accessibility to climbing through indoor facilities, it is no wonder that rock climbing is one of the outdoor industry's fastest-growing sports.

This chapter addresses the foundational aspects of rock climbing, serving as an introduction to the rest of this book. Approach this chapter as a type of ground school, an experience commonly used in introducing fundamentals or new technical skills to those eager to improve their climbing ability before they leave the ground. Topics discussed in this chapter are history of rock climbing, styles of rock climbing, finding places to climb, benefits of rock climbing, outdoor ethics, information on basic access, and getting started on rock climbing.

History of Rock Climbing

As early as 400 BC, Chinese artists painted watercolor depictions of men climbing rocks. The first (and the most skilled) rock climbers in North America were believed to have been the Anasazi. Though more commonly known as the cliff dwellers of the American Southwest, the Anasazi thrived in this harsh climate up until the 1300s. David Roberts, author of *In Search of the Old Ones* (1997, p. 75), remarks, "Without question, the Anasazi were the finest prehistoric climbers ever to inhabit the United States. The Navajo, arriving on the Colorado Plateau more than a century after the abandonment, were so dazzled by the vertical skills of their predecessors that they attributed their technique to magic."

The earliest rock climbing by Europeans was initially practiced as part of mountaineering expeditions when steep terrain required climbing vertical routes as the party sought to reach the summit. In the decade of 1880, the sport of rock climbing became independent of mountaineering in three geographic areas: the Lake District and Wales in Great Britain, in Saxony near Dresden in Germany, and in the Dolomites in the Italian Alps.

Walter Parry Haskett Smith, a 22-year-old Oxford graduate in the classics, was widely recognized as the father of rock climbing in the British Isles when in 1882 he explored the fells of the Lake District with his younger brother. Alan Hankinson wrote the following account of Haskett Smith's climb in *The First Tigers* (1972, p. 2): "They walked up the fells on morning, turned off the footpath to take a closer look at one of the great cliffs, inspected a dark, broken gully that split the precipice from top to bottom, began to scramble up, then to climb, and finally emerged triumphant at the top." Other young men soon followed Haskett Smith to the crags around Wasdale Head in the Lake District, calling themselves rock climbers and cragsmen, ushering in what has come to be called the golden age of rock climbing in the Lake District. Just five years later, in 1887, Georg Winkler, a 17-year-old high school student from Munich, Germany, made a solo first ascent of Die Vajoletturme, leading the way to the development of rock climbing as a sport in the Dolomites in the northern Italian Alps.

Rock climbing was also catching on as a sport in Saxony near Dresden, Germany. Referring to this area, J. Monroe Thorington (1964) wrote, "By 1890 rock climbing in this region had become a pure sport. It was no longer a question of getting up by any available means, but of how it was done. By 1898 a large number of summits had been gained by more than one route, O. Schuster and F. Meurer being pioneers." In 1902, an American by the name of Oliver Perry-Smith learned of this area after sailing from Philadelphia to join his mother in Dresden and soon gained recognition as one of the finest climbers in Europe.

While the history of climbing rightly focuses on climbers, a significant byproduct of World War II that affected rock climbing was the development of inexpensive army-surplus pitons, carabiners, and nylon rope, perhaps the most significant contribution. Royal Robbins, Chuck Pratt, Tom Frost, Yvon Chouinard, and others drew on these innovations to ascend the big Walls of Yosemite in the 1960s.

A new style of lead climbing, called sport climbing, was developed in the 1970s in France. See Sport Lead Climbing later in this chapter for a more detailed description of this style.

The next 30 years continued to see additional advancements in specialized gear. In 1971 Tom frost and Yvon Chouinard designed hexcentrics, usually called *hexes,* now commonly used in traditional climbing (also called *trad climbing;* see Traditional Lead Climbing later in this chapter for a more detailed description of this style). In 1978 Ray Jardine invented the first modern spring-loaded camming device (SLCD or cam) designed to maintain a constant camming angle with the rock, also used in trad climbing.

In 1994 the first one-day free-climbing ascent of the 3,000-foot Nose Route of El Capitan was made by Lynn Hill, American rock climber and former world champion sport climber. According to Ament (2002), Hill's ascent entirely without artificial aid had long been the most coveted accomplishment in the world of rock climbing. (The Nose Route has a Yosemite Decimal System, or YDS, difficulty rating of 5.13, one of the highest ratings. See chapter 4 for more information about the YDS rating system.) Chris Sharma, Ramón Julián, and Dani Andrada are the preeminent climbers in the world today, each with climbs of over 5.15 on the Yosemite Decimal System. To appreciate the difficulty of the climbs they have completed, the YDS was originally intended to rate climbs only up to 5.9.

The significant increase in participation in rock climbing in the past 30 years has caused the sport to gain broader acceptance, becoming the stuff of magazine and billboard visual advertisements for everything from sport drinks to SUVs. The variety of entry points to rock climbing has also increased with the advent of mobile climbing walls and indoor climbing gyms, climbing outings sponsored by college campus outdoor programs and summer youth camps, and climbing clubs and corporate-sponsored weekend competitions. The variety of climbing venues, both natural and artificial, has made rock climbing for a variety of skill levels more accessible than ever before. If you are a newcomer to rock climbing or you want to be more intentional about learning the skills that will help you enjoy climbing more, you have selected a great time in the development of the sport.

Styles of Rock Climbing

Most current styles of rock climbing are considered free climbing, which is climbing using only the climber's physical strength of hands, feet, and body to ascend while the climbing protection is used only to prevent a fall and not to support the climber's body weight.

By contrast, the climber engaged in aid climbing uses artificial aids to support his or her body weight or to assist in ascending the rock. Soloing is climbing a route without a rope for protection. Should the climber fall, serious injury or death can and often does result.

Free climbing is usually divided into several styles that can be distinguished from one another depending on the equipment used and the configurations of the belay, rope, and anchor systems employed to provide protection for the climber. In one sense, rock climbing can be viewed as a contest between climber and gravity. Since gravity is a worthy opponent, to say the least, it is wise to incorporate forms of protection to prevent serious injury when gravity wins out. In other words, climbers need to be proactive in minimizing risk.

Different forms of climbing involve different forms of protection, which have been influenced by many factors during the development of rock climbing, including the type of rock climbed, formation of the rock, and accessibility of anchor placement. The four styles of rock climbing presented in this section are bouldering, top-rope climbing, traditional lead climbing, and sport lead climbing. Popular locations to engage in each of these styles of climbing in the United States are listed after each section. Suggestions for international climbing sites are provided later in the chapter and include samples of each style of climbing.

Bouldering

Bouldering, in a broad sense, is rock climbing without the use of a belayer and belay rope for protection. The climber engaged in bouldering remains close enough to the ground so that a fall would not result in serious injury or death. Sound judgment is the most critical protection against injury in all forms of rock climbing. Accurately assessing your skill, surveying the area for hazards when selecting a bouldering site, and being wise in where you boulder and how high you climb when bouldering are all important factors to consider. Boulders (both large and small), low horizontal cliff sections, and the bases of taller cliffs provide prime bouldering opportunities.

A man bouldering, which is rock climbing without the use of a belayer or belay rope. His friends are spotting him for protection.

A static form of protection can be provided by a bouldering crash pad that softens the impact of a fall. A crash pad generally consists of a nylon-covered foam pad 3 to 6 inches (9.5 to 15 cm) thick and 3 or 4 feet (1 to 1.2 m) wide by 4 to 6 feet (1.2 to 2 m) long. Most crash pads will fold to smaller dimensions to facilitate ease of transport and storage. Proper placement of the crash pad is critical in order for climbers to benefit from this form of protection should a fall occur. Take care when placing crash pads to avoid causing damage to adjacent plant life.

A second type of protection takes the form of a spotter or spotters, a more dynamic form of protection. Spotters are used in bouldering in a manner similar to gymnastics, where the intent is not so much to catch the climber or prevent falls but to guide the climber to a relatively safe landing. A spotting stance providing the most stability for the spotter and therefore one that maximizes the effectiveness of spotting involves positioning the feet shoulder-width apart with one foot slightly forward and the other foot slightly back. Hands are held up with fingers together like spoons rather than spread apart like the tines of a fork. Focus on protecting the climber's head, neck, and spinal column from injury by wrapping your arms around the falling climber to maintain a vertical landing while absorbing the shock of the fall as you guide the climber safely to the ground.

Bouldering provides excellent opportunities to practice moves close to the ground, generally no higher than 15 feet. More difficult bouldering challenges, commonly referred to as bouldering problems, allow climbers to practice or perfect their technique, which can help them improve their overall climbing ability. Some climbers value bouldering for the sense of freedom and sheer joy of climbing without gear.

WHERE TO GO BOULDERING

If you are serious about bouldering, here are some prime spots in the United States that you might want to check out:

Rocky Mountain States
Jenny Lake Boulders,
Grand Teton National Park
in Wyoming
Flagstaff Mountain, Colorado

California
Mount Rubidoux in Southern California
Joshua Tree National Monument in Southern California
Indian Rock in Northern California
Yosemite Valley in Northern California

Northwest
Smith Rock State Park in Oregon
Minnehaha in Washington

Southwest
Huecco Tanks in Texas
Moab in Utah

Central States
The Needles in South Dakota

Northeast
Rumney in New Hampshire
The Shawangunks in New York

South
New River gorge in West Virginia
Blowing Rock in North Carolina

Top-Rope Climbing

A second style of climbing is called *top-rope climbing,* which is often the first exposure to rock climbing for many climbers. Whether climbing the artificial holds at your local climbing gym or climbing routes on natural rock features at your favorite crags, top-rope climbing is a great introduction to rock climbing that can prove both challenging and fun for people of all skill levels.

Top-rope climbing is appropriate when the rock you want to climb is high enough that an unprotected fall could result in serious injury or death. A rope and an anchoring system provide that all-important level of protection. Unlike indoor climbing walls where you pay your entrance fee and find routes that are set up in anticipation of your arrival, at the crags you must provide your own rope and gear and be prepared to build your own anchors for the routes you select. Top-rope climbing can be used when the height of the rock face is roughly 20 to 70 feet (6 to 21 m) and the top can be accessed safely so that anchors can be built to secure the rope at the top of the

Top-rope climbing is a challenging and fun introduction for many climbers.

climb—thus the name *top-rope.* Natural features, such as rock horns or sturdy trees, can be used as anchors, as well as mechanical devices designed to be wedged into the rock. The subject of anchors is examined at length in chapter 8.

When the rope is attached to the anchor system at the top of the climb by spring-gated aluminum carabiners, and both ends of the rope are at the base, the setup is referred to as a *slingshot belay.* One end of the rope is tied to the waist harness of the climber while the other end is managed by a partner, called a *belayer,* who feeds the rope out or takes the rope in as needed during the climb. The most important responsibility of the belayer is to stand ready to apply a braking force that enables the rope and anchor system to hold or catch a fallen climber. With the anchor above the climber, as long as the belayer is properly managing the rope, a fall by the climber will be limited to the length of the slack in the rope. Some rope stretch occurs in dynamic climbing ropes as a way for the rope to absorb some of the force of the fall, reducing the transfer of that force to the climber.

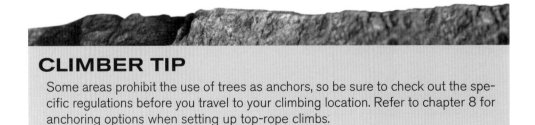

CLIMBER TIP

Some areas prohibit the use of trees as anchors, so be sure to check out the specific regulations before you travel to your climbing location. Refer to chapter 8 for anchoring options when setting up top-rope climbs.

WHERE TO GO TOP-ROPE CLIMBING

Check out www.rockclimbing.com; this site includes a huge database of climbing routes throughout the world. Searches can be conducted by geographical location (Africa, Asia, Australasia, Europe, North America, and South and Central America) and type of climbing (bouldering, top-rope, sport, and traditional). Additional information includes difficulty rating for routes, nearest town, directions, brief description, and titles of available guidebooks.

TOP-ROPE, TRAD, AND SPORT: WHAT'S THE DIFFERENCE?

Traditional lead climbing and *sport lead climbing* each have the leader (that is, the first climber) establish intermediate anchors as protection for the rope as he or she climbs. Trad or sport climbing may be chosen over top-rope climbing when there is no path available to access the top of a rock face to set up a top-rope climb. Other climbers choose trad or sport climbing for the added challenge and technical skill required.

Traditional Lead Climbing

In *traditional lead climbing*, the first climber places artificial anchoring devices to provide protection en route. Trad routes most often follow cracks that allow a more secure placement of anchors. The lead climber carries an assortment of devices on a sling or harness gear loops. Some trad routes also have bolts incorporated into the terrain.

Once the leader reaches the top of the route or pitch (a pitch is the distance between two belay points or one rope length), a belay anchor is built and the leader then belays his or her partner, known as the second, who recovers the protection placed by the leader on the route. Upon completion of the first route or pitch, the climbers can choose to continue climbing if the rock face has multiple pitches (that is, more than one rope length). They may also choose to descend by walking down if a path is available or belay to the ground. The topic of descending is presented in chapter 10.

Preparing to place an anchoring device in the rock for traditional lead climbing.

TRADITIONAL CLIMBING IN THE UNITED STATES

The United States offers a broad range of rock types and settings for trad climbing. Following are a few of the more prominent locations (and their corresponding Web sites) for trad climbing.

Northeastern U.S. Climbing
Shawangunks, or "Gunks," are located in southeastern New York and are touted as the cornerstone of Eastern trad climbing. Visit the Web site www.gunks.com.

Southeastern U.S. Climbing
The big stone of western North Carolina is one of the preferred locations in the Southeast for trad climbing. Looking Glass Rock, Table Rock/Linville Gorge, and the big walls of Whitesides Mountain offer many classic lines. The Web site www.southeastclimbing.com/faq/faq_guidebook.htm lists several guidebooks for prominent trad climbing in the southeastern United States.

Western U.S. Climbing
California has some outstanding trad climbing, including Joshua Tree National Park, with thousands of routes rated for the beginner up to the advanced climber. Yosemite National Park is one of the world's most famous rock-climbing areas with big walls soaring hundreds of feet and trad routes that are more appropriate for intermediate climbers. The Web site http://home.flash.net/~cfoster2/climbing/trad.html provides information on these and other climbs in the West.

Preparing to secure climbing rope to the hanger for sport lead climbing.

Sport Lead Climbing

Sport lead climbing is a style in which the lead climber secures the climbing rope to specially designed steel plates, called *hangers*, which are bolted to the rock face as he or she ascends. The lead climber on a sport route clips into the bolts using two carabiners (or biners) fastened together by webbing called *quickdraws*. One biner on the quickdraw is attached to the bolt and the climbing rope is then attached to the second biner on the quickdraw. Once the top has been reached, the rope is secured into a top anchor and the leader is lowered to the ground, collecting the draws that were placed during the ascent.

In both trad climbing and sport climbing, a partner belays the lead climber from below. Since the lead climber clips the rope into anchor points during the climb, unlike top-rope climbing where the anchor securing the climbing rope is at the top of the climb, a fall by a climber in trad lead climbing or sport lead climbing has greater consequences. When trad or sport climbing, you have no protection until you attach yourself to your first anchor. Should

SPORT CLIMBING IN THE UNITED STATES

Northwestern U.S. Climbing

Smith Rock State Park, Oregon, encompasses 651 acres in the high desert of Central Oregon. Ponderosa pines, juniper, and sage line the Crooked River surrounding the colorful cliffs and towers of Smith Rock, creating an exceptional setting for climbing. Known throughout the world as the birthplace of sport climbing in the United States, with over 1,000 high-quality routes, Smith Rock is an international sport climbing destination. The majority of the rock formations are composed of basalt, a common extrusive volcanic rock, which is ideal for rock climbing of all difficulty levels. Check www.spiritone.com/~summit/oldsmithrock/smthtoc.html for more details.

Western U.S. Climbing

Grizzly Dome-Feather River Canyon, Northern California, is located off Highway 70, just east of Chico. It has approximately 25 bolted sport routes along with a few trad and mixed trad and bolt routes. Grades range from 5.6 to 5.12a. Check www.rockclimbing.com for more details.

Big Cottonwood Canyon, outside of Salt Lake City, Utah, offers a heavy concentration of sport routes in the S-curve area. The area is on the north side of the canyon and just east of the Pile. The area is named for the S-curve formed by the road below the climbing area. Check www.rockclimbing.com for more details.

Southeastern U.S. Climbing

Muir Valley in the Red River Gorge, Kentucky, is privately owned and requires climbers to fill out a waiver. The Red has a lifetime of routes—traditional and sport as well as a few aid routes. If you are into exposure, then you will definitely fall in love with the climbing here. For more information, go to www.muirvalley.com/warnings-rules.php.

Horseshoe Canyon Ranch, Arkansas, is a 350-acre dude ranch just south of the scenic Buffalo National River. Surreal sandstone climbing is available on the 350-plus bolt-equipped routes along the many cliffs that line the canyon. The excellent rock has diverse features and loads of easy routes. Bring a rope and a light rack. Check www.gohcr.com/rock_climbing.htm for more details.

a fall occur, the lead climber falls the distance between himself and the last anchor plus that distance again as the fall continues past the anchor and the rope becomes taut. This makes the proper placement of artificial protection in trad climbing and secure clipping in to hangers for sport climbing all the more important so that the belay rope will catch the climber if he falls. An in-depth treatment of trad climbing and sport climbing is presented in chapter 11.

Finding Places to Climb

Some climbers have favorite local crags they visit on a regular basis, while other climbers enjoy the challenge of exploring new climbing areas during college breaks or summer vacations. One of the first things you should do in selecting a new climbing area is determine your preferred style of climbing (bouldering, top-rope, sport, or traditional). Many destinations offer several climbing styles, while the rock features at other locations may support only one or two climbing styles. The local climbing culture of a given area also has a significant influence on the styles of climbing available. For example, some areas have a longstanding history of trad climbing and discourage the establishment of bolted sport routes.

INTERNATIONAL CLIMBING SPOTS

These locations represent a variety of climbing styles.

North America

British Columbia, Canada

www.rockclimbing.com/routes/North_America/Canada/British_Columbia

British Columbia has the third-largest single rock face in continental North America, Canada's hardest sport route, Canada's hardest boulder problems, unlimited alpine and ice climbing, endless trad routes, and plenty of easier single-pitch routes. BC also has Canada's mildest weather in the lower mainland, allowing for almost year-round climbing. British Columbia's Provincial Parks offer some of the most popular climbing destinations.

Golden Horseshoe, Milton, Ontario, Canada

www.climbers.org

www.rockclimbing.com/routes/North_America/Canada/Ontario

Ontario is fortunate enough to be the home of the Niagara Escarpment, a 700-kilometer stretch of limestone. It offers many climbing areas from the powerful bouldering in the Niagara Glen to the trad routes of the Milton area to the exposed sport climbing with hanging belays at Lion's Head. There are various difficulty levels and some great spots for rappelling.

Europe

Central Lowlands: Traprain Law, East Linton, Scotland

www.rockclimbing.com/routes/Europe/Scotland/Central_Lowlands/Traprain_Law/Overhang_Wall

This is all trad climbing but varies in difficulty for the newest beginners to the most hardcore experts. The southerly aspect of the crag keeps it warm for most of the summer days, but be warned that there are a few who believe this to be the most polished crag in Britain.

Burbage North, Hathersage, England

www.rockclimbing.com/routes/Europe/England/Peak_District

This is probably the best rock in the area and fantastic bouldering for any grade. There are about 150 routes in all grades, up to 40 feet tall; these are very good for the lower-grade climbers. This site is just a stone's throw from the road.

Sport Climbing Routes in England

www.sportsclimbs.co.uk

This Web site provides information on sport climbing routes in Wales and England and includes photographs, maps, and general information on crags.

South America

Urca, Rio de Janeiro, Brazil

Urca is the area where Pão de Açucar is located. This is one of the most famous tourist sights of Rio. Urca is a popular climbing area with three main domes that include sport routes and boulder areas. A guidebook written in Portuguese, titled *Guia de Escaladas da Urca,* is available at www.guiadaurca.com.

Africa

Silvermine, Capetown, South Africa

Silvermine is about a 20-minute drive from Cape Town. The climbs are primarily long, single-pitch climbs and level of difficulty ranges from beginner to advanced.

Lukenya, Nairobi, Kenya

Lukenya is one of the most popular crags in Kenya, especially for weekend climbing. The cliffs are located on land and owned by the Mountain Club of Kenya, so you will need to purchase a daily membership ($2.50 US) or a temporary membership ($20 US) that lasts for three months.

Asia

Ha Long Bay, Vietnam

www.slopony.com/index.php

More than 2,000 limestone cliffs rise from the turquoise water of Ha Long Bay. With over 100 established sport routes, you will have lots of options. Additional routes continue to be added.

Web Sites on Climbing

Web sites are a great source of information on potential climbing sites, but remember that some Web sites are more reliable than others. Access to certain climbing areas may change for a variety of reasons, such as temporary closing due to wildfires or seasonal closing due to sensitive peregrine falcon habitats during nesting season.

When planning a climbing trip located on publicly managed land, contact the particular agency to learn the current status of the area you plan to use. Land management agencies in the United States include federal, state, and local agencies. Contact information is often available through the agency's Web site.

Climbing Guidebooks

Guidebooks continue to be a primary source of information on established climbing areas; most areas have at least one published booklet. Climbing magazines often highlight popular climbing areas and provide abbreviated information drawn from the primary guidebooks.

The purchase of a climbing guidebook is well worth the price when considering the wealth of information at your disposal, including driving directions, access information, and maps of the rocks. Refer to chapter 4 for additional information about guidebooks.

Climbing Periodicals

As you look for places to climb, climbing periodicals are another great source, such as *Climbing* and *Rock & Ice*. These climbing magazines highlight classic climbs located across the United States and around the world, often providing route information with topographical features, gear lists for specific routes, and background information and directions to the climbing sites.

CONSUMER TIP

Looking for a place to climb? Check out www.recreation.gov. This site provides a searchable database of U.S. agencies that manage recreation areas with 20 popular outdoor activities, including climbing. Searches can be conducted by key word or phrase; state, agency, and recreational activity. A search conducted on this site of "climbing" locations displayed 26 states (11 east of the Mississippi River and 15 west) overseen by 5 U.S. land management agencies (Bureau of Land Management, Bureau of Land Reclamation, National Park Service, USDA Forest Service, and U.S. Army Corps of Engineers) and yielded 139 recreation areas (each area having multiple climbing options), furnishing the following information for each area: state, agency, brief description, address, and Web site.

Local Climbing Organizations

Climbing enthusiasts in many areas have formed climbing clubs that go on weekend climbs. Many university campuses have outing clubs that include rock climbing among the various outdoor trips offered. Universities frequently offer activity classes in rock climbing at the introductory and intermediate levels, which usually include day or weekend climbing trips. Wilderness stores also sponsor climbing trips or have bulletin boards with news about rock climbing in your area. Networking with reputable organizations can help you get connected with the climbing community in your area. Check out the Web resources at the end of this book for information on these and other sources when looking for places to climb.

Benefits of Rock Climbing

Rock climbing has an intrinsic appeal to many people at a multitude of levels. Benefits associated with rock climbing are physical, psychological, social, and spiritual.

Physical Benefits

Physical activity is critical to achieving and maintaining optimal personal health. Be honest: You know that you are more likely to engage in physical activity when you enjoy what you are doing. Rock climbing provides workouts that are both physically challenging and enjoyable. When you enjoy an adventure pursuit like rock climbing, you gain incentive to engage in physical training so you can improve as a climber. As you get into rock climbing more, you find yourself motivated to do push-ups and other strength-training exercises on your own in order to perform better when you climb.

A healthy lifestyle is all about establishing positive, sustainable habits. Whether you are scaling a route on an indoor climbing wall, bouldering at a local park, or spending a weekend on a granite rock face, engaging in the physical act of climbing can improve your strength, balance, and agility and lead to a lifelong pursuit of adventure.

Psychological Benefits

Climbing has an obvious physical aspect, but it also includes a mental component. As you take your first step off the ground, you are faced with multiple decisions: Which hold will I grasp with my right hand? What is the best line for me to follow? Like a chess match with a seasoned grandmaster as your opponent, the rock face demands your concentration as you focus on the stone "board" to determine your next move.

Your mind and body work in tandem as you advance upward. Your confidence grows as you reach beyond your self-imposed limits to push against your ever-expanding limits. Self-confidence is gained from the many small successes you achieve. A momentary setback does not defeat you but challenges you to review your decisions as you replay your movements, weighing the wisdom of each to devise your strategy for your next attempt.

The lessons about confidence and tenacity learned on the rock are just as valuable in school, business, relationships, and countless other aspects of life. As Italian alpinist Walter Bonatti says, "Climbing is not a battle with the elements, not against the law of gravity. It's a battle against oneself." Most climbers agree that you can learn lessons about yourself through rock climbing that cannot be learned anywhere else.

Social Benefits

One of the attractions of rock climbing is that it can be enjoyed with a group as well as with just one other person. The camaraderie of fellow climbers or a climbing partner adds to the overall enjoyment of climbing. The relationship between a climber and a belayer is a bond of trust that is rarely duplicated in other settings. A belayer provides protection that allows the climber to attempt moves that he or she would be foolish to try when not belayed.

Take care as you select your climbing companions, especially your climbing partner. You want to be certain that he or she is someone who is safety conscious and technically proficient. Checking and double-checking harnesses, knots, anchors, and gear should not be left to a single person but should be consciously and intentionally shared because two sets of trained eyes are better than just one set. Each member of the climbing party should learn to develop and exercise sound judgment.

Your belayer's words of encouragement as you climb can urge you beyond your self-imposed constraints. When you have just completed a hard climb, you can appreciate the effort your climbing partner is exerting, and the words of encouragement you share are a valued gift.

Communication between belayer and climber is not dependent on electronic text messages, e-mail, or the Web. It is accomplished through intentional one-on-one speech. You want to climb with someone whom you can communicate with as well as trust.

Rock climbers having fun and gaining physical activity.

Spiritual Benefits

Adventure pursuits, which occur in natural and often remote settings, have long been recognized as activities that provide a context for pondering the significant questions of life. Even beyond the beauty of the natural setting, there is something about rock climbing that helps people become more receptive to learning new lessons.

Climbing, your belayer not withstanding, provides a unique solitary experience: just you and the rock. In that moment you have a measure of solitude that elevates the substance of personal thoughts. Through climbing you are faced with powerful metaphors for life, as you consider the trust you place in your belayer and the effort of each small gain that ultimately enables you to reach the summit.

Outdoor Ethics

Leave No Trace Center for Outdoor Ethics, or LNT for short, is a nonprofit educational organization dedicated to the responsible enjoyment and active stewardship of the outdoors by all people worldwide. The center is based in Boulder, Colorado, and focuses its efforts on reaching recreational enthusiasts through a variety of programs. LNT has a research division, the PEAK program (Promoting Environmental Awareness in Kids), numerous teaching resources, grant opportunities, a frontcountry program, and traveling trainers who tour the United States educating others to be better stewards of the environment. LNT also works with organizations such as Wilderness Education Association (WEA), National Outdoor Leadership School (NOLS), Appalachian Mountain Club (AMC), Landmark Learning (LLC), Boy Scouts of America, and USFS Ninemile Wildlands Training Center to offer five-day master educator courses. Other courses available are two-day trainer courses and one- to eight-hour workshops.

LNT began with the United States Forest Service in the 1960s but officially became the LNT Center for Outdoor Ethics in 1994. Volunteers and employees of the Forest Service, National Park Service, Bureau of Land Management, and NOLS worked together to form the present-day seven principles of Leave No Trace. The principles are based on scientific research and support ethical programmatic approaches to resource protection for the natural world (see sidebar).

PRINCIPLES OF LEAVE NO TRACE

1. Plan ahead and prepare.

2. Travel and camp on durable surfaces.

3. Dispose of waste properly.

4. Leave what you find.

5. Minimize campfire impacts.

6. Respect wildlife.

7. Be considerate of other visitors.

Leave No Trace Seven Principles are reprinted, by permission, from Leave No Trace.

The seven principles are easily applied to recreational activities in both frontcountry and backcountry settings. Leave No Trace provides educational material for specific natural environments (desert, canyons, alpine) as well as activity-specific guidelines (rock climbing, caving, mountain biking). These resources are available online at www.lnt.org. By educating yourself and practicing these principles, you will help ensure that local climbing sites have the best chance to remain pristine and accessible for all to enjoy.

Since the seven principles serve as guidelines and not rules, there are specific applications that relate to rock climbing. The Leave No Trace climbing principles apply most directly to outdoor settings on natural rock. In an outdoor setting, the environment is dynamic and unpredictable, requiring you to be more aware of your surroundings and to plan accordingly.

Plan ahead and prepare. One of the first considerations for minimizing your impact on the environment where you climb is to plan ahead and prepare. Begin by selecting a climbing site that best suits your skill level. By planning for your trip, you will also be less likely to leave gear at the climb site. Educate yourself on the climbing destination and bring the proper equipment for the type of climbing available at the site. It is recommended that you purchase a guidebook, research each climbing site online, or talk with other climbers who climbed there before. Remember that information in books and on Web sites can become outdated regarding permit requirements, accessibility, and other important issues.

By assessing your skill level, you can select a climbing site that will be challenging but within your ability. You do not want to attempt a multipitch climb if you have never climbed on real rock before, nor do you want to show up expecting to sport climb only

This is a dynamic and unpredictable environment where you should be aware of your surroundings.

to discover that there are no bolted sport routes when you arrive. Bring the appropriate equipment to ensure that you are able to climb safely, and commit to packing out everything that you pack in. This will help keep the area free of items that are not natural to the environment.

Travel and camp on durable surfaces. A negative impact can be nonreversible. In a highly concentrated area, stay on trails and worn areas. This reduces the spread of unnecessary paths and destruction of vegetation. Climb on dry rock; climbing on wet rock can leave permanent scarring. Be aware that the rock ledges are also vulnerable to scarring because of the placement of anchors or even rope friction. Place the masterpoint of your anchor just below the ledge (see chapter 8 for more information on the masterpoint). When descending, walk or scramble down to avoid leaving gear behind. Avoid moving rocks or altering the natural environment in any way. Vegetation is very fragile at the base of the climb. Do not trundle rocks, scrub lichen, clear or trim vegetation, or alter the environment in any way. Instead, find another place to climb or boulder, leaving the area wild and untainted.

Check with the local land managers to determine the appropriate methods for anchoring and setting up climbs for the area you have selected. Many state and provincial parks do not allow the use of trees for climbing anchors because of the potential damage to tree bark. Most climbers prefer to use chalk, but it does leave a residue on the rock surface. The best method is not to use chalk at all or use an ecco ball. If you do plan on using chalk, check to see if the area permits the use of it. Some areas limit the number of climbers in a party or require a certified instructor if you are climbing with an organized group.

Dispose of waste properly and minimize campfire impacts. These principles are pretty straightforward. Some big walls require you to pack out your waste, but in most cases digging a cathole 6 to 8 inches (15 to 20 cm) deep and burying your waste is sufficient. For cooking, stoves are better than fires. Fires have an impact and require skill and responsibility. If at all possible it is ideal to light a candle or use a lantern in lieu of a camp fire. If you

Respect and be aware of wildlife in the area of your climbing site.

choose to make a fire, keep it small and manageable by using only dead wood that you can break by hand. Use existing fire rings so that you do not create new ones that scar the land. If there are no established fire rings, make a mound of mineral soil about 5 inches (13 cm) thick (sand from a dry streambed works well) and build your fire on top. This protects the microorganisms in the soil from the heat of the fire.

Respect wildlife. You will most likely see various birds, insects, sheep, and goats when you go outdoors to climb. The rock is home to the wildlife. As you select your climbing site, be aware of wildlife in the area and do not disturb their habitats. The best action you can take when seeing wildlife is to respectfully keep your distance or choose not to climb in that particular area. Be especially careful during sensitive times: mating, nesting, raising young, and winter. Maintain a buffer area around wildlife you might encounter so that you and the permanent residents can share the environment in harmony. Some climbing areas close down during nesting and mating seasons. Before your trip, check with the land managers to determine if the desired climb site is closed.

Leave what you find. This principle has direct application to climbing. Do not clean an area and remove vegetation for a more convenient and comfortable climb. It is also important to clean your gear after climbing to avoid spreading non-native plants and animals to the next climb site you visit. Many climb areas are near historical structures and artifacts. Though it is tempting, completely avoid climbing in areas that have prominent historical artifacts or areas that are considered archeological sites. Once again, by planning ahead and checking with land managers, you can help preserve our rich history.

Be considerate of other visitors. In addition to demonstrating respect for the land and local wildlife, you are encouraged to respect other visitors. Respecting others is simple: Do to others as you would like others do to you. Ensure a good experience for all by keeping your voice down, wearing earth-tone clothing, and being discrete in urinating and

Climbers should avoid areas with historical artifacts to preserve history.

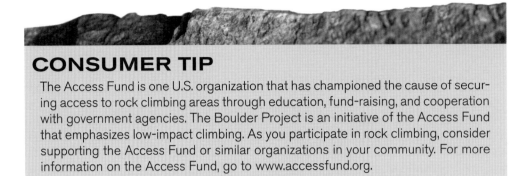

CONSUMER TIP

The Access Fund is one U.S. organization that has championed the cause of securing access to rock climbing areas through education, fund-raising, and cooperation with government agencies. The Boulder Project is an initiative of the Access Fund that emphasizes low-impact climbing. As you participate in rock climbing, consider supporting the Access Fund or similar organizations in your community. For more information on the Access Fund, go to www.accessfund.org.

defecating. Be courteous when you encounter others. Respecting others also requires that you respect private land. Never climb on private land or cross over private land without permission from owners. If the climbing area requires a permit, obtain one through the right sources.

To protect the natural area and to ensure an enjoyable and safe experience, follow the Leave No Trace principles in any activity you do—climbing, biking, and walking. Continue to educate yourself and practice these principles in hopes that others will follow your example.

Information on Basic Access

As with other outdoor pursuits in natural settings, as climbing becomes more popular, issues of accessibility become more critical. Locations for climbing can be closed to the public if climbers fail to respect the land as a resource to be shared with others engaged in various activities. Many established climbs are on government-managed lands, whether national forests; provincial, state, or municipal parks; or other government agencies like the Bureau of Land Management. The continued use of climbing sites on public lands often depends on the appropriate behavior of climbers demonstrated by observance of the Leave No Trace principles and local guidelines. Remember that your actions influence the ability of others to enjoy valuable climbing areas.

As demand on natural resources increases, monitoring and limiting the number of users at a given time require the establishment of climbing permits for certain heavily used areas or areas where the environment is especially fragile. Check to see if a permit is required and learn the process of securing a permit before you travel to a new climbing area. Chapter 4 covers this process in more detail.

Getting Started in Rock Climbing

A word of caution needs to be shared up front. Climbing can be enjoyed at a variety of skill levels, but by its very nature rock climbing has inherent risks and requires strict adherence to fundamental practices when setting up anchors and using harnesses, ropes, and

SAFETY TIP

Contact the American Mountain Guides Association or the Professional Climbing Guides Institute in the United States, or the Alpine Club of Canada, the New Zealand Alpine Club, the British Mountaineering Council, or other established rock climbing organizations for help in identifying qualified rock-climbing instructors or guides in your area. Contact information for each of these organizations is listed in Web Resources on page 288.

specialized gear. Although this book presents you with the fundamentals of climbing using various forms of protection, selecting and using equipment, and training to increase your physical ability, this book is not intended as a substitute for personal instruction from a qualified climbing instructor or guide. Should you misinterpret or incorrectly practice essential safety procedures presented throughout this book, the consequences could be serious or fatal.

No book on rock climbing, no matter how well written, can be a substitute for personal instruction. Many colleges and universities that offer introductory rock-climbing courses are affiliates of the Wilderness Education Association. A list of WEA affiliate schools appears at www.weainfo.org. Local climbing clubs and climbing organizations may also offer weekend workshops and informal classes. A good source for information on such events in your area is your local outdoor equipment store.

Indoor climbing walls have a more controlled environment and are good for beginners and training.

Climbing gyms or indoor climbing walls are also a good place to explore rock climbing in a more controlled environment. Most indoor climbing facilities offer an orientation session for beginners and training in belaying skills and lead-climbing clinics. Staff members are generally quick to offer additional guidance when asked. Though indoor gyms do not fully prepare you for an outdoor climbing experience, the skills taught are in a controlled environment and can help prepare you to accompany more advanced climbers to the crags.

Summary

Climbing is an outdoor pursuit that you can enjoy for a lifetime. Reading this book is a great first step. Take the time to get specific training so that you can put into practice the concepts in this book under the watchful eye of an experienced and trained rock climber. As the saying goes, "There are old climbers and there are bold climbers, but there are no old, bold climbers."

CHAPTER 2

Climbing Into Fitness

The best climber
in the world is the
one who is having
the most fun.

Alex Lowe

The opportunity to enter the world of rock climbing is open to anyone with a penchant for adventure and self-discovery. The act of gliding over natural rock faces or artificial walls is without equal as you become immersed in your physical well-being. Whether you hike into a coveted climbing area or take a short walk into a climbing gym, your body needs to be fit and ready to cling to small, tenuous holds.

This chapter covers the components of fitness, including cardiorespiratory fitness, body composition, muscular fitness, and flexibility. Proper nutrition and hydration for optimal performance in climbing are also discussed, along with physiological responses to climbing. If you're not properly fueled, your physical performance will show it! In addition, specific training programs for rock climbers are presented in this chapter. These training programs are designed to improve muscular fitness and cardiorespiratory endurance. With these programs, you can clearly define your training goals and plot a structured training course that will enable you to advance your skills and prevent injuries.

You may have observed the experts effortlessly climbing up, around, and over seemingly glasslike walls. You probably wonder how they hang on. Are they naturally talented? Can you train to climb as smoothly as these elite, world-class climbers? Your ability to become good at rock climbing depends not only on natural talent and a high level of desire, but also on consistent training and practice. To advance in the sport of rock climbing, you must commit to progressive and structured training.

The most important recommendation of any training program is to have fun. If you do not truly give yourself up to the process of training and progressing for the pure fun of it, then the toil of training can become drudgery. Thus, as you embark on a more disciplined fitness program to train for rock climbing—and as you use your newfound strength and fitness during unbridled ascents of novel and exciting routes—remember to always convey how much fun you're having along the way. The late Alex Lowe, dubbed the world's best climber posthumously by *Outside Magazine,* had an unquenchable and invincible spirit. Lowe gave this advice: "The best climber in the world is the one who is having the most fun." *Outside Magazine* further stated, "No matter how jaw-dropping his routes, Lowe's real genius grew out of the way he combined physical accomplishments with an indomitable spirit." The message is clear: Get ready for fun as you hone your physical skills.

What Constitutes Fitness?

To properly devise a training program that enhances overall climbing fitness, you need to have common knowledge about exercise. In general, fitness components include the following: body composition, muscular fitness (includes strength and endurance), cardiorespiratory endurance, and flexibility (ACSM, 2006; Heyward, 2002). Together, these components ensure that muscle groups and soft connective tissues pulling on the skeleton are properly trained to undergo constant stress and strain patterns. Also, with better overall fitness, you will have less chance for injury as well as a faster recovery from hard days at the crag.

In addition to the stress and strain placed on muscle, bone, and connective tissue when a person is rock climbing, the cardiorespiratory system is frequently taxed during this activity. Therefore, this system should not be overlooked when training for the sport of rock climbing. The cardiorespiratory system includes the heart, lungs, and blood transport system, which work in concert to deliver oxygen to muscles, especially during

TECHNIQUE TIP

Note that various measures exist that quantify body composition; one such measure is termed body mass index (BMI) and determines the ratio between your weight (in kilograms) and height (in meters squared). Normal or healthy BMIs fall below 25.0. Another measure of body composition is based off of subcutaneous fat (or fat just below the surface of the skin) through the use of skin calipers, which measure the thickness (in millimeters) of certain body fat skinfold sites to determine an overall percentage of body fat. Percent body fat, however, is not normally a good indicator of rock climbing ability, but rather a measure that can help you track the progress of your fitness level. Thus, establishing a baseline body fat percentage and tracking this number to determine if it is decreasing may provide information that you're adding muscle mass and losing body fat.

hard exertion such as rock climbing. If the cardiorespiratory system is not adequately trained, a person's ability to climb a long route is compromised. Additionally, the muscular system will not be able to adequately maintain a constant muscle action without a well-trained cardiorespiratory system. Remember, to move effortlessly against gravity, you must achieve a base of general fitness, including cardiorespiratory endurance.

Body Composition

Body composition and rock climbing tend to go hand-in-hand because having a lower percent body fat implies a greater percent of muscle mass. The goal, then, is to train to increase muscular strength and endurance so that climbing feels easier. Note that 5 pounds (2.3 kg) of fat is not as functional as 5 pounds of muscle tissue. The ratio of fat to muscle tissue is not of importance the first time you go out to the gym or crag to climb, but as you advance in your skills your goal should be to reduce fat tissue and strengthen existing muscle mass. The underlying message is that you should train your body to be strong and healthy while climbing to the best of your ability at any given time.

Overall, you should focus on becoming physically fit with greater muscle mass. This will enhance your climbing ability and your efficiency of movement. It's interesting to note that body composition may not be the best indicator of rock climbing performance and instead a beginner climber should focus more on developing finger and overall body strength.

Muscular Fitness

The main ingredient in rock climbing tends to be muscular fitness (encompassing both muscular strength and muscular endurance) (ACSM, 2006). Without a high level of muscular fitness, a rock climber will not progress to a higher level of difficulty. This is true for recreational and novice rock climbers (as well as experienced, competitive, and elite climbers). One pitfall to avoid is dedicating too much time to nonspecific strength and cardiorespiratory training in the gym while failing to incorporate climbing-specific exercises into your workout routine. Another pitfall that can be even more detrimental is not using indoor or outdoor climbing venues on a regular basis, especially during your "off-season." In short, to become a better climber, you must develop *specific* muscular fitness. This can be done through frequent climbing and by using climbing-specific exercises designed for muscular improvement and proper skill development.

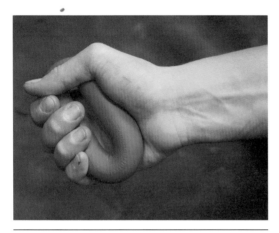

Figure 2.1 Donut trainer.

Figure 2.2 Using a campus board.

A majority of the studies conducted to measure muscular fitness in rock climbers have primarily assessed strength and endurance of the forearm, hand, and fingers via dynamometry (mechanized gauges). Handgrip strength is defined as a gripping motion, and finger strength is measured using climbing-specific finger positions. Forearm endurance (sometimes coupled with handgrip) is assessed via sustained and repetitive dynamic actions as a percentage of maximum voluntary contraction (MVC). When implementing a strength training program, you will most likely choose dynamic (shortening and lengthening of the muscle) exercises that involve a push and pull. You will also likely choose isometric (static) exercises (without shortening or lengthening of the muscle) that involve hanging on or maintaining a body position without movement, such as clinging to a small hold for a period of time or "resting" in a precarious position before climbing beyond a crux move. To train yourself to maintain the aforementioned dynamic or static positions that at times involve insecure holds, purchase a donut (see figure 2.1) or use a campus board (see figure 2.2) at home or your local rock gym. Practice squeezing and holding the donut for a few seconds at a time and with daily practice up to 60 seconds; then work to 3 to 5 sets of 25 to 30 repetitions. Likewise, hang on the campus board for a few seconds and up to a few minutes per use with progression. These two simple exercises, if implemented on a regular basis, will provide a baseline of strength, progression, and preparation for the training and climbing ahead.

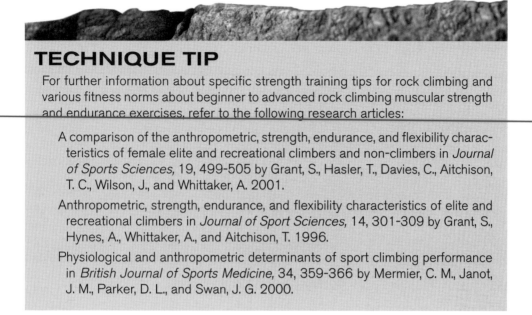

TECHNIQUE TIP

For further information about specific strength training tips for rock climbing and various fitness norms about beginner to advanced rock climbing muscular strength and endurance exercises, refer to the following research articles:

A comparison of the anthropometric, strength, endurance, and flexibility characteristics of female elite and recreational climbers and non-climbers in *Journal of Sports Sciences,* 19, 499-505 by Grant, S., Hasler, T., Davies, C., Aitchison, T. C., Wilson, J., and Whittaker, A. 2001.

Anthropometric, strength, endurance, and flexibility characteristics of elite and recreational climbers in *Journal of Sport Sciences,* 14, 301-309 by Grant, S., Hynes, A., Whittaker, A., and Aitchison, T. 1996.

Physiological and anthropometric determinants of sport climbing performance in *British Journal of Sports Medicine,* 34, 359-366 by Mermier, C. M., Janot, J. M., Parker, D. L., and Swan, J. G. 2000.

Good muscular strength and endurance in the fingers, hands, and forearms (i.e., the ability to sustain many contractions over time) are required when climbing. Also, excellent muscular endurance in the shoulders, chest, and back is a great goal. Many beginning rock climbers think that climbing involves only the upper body, but in reality the upper and lower body work in harmony while climbing. Therefore it is important to train the upper and lower body to be not only full of muscular endurance and strength, but to have a great amount of explosive power. Limb length, body height, and body weight are not necessarily barriers to achieving higher standards in rock climbing (Sheel, 2004).

Whatever the case, muscular fitness is important for rock climbing, and people may develop a suitable level of muscular fitness through regular participation in a fitness routine. The challenge is designing a sport-specific training program that targets the muscle groups commonly overloaded while rock climbing and that allows you to progress in difficulty as a climber.

Flexibility

For a rock climber, flexibility is important because of the various leg and arm positions required for reaching various handholds or footholds and for ascending routes that are progressively more difficult. For instance, a common practice in climbing is bridging (also known as stemming), which requires a moderate amount of hip flexibility and strength as a climber does a variation of the splits. Being flexible implies that you have a range of motion (ROM) that is adequate for your desired level of climbing. Adequate ROM encompasses all the major joints of the body: the shoulder, elbow, wrist, hip, knee, and ankle. Even neck flexibility is needed in order to maintain a high level of functioning.

SAFETY TIP

When performing stretching exercises, don't stretch to the point of pain. You should feel a slight discomfort in the targeted tissue and hold the stretch for 10 to 30 seconds. Repeat each stretch several times, and always breathe! Remember, it is best to apply static stretching *after* you workout or climb for the day. Use a dynamic warm-up (e.g., easy traversing and/or large muscle group actions of the arms and legs) prior to all training or climbing which ensures that your muscles maintain strength.

Another common climbing practice, high stepping, requires a climber to bring a foot up to match with a handhold or to gain better footing (see figure 2.3). To perform this movement, a climber must maintain flexibility of the hip and knee (Giles et al., 2006).

As mentioned in the safety tip, ideally, you should spend 15 to 20 minutes, two or three times per week (or most days of the week) stretching the major muscle groups of the body. Think *toe to head,* stretching the ankle, calf, thigh (front and back), hip, torso (abdomen, chest, and back), wrist and forearm, upper arm, shoulder, and neck. Hold each stretch for a minimum of 10 seconds and up to 30 seconds. You should feel a mild discomfort or strain in the targeted muscle group so that the muscle and connective tissue become more elastic. Don't stretch to the point where you feel pain.

Repeat each stretch up to four times, alternating through the order each set for maximum benefit (ACSM, 1998). Note that the American College of Sports Medicine (ACSM) indicates that a prestretching warm-up (gentle walking, cycling, running, and so on) does not appear to provide additional benefit over stretching alone. However, stretching *after* a workout is usually recommended. When stretching after a workout, you should focus on breathing and relaxing each muscle group during each stretch. The following stretches provide a suggested full-body stretching routine for climbers, preferably completed after a workout or 3- to 5-minute gentle aerobic warm-up using large muscle groups.

Figure 2.3 The author of this chapter high stepping during an ascent of Edge of Time near Rocky Mountain National Park, Estes Park, Colorado.

Achilles Tendon Stretch

Description. Stand erect and place one set of toes on a vertical surface with the heel firmly on the ground. Maintain this position with the knee flexed at 10 degrees. The other leg should remain back and straight with the foot flat on the ground. Breathe slow and easy. Repeat with other side.

Duration and frequency. Pain-free stretch; hold for 10 to 30 seconds and repeat 4 times. Do this most days of the week.

Achilles Tendon and Calf Stretch

Description. Stand on ground with feet flat and both legs straight; keep one leg straight behind the body while bringing the other leg forward while bent. Feel the stretch in the calf and Achilles tendon of the straight leg. Breathe slow and easy. Repeat with the other leg.

Duration and frequency. Pain-free stretch; hold for 10 to 30 seconds and repeat 4 times. Do this most days of the week.

Calf Stretch

Description. Stand erect with both knees back and straight. Feet are flat. Maintain controlled breathing. Feel the stretch in the targeted muscle.

Duration and frequency. Hold stretch for 10 to 30 seconds and repeat 4 times. Do this most days of the week.

Hamstring Stretch

Description. Sit upright on the ground with both legs straight in front of you. Bend forward at the waist and reach for your toes. Feel the targeted muscle and breathe slowly.

Duration and frequency. Hold stretch for 10 to 30 seconds and repeat 4 times. Do this most days of the week.

Quadriceps Stretch

Description. Stand erect and grab an ankle with knee pointed down toward the ground. Pull foot toward buttocks. Feel the targeted muscle region. Breathe slow and controlled. Repeat with other leg.

Duration and frequency. Hold for 10 to 30 seconds and repeat 4 times. Do this most days of the week.

Cobra Stretch

Description. Begin by lying facedown on the ground. Place hands on ground wider than shoulder width. Gently press up until tension is felt in the abdominal region. Do not feel pain in the low back, only slight tension. Feel the stretch in the abdominal region. Over time, progressively increase the height of your torso off the ground. Maintain slow, rhythmic breathing and relax the back and abdominal area.

Duration and frequency. Hold for 10 to 30 seconds and repeat 4 times. Do this most days of the week.

Chest Stretch

Description. Stand or sit on the ground with legs gently crossed. Clasp hands behind your back with thumbs down and arms straight. Gently pull arms up. Feel the stretch in the chest region. Always maintain gentle breathing.

Duration and frequency. Hold for 10 to 30 seconds and repeat 4 times. Do this most days of the week.

Shoulder Stretch

Description. Stand upright or sit comfortably and pull one arm across your chest with the other hand. Feel the targeted muscle group. Maintain controlled breathing.

Duration and frequency. Hold for 10 to 30 seconds and repeat 4 times. Do this most days of the week.

Low Back Stretch

Description. Sit upright on the ground with both legs straight in front of you. Cross one leg over the other and place opposite arm against the bent knee to assist with torso rotation. Feel slight tension in the low back. Focus on easy and gentle breathing. Repeat on the other side.

Duration and frequency. Hold for up to 30 seconds and repeat 4 times. Do this most days of the week.

Neck Stretch

Description. Standing or sitting, look down at your shirt. Then, while looking straight ahead, rotate your head to the left, then right, as if trying to peer behind you. Finally, bring your ear toward your shoulder. Be gentle. Do not feel pain. Breathe slow and controlled. Feel the stretch each time.

Duration and frequency. Hold each position for 10 to 30 seconds and repeat up to 4 times. Do this most days of the week.

Wrist and Forearm Stretch

Description. Hold one arm out in front of you with elbow locked. With the other hand, flex the wrist with palms down. Next, turn the palm up and again push down on the hand. Both times, fingers should point toward the ground. Feel the stretch in the wrist and forearm. Repeat with other arm and wrist. Maintain controlled breathing.

Duration and frequency. Hold each position for up to 30 seconds and repeat 4 times. Do this most days of the week.

Yoga and Pilates also provide excellent fitness training for climbers. These methods of exercise can supplement or replace the suggested stretches. Yoga and Pilates allow you to focus on body movement, which is directly connected to various movements in climbing. Attending regularly scheduled classes at a local fitness facility will provide you with a set time to practice these strength and stretch exercises. Be sure to use a program that involves training two or three times per week in order to achieve and maintain tissue adaptations. Going to a class less often—such as once every other week—will not enable you to become stronger and more flexibile. To achieve the desired benefits, you must be consistent in your training. Of course, climbing or bouldering provides some of the best training adaptations as you slowly traverse a wall using exaggerated movements.

You should always focus on your breathing whenever you are engaged in stretching exercises. Breathe in deep and slow, then exhale the same way. Continue this pattern throughout your routine. In a yoga or Pilates class, the instructor should cue you into your breathing, usually suggesting slow, rhythmic respirations. Breathing out slowly helps slow your heart rate and puts you in a more relaxed state. Meditation of this type can heighten your concentration level and provide for more relaxed muscles, which in turn can ease your mind and increase your focus on difficult climbing moves. Typically, beginning climbers think that climbing is about 90 percent physical and 10 percent mental. However, the best viewpoint may be that climbing is 100 percent mental and 100 percent physical; thus, you need to learn to train both. This includes learning to breathe in a slow and controlled manner and progressing to sustained focus and concentration during your climbing ventures.

Climbing and yoga are connected. In both you must concentrate on controlled breathing and body movement.

Proper Nutrition and Hydration for Climbing

Fuel efficiency, especially in the specific muscles used during climbing, is needed for optimal performance. Efficiency means that fat and carbohydrate are plentiful to fuel your climbing progress and that your energy systems are highly trained. For example, without sufficient fuel processing, fatigue will occur prematurely and hamper your climbing performance. Furthermore, without adequate and timely food and water intake, your recovery from hard bouts of climbing will be hampered. Thus, plan to be wise about fueling up before, during, and after training in order to optimize performance, minimize fatigue, and speed recovery. The goal should be not to maintain your fuel stores so that your body is able to drive you farther when you most need it. See table 2.1 for daily diet recommendations for climbers.

Table 2.1 Daily Diet Recommendations for Climbers

Macronutrient	Timing and Suggested Intake of Various Foods
Carbohydrates (55-60% of total diet)	3-4 hours before climbing: A few handfuls of granola, 1 bagel, 1 sport bar, or 1 liter of sport drink with bar
	30-60 minutes before climbing: 1 sport bar, handful of gummy candy, or 1 sport drink (16-20 ounces)
	Immediately before climbing: 1 handful of raisins or trail mix, ½ liter of sport drink, or 1 sport gel packet
	During climbing bouts (every hour): 1 gel, several candies, 1 sport bar, or a handful or two of raisins or trail mix
	Recovery, after climbing: within 30 minutes intake a handful of crackers, 1-2 glasses of fruit punch, a bowl of sweetened cereal, a few handfuls of gummy type candies, or 1-2 glasses of orange juice, then continue this type of food intake every 2 hours for up to 4-6 hours if a bigger meal is not planned
Fat (20-25% of total daily diet)	Daily intake: desired weight (in pounds) × 0.45 = number of fat grams per day based on a desired body weight in order to keep overall fat grams low: intake butter, margarine, and oil sparingly along with nuts, nut butters, chips, and lean meats
Protein (15-20% of total daily diet)	Daily intake: 1.2-1.8 grams/kilogram body weight: intake poultry, vegetables, fish, eggs, grains, some cheese, dry beans, soy products, milk, yogurt, or nuts and seeds
Water	Daily intake: 3-10 liters per day, especially if ambient temperature is hot or exertion is high intensity
	Before climbing: 0.5-1.0 liter
	During climbing: 150-350 milliliters every 15-20 minutes so that 600-1,200 milliliters per hour is maintained
	Recovery: approximately 1-2 liters in the first few hours and regularly throughout the day

Adapted from Bonci, L. (2007, March). Sports nutrition—nutrition for optimal performance. Special Selections—Training Room. Retrieved April 1, 2007, from http://espn.go.com/trainingroom/s/2000/0324/444124.html; Wildman and Miller, 2004; Jeukendrup and Gleeson, 2004; ACSM Joint Position Stand, 2000; and McArdle, Katch, and Katch, 1999).

MyPyramid

The MyPyramid plan lists the recommended daily intake of grains, vegetables, fruits, milk, and meat and beans according to your age, sex, height, weight, and physical activity level. For details about this plan, go to www.mypyramid.gov/mypyramid/index.aspx.

Climbers can lose energy if they become dehydrated. Therefore, you should consume anywhere from 3 to 10 liters per day of water and sport drinks if you're at rest. You'll need 3 to 6 liters per day if you're exercising or climbing at a low-intensity work rate, and you'll need 6 to 10 liters per day if you're climbing at a high-intensity rate (Jeukendrup and Gleeson, 2004). As shown in table 2.1, even during rest days, your body requires a fair amount of liquid nourishment. When you add exercise, the requirement goes up quickly with high-intensity work and even with increasing ambient air temperature.

Vince Anderson, a world-class mountaineer and rock climber, is a good example of a climber who tailors workouts based on the use of muscle fuel. (Anderson is discussed in more detail in the next section.) To take advantage of his fat metabolism (used at low to moderate intensity), Anderson purposely paces himself to go slow during long- or short-approach hikes to ice or rock climbs so that his breathing and heart rate are low to moderate. He may not be able to sprint up a mountain, but he can go all day, primarily because he's able to maintain endurance while his body conserves stored fuel.

Overall, energy balance is essential to maintaining lean mass, immune function, and athletic performance. Energy balance occurs when energy intake (from foods, fluids, and supplements) equals energy expenditure. If the body has inadequate intake of nutrients, then the benefits of training are diminished, and performance decreases to a greater degree. The body will begin to consume itself (i.e., lean mass), and a continuous loss in strength and endurance will occur if nutrient intake is insufficient for maintaining energy balance. Finally, if you are making a point of eating a variety of foods, as suggested in the MyPyramid tip, then the use of nutritional supplements is not advised (ACSM Joint Position Stand, 2000).

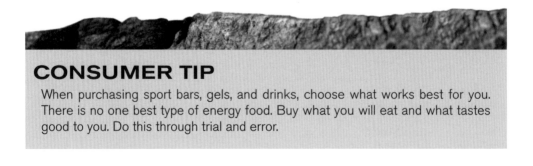

CONSUMER TIP

When purchasing sport bars, gels, and drinks, choose what works best for you. There is no one best type of energy food. Buy what you will eat and what tastes good to you. Do this through trial and error.

Physiological Responses to Climbing

Before embarking on a training schedule for rock climbing, you should understand a few key elements about your program related to how your body operates under the stress of exercise. This is the same as beginning a long climbing expedition to a remote mountain region, which first requires research and inquiries about what you're up against. The same is true now as you learn the basic language and variables included in your training plan.

While climbing, at times you feel out of breath with a high perceived effort and a great sense of muscular overload, which can be measured as rating of perceived exertion. Being out of breath and feeling a tremendous sense of muscular fatigue indicate that your body is becoming more anaerobic (high intensity) than aerobic (low to moderate intensity). Keep in mind that anaerobic literally means "without oxygen" and aerobic indicates "with oxygen." Once you cross the threshold into the realm of a high perceived effort, breathlessness, and a sense of constant high muscular force generation (or feeling more anaerobic), your muscles' ability to sustain a great workload is becoming maxed out. This photo illustrates high intensity, muscular overload, especially for the muscles of the arms and shoulders. This position, with the elbow joint fully extended and shoulders flexed, is the proper way to hang or rest prior to conducting a pull-up like motion, but still requires a large muscular effort. Thus, be prepared to scope your next move quickly and accurately. Proper training then allows your body to use metabolic fuel (especially carbohydrate and fat) and hang longer and more efficiently so that you can continue working for a long time and be able to overcome high intensity, muscular overload moves.

A novice climber in a static state while scoping the next hold. The elbow is straight or extended and the shoulder partially flexed, which minimizes muscular overload. However, it pays to stay rock-climbing fit so that your muscles will maintain power longer, even when "hanging out" on a move.

Whatever your training, skill, or ability level, how well and when your body uses a particular energy system also depends on the difficulty, terrain, and weather found on a particular route. As stated previously, you go through many sensations while climbing, such as periods of breathlessness, high muscular overload, and great perceived effort. You even have times when everything feels easy or moderate in nature. Following are descriptions of the three energy systems. The major outcome of all three systems is the production of adenosine triphosphate (ATP), the only molecule in your muscles that allows for contraction when produced in any of the three energy systems (Jeukendrup and Gleeson, 2004; Sharkey and Gaskill, 2006).

1. The ATP-PCr system is used for bursts of power that last 15 seconds or less. It uses phosphocreatine (PCr), which helps produce very quick energy in the muscle without the need for oxygen (very high-intensity training with feelings of breathlessness and a great sense of sudden fatigue known as anaerobic metabolism).

2. The glycolytic system is favored as a primary fuel source for intense efforts lasting 15 to 90 seconds. It uses glucose (sugar) breakdown in muscle fiber via a process termed *glycolysis*, which equals fast to moderately fast energy production without the use of oxygen (high-intensity training with feelings of breathlessness and severe fatigue, also known as part of anaerobic metabolism).

3. The aerobic system is favored as a primary fuel source for bouts of activity lasting 90 seconds or greater (up to several hours). It uses continued carbohydrate and fat breakdown with constant oxygen uptake and processing (low- to moderate-intensity training with feelings of steady breathing, little fatigue, and moderate perceived effort).

HOW FIT IS VINCE ANDERSON?

Vince Anderson, a world-class climber from Ridgway, Colorado, recently completed a new route on Nanga Parbat in Pakistan with climbing partner Steve House. This great accomplishment was featured on the cover of *Outside Magazine*. Through hard work and dedication to training, Anderson maintains an excellent aerobic base at age 37 despite being compared to athletes (such as distance runners) who are specifically trained to have high aerobic capacities. His major training emphasis is long-duration activity (running, cycling, swimming, and so forth) interspersed with weekly powerful and high-intensity workouts (plyometric training, strength training, or rock climbing). He also uses a well-planned periodized training scheme (discussed later in this chapter) to overload his cardiorespiratory and muscular systems for optimal climbing fitness.

Regarding energy systems, you need to understand that continuous rock climbing is a highly aerobic activity that is interspersed with periodic bouts of powerful and high-intensity movement. In the long run, then, a beginning climber who wishes to progress in fitness and skill will need to incorporate intense climbing-specific exercises into a training regimen while at the same time developing and maintaining an aerobic base (low to moderate intensity). Caloric expenditure tends to increase as route angle and difficulty become greater even though the body tends to favor *both* fat and carbohydrate.

Musculoskeletal Injuries and Rock Climbing

Inherently, rock climbing and the process of training for climbing can lead to injuries in muscle and connective tissue, such as muscle strains, sprains, or even bruises. Additionally, overuse injuries such as tendinitis or a pulled ligament (or tendon) can occur. As mentioned previously, these injuries are usually caused by repetitive trauma or overuse of a particular muscle, joint, or combination of these because of weakness (such as infrequent training or genetic differences). The best defense is a good offense. In other words, you need a planned and progressive training program that takes into account your body's strengths and weaknesses, which are usually different for each person. In general, if your body is always in a state of high fitness because you climb frequently along with strength and aerobic training on a regular basis, then your tendons, ligaments, and surrounding muscle groups should be resistant to injury. On the flip side, if you engage in very little training and are a sporadic climber, then you become less resistant to injury. Remember, you're only as strong as your weakest link.

To combat injury in rock climbers, Tim Poppe—a physical therapist at Physiotherapy Associates in Gunnison, Colorado—recommends weekly strength exercises specific to climbing. He also recommends that climbers use dynamic movement, such as light bouldering or traversing on a wall, to warm up before climbing. If an injury does occur, you should stop climbing in order to evaluate the severity of the damage (and have it evaluated by a trained medical professional if necessary). Pain should always be your guide. Continuing to climb while injured can exacerbate the damage; thus, rest is usually advised, followed by specific stretching or strengthening exercises (normally prescribed by a physical therapist or athletic trainer) to rehabilitate the injured area. Light, specific bouldering exercises may help with the recovery process as the injured area gains strength and becomes less prone to reinjury and pain.

As mentioned, the first thing to do when an injury occurs is usually to stop the activity that caused the damage. Next, it's recommended that you ice the inflamed region for 15 to 20 minutes along with painless compression. Elevation of the injured site may be warranted to help reduce swelling and pain. This is the RICE principle (rest, ice, compression, and elevation). Also, anti-inflammatory medication may be helpful and should be taken according to the manufacturer's recommended dosage. Remember, you should seek advanced medical advice if an injury is severe, is painful, and hinders normal movement. Otherwise, you may just need to apply the RICE principle, emphasizing the need to rest the injured region, followed by a planned, progressive strengthening routine to get back to form without rushing the healing process.

If a bone is broken or a serious tendon or ligament pull occurs—especially in the hand or fingers (a very common injury region for climbers)—then expert medical evaluation and rehabilitation are necessary. Surgery may even be needed to set the bone correctly or to scrape away scar tissue. Also, specific taping or splinting measures can be undertaken (according to the advice of a professional) to help stabilize an injured area after recovery. You must carefully evaluate all injuries—no matter how insignificant they may appear— in order to avoid future flare-ups caused by overuse or inadequate training. Nothing substitutes for and makes you injury resistant like the specificity of training achieved by climbing on a regular basis. If you know that you're not fit, you should begin at an easy to moderate grade. Don't be afraid to back off an overly strenuous situation—you can return when you're fitter and ready to face the demands. The rock or route will always be there!

Muscular Fitness and Cardiorespiratory Endurance Training for Rock Climbers

In this section, generalized strength and endurance programs are introduced. The concept of periodization involves identifying various training schemes throughout each year of training. This may sound cumbersome and uninteresting at first glance; however, the concept of periodization will enable you to see the big picture of training along with the minute details needed to achieve optimal success. This concept can help you achieve adaptation to training, progress, and realization of goals. For an in-depth view of periodization (beyond the scope of this chapter), refer to Tudor Bompa's text *Periodization: Theory and Methodology of Training, Fifth Edition* (Champaign, IL: Human Kinetics, 2009). In short, periodization emphasizes that an athlete should see the big picture of strength and endurance training by using the principles of progression, specificity, and overload. The intensity of the athlete's workouts should move from light to moderate to high throughout an entire yearlong cycle (the cycle may be shorter depending on goals and athlete ability). Also, within a periodized program, rest, relaxation, and cross-training are frequently incorporated to allow for adequate metabolic adaptations of the muscles. Thus, when designing your training schemes—including the use of year-round climbing—you should frequently change your routine from light to moderate to high intensity. You should also remember to schedule rest and episodes of cross-training (different than your normal grind of training).

For rock climbers, year-round climbing is now possible on indoor walls. This will be the cornerstone of any training program used to maintain specific muscle adaptations and the range of motion of joints. Rock climbers wishing to progress should focus on the following: high aerobic power, specific muscular strength and endurance, developing energy systems related to muscular power, and some minimum range of motion for leg and arm movements (Watts, 2004). Based on this, climbers should aim for overall muscular and cardiorespiratory fitness along with specific strength (i.e., muscular strength and endurance) that will enhance climbing ability.

Aerobic ability can be developed by using a variety of modalities or situations, including treadmills, stationary cycles, elliptical trainers, hiking with a backpack, run-

Indoor running or walking is a great cardiorespiratory workout. Improving your aerobic power will enhance your climbing ability.

ning on mountain trails, and mountain biking. In general, running creates the most effective cardiorespiratory (and muscular) overload and requires greater energy input compared to walking or cycling for the same duration. Trail running on undulating terrain is especially stimulating to the cardiorespiratory system and the muscular system of the lower body. When choosing an aerobic activity, be sure it is something you enjoy, and feel free to change up your activities frequently to maintain interest and tissue adaptations. Don't forget to vary the intensity from day to day, week to week, and month to month.

Aerobic Training Program Recommendations

Aerobic training teaches your body how to take up and use more oxygen in muscle so that you avoid premature fatigue when climbing. Your body will fatigue less if you use a solid aerobic training base that is consistent and varied. Understanding the following definitions will help you piece together an effective training program from year to year. These key words are important components of any aerobic training program. Now the fun begins! See table 2.2 for recommendations on aerobic base training and periodization.

INTENSITY DEFINITIONS FOR AEROBIC TRAINING

rest—The lowest heart rate recorded of those taken on several occasions when the person is first waking up in the morning or is sitting quietly for 10 minutes.

easy—Low-intensity training (a conversational pace).

moderate—Medium-intensity training (can still talk but not easily).

hard—High-intensity training (hard to talk with high breathing rate).

Suggested Strength Training Routine

Before starting your personalized strength training routine, you should review the definitions of key words related to strength training. Recall that you need to use progression, overload, and specificity in a periodized routine. Also, you need to understand the specific definitions of muscular strength and muscular endurance, which are collectively known as muscular fitness but require different training stimuli. Moreover, muscular power has its own distinct definition and operates at a higher speed of movement than normal muscular fitness. Regardless of these different components, you should keep in mind that simply altering your strength training routine periodically will enhance your training and ultimately your climbing fitness. Work to incorporate the training suggestions in this chapter over a period of time so that you can build on your specific rock-climbing progress from year to year. See table 2.3 for recommendations on strength training for muscular fitness and periodization. For specific training for the various seasons (or phases) please see your gym supervisor, personal trainer, or experienced guide.

Table 2.2 Aerobic Base Training and Periodization Recommendations

Goal	Length	Mode	Frequency	Duration	Intensity	Progression
Phase 1: Active rest and off-season (late fall and winter)						
Recovery and maintenance	12 weeks	Run, walk, hike, cycle, swim, Nordic ski	3-5 × week	30-45 min; 1 × week for 60 min	Low to moderate intensity	Increase duration before intensity
Phase 2: General training and off-season (late winter and spring)						
Gradual increase in aerobic base; get ready for climbing season	12 weeks	Run, walk, hike, cycle, swim, mountain bike	General frequency: 4-6 × week	30-60 min	Moderate intensity	Increase duration before intensity; stay at lower end of ranges first 6 weeks
Overload session (general training period)						
Gain anaerobic and aerobic power		Tempo run on treadmill (TM) or trail	1 × week (include as part of general frequency)	20 min + 5 min warm-up and cool-down	High moderate to hard intensity	Add 1 min each week
Phase 3: Specific training (summer and early fall)						
Maintain aerobic base; increase overload; increase intensity and power energy systems	12-18 weeks	Run, walk, hike, cycle, swim, mountain bike	General frequency: 4-5 × week	30-50 min	Moderate to very hard intensity	Stay at lower end of ranges first 6 weeks; then begin overload sessions
Overload session 1						
Overload aerobic system; increase aerobic power		TM, trail, hilly terrain	1 × week; do during even # weeks in this period (include as part of general frequency)	30-45 min + 10 min warm-up and cool-down	Hard intensity	Stay within given range

	Duration	Surface	Frequency	Volume/reps	Intensity	Focus
Overload session 2						
Overload anaerobic and aerobic systems		TM, trail	1 × week; do during odd # weeks in this period (include as part of general frequency)	1 min bursts with 3 min easy = 1:3 duration; 5 min warm-up and cool-down	Surge at a hard pace	Progress to 2:3 or 3:5
Overload session 3						
Overload anaerobic and aerobic systems		Trail	1 × week; do during even # weeks in this period (include as part of general frequency)	1-2 min hill × 6-8	Very hard intensity	Focus on form, pump arms, push off hard, jog down easy
Phase 4: Peaking period (late summer and early fall)						
Maintain aerobic base; overload ATP-PCr system (anaerobic)	3-4 weeks	Trail, dirt	General frequency: 3 × week easy	30-40 min	Moderate intensity	Go easy on easy days
Workout 1						
Overload ATP-PCr system (anaerobic)		Track	1 × week (include as part of general frequency)	Varies; 15-20 × 100 m with 100 m jog recovery; 4 × 200 m "zooms" with 200 m jog recovery; 10 min warm-up and cool-down	Very, very hard intensity, close to max effort	Focus on feeling "faster" each week; strive for good form
Workout 2						
Overload ATP-PCr system (anaerobic)		Dirt, grass	1 × week (include as part of general frequency)	Varies; hill repeats: 15-20 sec hill × 15 on dirt or grass; 10 min warm-up and cool-down; jog down	Very, very hard intensity	Accelerate quickly, focus on leg push-off and "smooth" arm swing

Table 2.3 Recommendations on Strength Training for Muscular Fitness and Periodization

	Phase 1: Active rest (October–December)	Phase 2: Off-season (January–March)	Phase 3: Preseason (April–May)	Phase 4: In-season (June–September)
Objective or goal of phase	Recovery from competitive or specific climbing season. Maintain a general base of cardiorespiratory and muscular fitness.	Develop muscular strength and some endurance. Focus on slow, controlled movement through a full range of motion.	Develop climbing-specific strength and endurance. Increase speed of movements and overall body climbing fitness.	Develop peak muscular strength and endurance specific to climbing goals.
Suggestions for strength training routine	General strength and endurance maintenance: Lift 2-3 days per week with 1-3 sets of 12-15 repetitions with a moderate weight on all body parts ("head to toe").	Strength development, full body: Lift 2-3 days per week with 3 sets of 10 repetitions at a moderate weight. Lift to muscular failure each set. Spend an additional 1-2 days per week on a climbing and campus board along with bouldering for 15-20 minutes per session traversing, ascending, and descending.	Strength development, full body: 2 sessions per week; 2-3 sets of 6-8 repetitions at a challenging weight that feels hard. Power and speed on select upper and lower body parts: 3-4 sets of 3-5 repetitions at a relatively easy weight for power exercises; Plyometric exercises incorporated.	Maintain strength and power: Strength, full body: 2 sets of 6-10 repetitions with a moderate to hard weight. Power on select upper and lower body parts: 2-3 sets of 4-6 repetitions at a relatively easy weight for power exercises.

STRENGTH TRAINING DEFINITIONS

muscular endurance—The ability of a muscle or muscle group to exert submaximal force for extended periods (Heyward, 2002).

muscular power—The amount of work performed over time (i.e., increased work over little time equals high power) (Baechle and Earle, 2000).

muscular strength—The maximum force that a muscle or muscle group can generate at a specific velocity (Baechle and Earle, 2000).

one-repetition maximum (1RM)—The maximum amount of weight you can lift once.

overload—Training at a level that is greater than what a body system is currently accustomed to (Baechle and Earle, 2000).

progression—Advancing the training stimulus or loads (weight lifted) so that improvement continues over time (Baechle and Earle, 2000).

specificity—Adaptations in physiological (body) systems that are distinct or limited to the body structures overloaded during training (Baechle and Earle, 2000).

General Order of Strength Exercises

1. Begin lifting sessions with light warm-up sets focused on all muscle groups to be trained.

2. During a full-body workout (all muscle groups) done in one session, you should overload larger muscle groups before smaller ones, perform multiple-joint exercises before single-joint lifts, and conduct high-intensity exercises before lower-intensity exercises (Sharkey and Gaskill, 2006; Kraemer et al., 2002, ACSM Position Stand).

General Frequency of Strength Training

- Strength training should be performed three times per week with a minimum of one day of rest in between sessions (e.g., train on Monday, Wednesday, and Friday or Tuesday, Thursday, and Saturday).

- Phases of strength training for climbers can be as follows: phase 1 (active rest), phase 2 (off-season), phase 3 (preseason), phase 4 (in-season).

SAFETY TIP

When engaging in strength training, always move your limbs in a slow and controlled fashion—unless you are trying to specifically develop power and speed of movement, which requires quick response time. Don't forget to continually breathe throughout each repetition. Using the machines and exercises properly will lessen the risk of injury to the body. Seek the advice of a gym specialist or personal trainer.

Summary

Climbing with ease requires lean body mass, muscular fitness, and flexibility along with enhanced physiological responses to increased climbing intensity. Successful training and climbing always require dedication, an organized training plan, and a penchant for having fun. When organizing a training plan, remember to address progression, overload, and specificity using a periodized program for both endurance and strength routines. Frequent and well-planned training allows your body to accrue overall climbing fitness. This comes in the form of enhanced endurance, muscular fitness, and flexibility, as well as greater development of muscle mass relative to fat tissue. As you train and rock climb in a gym or at a local crag, remember to keep your body well fueled with sugars and some protein by consuming your favorite bars, gels, or sport drinks. Throughout the day and week before climbing (or around training), be sure to eat a well-balanced diet tailored specifically to your activity level (see www.mypyramid.gov). Most of all, make sure you incorporate rest periods into your training or climbing days. This will allow your body to recover properly from the degradative nature of continual exercise. Don't forget to become a student of climbing! Reading up on climbing technique, climbing often, and having a plan will make it easier for you to progress as a rock climber.

CHAPTER 3

Indoor Climbing

Climbing is not a battle
with the elements, nor
against the law of gravity.
It's a battle against oneself.

Walter Bonatti

With the advent of indoor climbing options, rock climbing is no longer limited to the rugged sandstone crags or granite cliff faces tucked away down dirt roads. Whether you are a beginner or a seasoned climber, you now have many more climbing options than in the past. These options enable you to climb for fun, fitness, skill acquisition, or sport-specific training. This chapter describes the development of indoor climbing, types of indoor climbing settings, anchors used indoors, climbing gym design, and the programs and services typically available at a climbing gym.

Inception of Indoor Climbing

The earliest forms of artificial climbing walls can generally be credited to the military. Vertical walls composed of odd-shaped blocks and cutouts have commonly been used to train soldiers how to climb obstacles during combat situations. The first commercial climbing gyms in America began to appear in the late 1980s. Indoor climbing facilities were initially created to help climbers develop and maintain their strength and technical climbing skills without having to travel great distances to outdoor climbing sites. Indoor climbing facilities were also designed to allow climbers to practice their sport without combating the whims of weather and limited winter daylight hours. Early gyms were often poorly designed and crudely constructed retrofits to existing buildings. Many of the early gyms failed to reach out to a diverse and mainstream user base because they were intended to exclusively serve the climbing population. Modern climbing gyms now incorporate a balance of social, active, programmatic, and maintenance elements into the overall gym layout and design. Well-planned designs offer a variety of climbing terrain, free-flowing traffic patterns, and high-visibility program areas for aesthetics and safety management. Climbing gyms, once merely a training arena for elite athletes, have become accessible to mainstream populations because of the addition of climbing walls to multiuse fitness facilities. Climbing walls now exist at commercial fitness clubs, public schools, summer camps, university recreation centers, military bases, and youth amusement parks. What was once perceived to be a fad has become a core offering of many recreation centers.

Indoor Climbing Facilities

Climbing gyms generally exist in two types of environments: stand-alone climbing facilities and inclusive fitness facilities. Stand-alone facilities are businesses that provide climbing services as their core offering. Typically, stand-alone facilities are private commercial businesses catering primarily to the climbing community. These businesses

CONSUMER TIP

When choosing a climbing gym to join, select one that offers the greatest amount of services relative to the monthly fee.

may incorporate nonclimbing areas such as meeting rooms, informal gathering spaces, and areas for free weights into the building design. These add-on features are perceived as bonuses to climbing patrons. Meeting rooms offer space for small events (e.g., slide shows and birthday parties), climbing education, and fitness programs such as stretching, yoga, or Pilates. Since the target market being served is people interested in climbing activities, the climbing portions of the facility need to be available during all hours that the facility is open; the supplemental services can be offered at varied times.

Inclusive recreation facilities maintain climbing gyms as a bonus feature to round out a complete recreation offering (see figure 3.1). Typically, inclusive facilities are commercial fitness clubs, university or municipal recreation centers, summer camps, or nonprofit community centers. Climbing programs in these facilities are a specialty area that enhances the total user experience of the facility. Increased visibility and the inclusion of climbing in cross-training promotions have increased the perceived value of climbing as a fitness activity. In these facilities, a patron might play a game of pickup basketball, followed by a swim and some light weightlifting, before his climbing workout. Unlike a commercial climbing gym, the hours of operation for the climbing features in an inclusive recreation facility may be limited solely to peak times of participation. Ultimately, the type of facility that a climber chooses to use will be based on the person's preferred recreational objectives, the facility location, the available services, the hours of operation, and the cost of a membership.

Figure 3.1 A rock-climbing facility in a big commercial gym can provide the most value for your dollar.

Types of Climbing Walls

Throughout the world, outdoor climbing areas differ by their location; their vertical relief; and the shapes, features, and textures associated with the rock type of the cliff area. Indoor climbing walls are designed to mimic natural geologic formations. Indoor walls typically incorporate a wide variety of angles, formed features, and textures to simulate an outdoor climbing environment.

Climbing walls are constructed in a two-part manner similar to constructing a house. Part 1 of constructing a climbing wall involves framing the walls of the structure. The framing is the part of the climbing wall that supports the weight of the structure and the forces generated by falling climbers. Steel is the preferred material used to frame modern climbing walls. Part 2 of constructing a climbing wall is the process of sheeting the structure. The sheeting is similar to the interior walls of a house because it provides the surfaces that you can see and touch.

The type of climbing surface will vary from facility to facility. The four main types of climbing surfaces are plywood, plywood covered in concrete, shelled concrete, and glass fiber reinforced concrete. The different surface textures lend themselves to different climbing opportunities. Plywood or "woody" walls are the most cost-effective form of climbing wall construction (see figure 3.2). These walls can often be found in locations such as public schools and municipal recreation centers. Plywood covered in

Figure 3.2 Plywood surfaces are most often found in public schools and municipal recreation centers because of their cost-effectiveness.

CONSUMER TIP

When purchasing your first pair of climbing shoes, you should ask the sales person which shoe would be the highest performing and most durable for the surface texture of your climbing gym.

Figure 3.3 Walls with surfaces made of *(a)* glass fiber reinforced concrete and *(b)* wood covered in concrete are commonly found at both universities and commercial climbing gyms.

concrete (see figure 3.3*b*), shelled concrete, and glass fiber reinforced concrete (see figure 3.3*a*) are premium surfaces and are commonly found at both universities and commercial climbing gyms. These materials are more costly to construct, but they provide wall surfaces that have many features and can look and feel like natural rock. Wall builders can use these materials to hand sculpt features such as pockets, cracks, edges, and bulges into the wall. Permanent sculpted features are integrated into wall designs because they offer climbers the opportunity to use different body movements and techniques that cannot be used with modular handholds. Many sculpted features are designed to pull the climber into the wall surface rather than suspend the climber off of the surface.

Climbing wall designers usually only incorporate a moderate number of features to the wall surface because these are permanent features that can become familiar and nonchallenging for climbers. Most modern climbing walls are built with a surface that allows for the use of modular handholds that can be repeatedly set and removed from the wall. This interchangeability of the handholds allows for an infinite number of route configurations. It is also one of the key differences between indoor and outdoor climbing. Within the same amount of space, an indoor climbing wall can offer millions of route possibilities rather than the 10 to 12 that may naturally exist at an outdoor cliff.

Climbing Wall Features

The features of most climbing facilities can be broken down into two basic categories: the wall features and the programs offered at the facility. In this section, we'll focus on the different types of wall features available. Later in the chapter, we'll address commonly offered programs and services.

Figure 3.4 Slab surfaces can help build confidence in beginner climbers.

Slab

Low-angle, less-than-vertical walls are an invaluable training surface for introducing new climbers to the sport (see figure 3.4). Climbing on low-angle slabs enables beginner climbers to gain confidence and helps them develop good climbing posture. Slabs help climbers focus on placing their body mass over their feet to maximize friction between their shoes and the wall surface. Slab surfaces are a natural starting location for new climbers, youth, and people with reduced upper body strength. Both introductory and advanced climbing routes can be set on slab terrain; however, because of the quick learning progression of most climbers, many climbing gyms do not incorporate large areas of slab surfaces in the design of their climbing walls.

Climbers need to recognize that the design and construction of an indoor climbing facility can unintentionally include a variety of safety hazards. Climbing wall designers take great care during the design stage to create the most challenging terrain with the least amount of risk to the climber, belayer, and other gym patrons. Unfortunately, many hazards are often identified after construction. Therefore, when visiting a new facility, you should always ask the staff of the climbing gym to identify any known gym hazards.

When inspecting a new facility for hazards, you should carefully look at the slab terrain and those areas with complex terrain features. During a fall on a slab surface, climbers might sustain cuts, abrasions, or other injuries as they slide down the wall surface. You can recognize potential hazards by looking at the wall to see if the slab surface extends partway or entirely up the wall. If the slab has vertical or overhanging terrain built above a low-angle wall, there is a chance that a climber could hit other climbers or hit the wall surface during a fall.

Vertical Terrain

Vertical terrain refers to climbing surfaces that are perpendicular (90 degrees) to the gym flooring (see figure 3.5). Climbing surfaces that are vertical offer a wide variety of training opportunities and challenges for beginner, intermediate, and advanced climbers. The angle of the vertical wall surface, similar to a ladder, can allow for an even distribution of the climber's body weight. Vertical terrain helps to further develop climber strength and technique because much of the climber's body weight begins to shift from the legs to the arms. Body awareness, positioning, strength, and endurance can be refined on vertical features. Most modern climbing centers will have a large percentage of vertical terrain included in their wall design because of the wide range of skills and abilities that this terrain can accommodate. Vertical terrain can also include more complex wall configurations, shapes, and features that help to maintain climber interest and challenge.

Overhanging Terrain

Overhanging terrain refers to wall surfaces that are past vertical (90 degrees) and angling back toward the floor of the climbing facility (see figure 3.6). In most modern climbing gyms, the overhanging terrain is 3 to 15 percent past vertical. These walls keep climbers challenged by the physical demands of fighting gravity as they ascend the climbing routes. For overhanging terrain, the route setting and the selection and placement of the modular climbing holds must be well thought out. Proper selection of holds relative to the desired route difficulty can create climbs on overhanging terrain that are accessible to the complete range of gym patrons. Unlike low-angle slab surfaces—where climbers may slide down the wall surface if they fall—the climber on vertical or overhanging terrain will generally fall cleanly and safely straight down or away from the wall surface.

Figure 3.5 Vertical terrain offers a wide variety of training opportunities and challenges.

Figure 3.6 Overhanging terrain keeps climbers challenged because they must fight gravity in addition to ascending the climbing route.

Figure 3.7 Complex plane breaks are incorporated into vertical surfaces to increase the variety of route setting.

Complex Plane Breaks

Vertical and overhanging walls that are flat in design are quick and cheap to build, but they limit the variability of route setting, which ultimately can limit climber challenges. Wall designers often use short triangular-shaped sections of wall surface to incorporate multiple plane breaks in one climbing area (see figure 3.7). The use of triangular-shaped building materials can create both gentle and dramatic changes in the relief of the wall surface. Also, climbing walls that incorporate multiple plane breaks increase the esthetic appeal of the facility because the undulating wall surface creates variations of shade and light. Wherever the edges of the triangles meet, new features such as inside and outside corners, arêtes (see figure 3.8), shelves, and overhangs can be created. All climbers enjoy a wide variety of surface textures, shapes, and angles because these features require the climber to use multiple body movements and techniques to ascend the walls (see figure 3.9).

Figure 3.8 Arêtes are formed where the edges of the plane breaks meet.

Figure 3.9 Highly featured walls provide all climbers (beginner through advanced) with many challenges requiring multiple moves and techniques to ascend the walls.

When climbing walls include complex plane breaks and overhanging terrain, there is always the potential that a climber may swing into other patrons, features protruding from the wall surface, or fixed objects such as benches, counters, and railings. During any fall, climbers have the potential to hurt deep tissue, bones, or ligaments as they collide with modular climbing holds or the surface of the wall; therefore, you should always ask the climbing gym staff and other patrons about known hazards.

Bouldering

Bouldering terrain often encompasses all of the terrain features previously mentioned; however, bouldering is generally done at heights below 14 feet (4.2 m) (see figure 3.10). Bouldering is the fastest growing element of the sport of rock climbing. Therefore, indoor climbing facilities are increasingly incorporating dedicated bouldering areas into their designs. Bouldering is a very social part of climbing because climbers navigate short, challenging sections of wall close to the ground without a rope for protection. A bouldering route that requires the climber to use a sequence of rock climbing moves is called a *problem.* Outdoor boulder problems can exist on isolated freestanding rocks or at the base of larger rock structures. Boulder problems can also be created within an indoor climbing facility.

Bouldering is one of the most dynamic and rewarding aspects of indoor climbing. Climbers commonly push themselves to their point of failure in pursuit of successfully completing a route or bouldering problem. When bouldering, you should always be aware that you do not have the benefit and safety of a climbing rope, especially when you are making difficult moves. All of the possible injuries from roped climbing can also occur when bouldering. Though bouldering is not immune from causing catastrophic injuries, the most common injuries attributed to indoor bouldering are twisted or broken ankles and wrists, dislocated knees, and skin abrasions. To protect climbers who are bouldering, many gyms supply climbers with portable pads that help protect against injuries when falling from low heights. However, many of the common bouldering injuries can be linked to the use of individual portable pads often called "drag" or "crash" pads. Drag pads are large pads that users can move around the gym floor to help protect themselves from large falls when attempting boulder problems. Climbers often stack pads to provide more cushioning against the forces of a fall, but these climbers sometimes end up receiving musculoskeletal injuries when they land on the edge of the pads.

To prevent injuries attributed to portable drag pads, many gyms have begun to have custom foam pads built to fit the shape of their wall surface. Asana Climbing is the manufacturer that pioneered these custom bouldering pad systems. The pads are constructed with the same multidensity

Figure 3.10 Boulder problems in an indoor facility can mimic outdoor boulder problems, but they are set at a maximum height of 12 to 14 feet.

foam components of a conventional drag pad; however, the pads are designed to connect to each other to create a uniform landing surface that contours to the shape of the climbing wall. These pads are also designed with reinforced fabric paneling that covers any edges or seams so that a climber cannot land between two pads. Custom uniform bouldering surfaces have increasingly become more prevalent in indoor climbing facilities because of their recognized ability to reduce the likelihood of many bouldering injuries.

Anchors for Indoor Climbing

Anchors are one of the facility-based items that can reduce climber risk. Artificial climbing facilities use bottom, top, and intermediary anchors to protect patrons. The exact locations and types of climbing anchors are based on the type of frame and surface used for the climbing wall. Regardless of the types of anchors used by a climbing gym, the anchors must be designed and engineered to significantly exceed the expected forces that will be placed on them by a falling climber. Historically, builders of climbing walls used the standards established by a now defunct organization called the Climbing Wall Industry Group (CWIG). In the absence of the oversight provided by this industry group, most builders and designers continued to use the standards set by CWIG. Recently, a new nonprofit trade organization was formed to set standards for the construction and operation of climbing facilities. The Climbing Wall Association has established a variety of standards and operating protocols that its members can electively adopt and use.

Anchors in a climbing gym are similar to the equipment that outdoor climbers use because they must be able to sustain impact forces that exceed those expected in a fall. Climbing ropes are intended to be the strongest part of the climber safety chain; therefore, most climbing gym designers and builders construct and install anchors that withstand forces exceeding the strength limits of the ropes used in the facility.

Top-Rope Anchors

Top anchors create a pulley or slingshot system that is often called a top-rope climbing situation. The design layout of most modern climbing gyms will include more top-rope stations than lead climbing stations. Top-rope climbing principles are easy to learn and readily accessible to the majority of the patrons. Three types of top anchors are generally accepted for climbing gyms: belay bars, chains or quickdraws, and auto belays. Regardless of the type of anchors used at a climbing gym, they must all be constructed so that they are attached to the load-bearing framing of the climbing wall and not just the climbing wall surface. Belay bars are large-diameter steel tubes (often 2 to 4 feet [61 to 122 cm] in length × 4 inches [10.2 cm] in diameter) that can be attached to the wall structure to provide a fixed point for the climber's rope to pivot around (see figure 3.11). Belay

Figure 3.11 Belay bars are one to several feet in length, allowing one anchor to provide protection for several climbing routes.

bars distribute the friction at the fulcrum point of the pulley system, thereby reducing the wear and tear on the ropes. Since belay bars are typically several feet in length, they allow one anchor to provide safety for several climbing routes. Belay bars can be very effective in protecting climbing routes that take an indirect path toward the top of the wall since the climber's rope can move left or right along the length of the belay bar. Climbers should be aware of their body position as it relates to the top anchors when climbing in a gym that uses belay bars. Routes are often set that wander (from side to side) up the wall surface, and these types of routes can place a climber in danger of a pendulum-type fall. In this situation, falling climbers might strike the wall, their belayer, other climbers, or spectators.

Traditional chains or quickdraws are used as a top anchor system by many climbing gyms because they are similar in design and function to the anchors that are used for outdoor climbing (see figure 3.12). Two anchors are fixed to the load-bearing framing of the wall, and either a set of steel chains or webbing quickdraws are attached (with steel rapid links) to these anchors. At the end of the chains or quickdraws, a set of steel carabiners are connected to the rope. A chain or quickdraw anchor provides climbers with two points of protection to arrest the forces of a fall. These anchor systems are designed to balance the forces generated in a fall between the two anchors. To maximize the safety of this anchor design, climbers should ascend the wall so that they are directly below that anchor. Climbing below the anchors will help to minimize any pendulum-type swings that a climber might take during a fall.

Auto belay systems are devices that were designed specifically for the recreational climbing industry. These devices work without the conventional climber–belay relationship because a mechanical system fulfills the role of the traditional belayer. Auto belays can be likened to a mechanical winch. A climber is attached with a steel carabiner to either a steel cable or a webbing strap. As the climber ascends the climbing wall, the winch moderates the amount of slack in the line to keep the climber taut and protected in the event of a fall. Once the climber reaches the top of the wall, the device engages and slowly lowers the climber to the ground. When used and maintained properly, auto belays can help reduce some of the risks associated with rock climbing; however, climbers need to recognize that these devices do not teach a skill set

Figure 3.12 Quickdraws (shown on the right) are used as a top anchor system in many climbing gyms because they are similar to the anchors used for outdoor climbing. An auto belay system is shown on the left.

that is transferable to other facilities or outdoor climbing environments. In addition, climbers must always be vigilant to examine the cable and the connecting hardware that is provided with the auto belay system to ensure that none of the components are visibly worn or damaged.

Lead Anchors

Many climbing facilities are limited to offering bouldering and tope-rope opportunities because of the type of framing used for the wall construction. Lead anchors can only be placed on climbing walls that have load-bearing framing—that is, walls that allow the impact forces of a falling climber to be transferred directly to the load-bearing frame of the wall rather than the top surface sheeting (see figure 3.13). The placement of lead anchors at a climbing facility enables the gym's patrons to practice and train for outdoor climbing scenarios. Outdoor sport climbing requires climbers to place their protection—by clipping into fixed anchors—as they ascend the rock face.

Most climbing gyms will have quickdraws securely attached to their wall to minimize the risk of patrons failing to properly clip into a fixed anchor with their own equipment. Lead anchors at a climbing gym usually consist of a four-part system: (1) a bolt and bolt hanger that are secured directly to the load-bearing framing of the wall, (2) a steel rapid link that is attached to a bolt hanger, (3) a webbing quickdraw, and (4) a steel carabiner for connecting a climbing rope. Lead climbers will

Figure 3.13 Lead anchors can only be used in indoor climbing facilities that have load-bearing framing.

clip into multiple anchors as they ascend a route in the gym. At the top of the route, the climber will need to clip into two final pieces of protection in order to be lowered back to the ground. At the top of lead climbing terrain, most gyms will use either two quick-draws (see figure 3.14a) or two Super Shuts (see figure 3.14b). Climbers using the quickdraws will clip their rope into the two carabiners before being lowered. Climbers using Super Shuts will simply pull their rope through the spring levers of the Super Shut before being lowered. Climbers must never climb above a pair of Super Shuts because they run the risk of accidentally unclipping from the system if they take an unexpected fall. Falling climbers have the potential to violently strike other climbers, the wall surface, or the gym floor. When you are preparing to lead a route at an indoor climbing facility, you will need to consider general floor traffic patterns, potential rope drag on the wall surface, swing angles during a fall, and lowering zones for leaders.

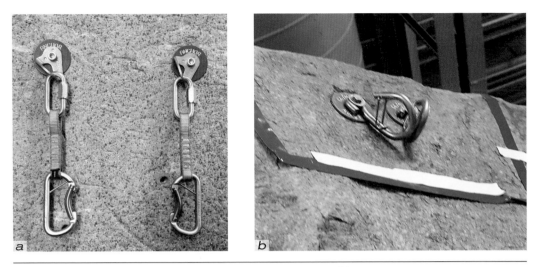

Figure 3.14 Lead anchors in a climbing gym are usually *(a)* two quickdraws with carabiners or *(b)* two Super Shuts at the top of lead climbing terrain.

Anchoring the Belayer

Floor anchors are another critical safety component for indoor climbing because they help prevent a beginner, lightweight, or lead belayer from being pulled off balance when arresting the force of a falling climber. Unsuspecting belayers can be pulled off their feet and flung either forward into the wall or vertically into an overhanging feature when their partner falls. Many climbers fail to use or simply forgo the benefits of a ground anchor when they climb outside; however, floor anchors are an invaluable and readily available safety feature in an indoor climbing facility.

Floor anchors can be fixed, mobile, or human depending on the design of the climbing facility. Fixed floor anchors are permanently attached to the floor of the climbing gym by an expansion bolt (see figure 3.15). A webbing runner and carabiner are then attached to the floor connection. This system allows a belayer to clip the carabiner into the bottom of his belay loop

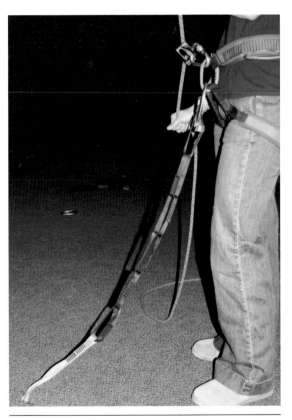

Figure 3.15 A fixed floor anchor is permanently attached to the floor of the climbing gym by an expansion bolt.

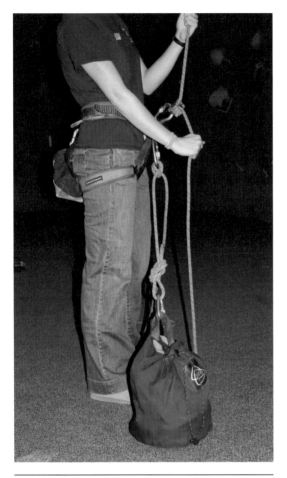

Figure 3.16 Mobile floor anchors can be made from anything soft, heavy, and portable. Climbers can carry these around the gym to the base of their selected climbs.

in order to counteract the upward forces of a falling climber. Specially designed webbing runners that are composed of a series of sewn loops allow a belayer to adjust the length of the anchor to his height. Adjusting the length of the anchor to the belayer's height helps minimize the distance the belayer will travel when arresting a falling climber. Note that fixed anchors that are permanently attached should be installed below the floor surface to reduce the chance that a falling climber might land on the anchor.

Mobile floor anchors can generally be made from anything soft, heavy, and portable (see figure 3.16). Soft-sided sandbags with attachment handles made of sewn webbing are a good example of a type of mobile floor anchor used by climbing gyms. Climbers can carry these mobile floor anchors around the gym to the base of their selected climbs. A human anchor is another means of anchoring a belayer to the ground. This low-tech solution is simple to do and can make a huge difference in helping a belayer arrest a falling climber. To form a human anchor, a second climber places her hands on the back of the belayer's harness. In the event of a fall, the additional weight of the second climber will counteract most of the falling forces (and the associated lift and tug) placed on the belayer.

Climbing Holds

The dramatic visual appeal of the climbing wall—including the shape, height, and texture of the wall surface—will be the initial draw for beginner and veteran climbers; however, the selection and distribution of climbing holds will be the component of an indoor facility that keeps climbers coming back for more. Indoor climbs are referred to as "routes." Like a music composer, route setters orchestrate the flow, rhythm, and difficulty of a particular route. Route setters are the individuals who maintain and rotate the modular climbing holds that are attached to the wall surface. Route setting is a complex art that integrates the selection and combination of proper handholds and footholds with the terrain, features, textures, and angles of a climbing wall surface. Indoor climbing routes can be designed to represent anything from a straightforward beginner route composed of an abundance of large handholds to a complex vein-popping feat of endurance.

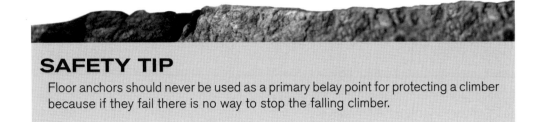

SAFETY TIP

Floor anchors should never be used as a primary belay point for protecting a climber because if they fail there is no way to stop the falling climber.

Routes are composed of a collection of modular handholds that are arranged and identified on the wall surface by a route setter. The handholds on any given route are usually marked with a colored strip of tape. This colored tape helps climbers identify the next handhold or foothold that they are to use in a particular sequence of climbing moves. New climbers will often climb to the top of a wall by using any available combination of handholds or footholds that allow them to successfully ascend the wall. As climbers progress in their strength and ability, they often begin to selectively limit their use of hand- and footholds to a particular sequence or combination of moves that have been placed and marked by a route setter.

Handholds and footholds can be purchased in any size or shape. Manufacturers make holds that can be as small as a silver dollar or larger than a human head. Climbing holds are typically created to resemble the textures, shapes, and characteristics associated with particular types of rocks. Along with recognized rock types (e.g., sandstone, granite, and limestone), climbing holds are also created to resemble the natural weatherization of rock that has happened at famous climbing areas such as Fontainebleau, France.

The wide diversity of shapes, sizes, and textures of climbing holds available helps route setters create a never-ending array of unique masterpieces. Popular climbing gyms can usually attribute their success to the rate at which they rotate or update their climbing routes. When gyms regularly update their routes, this enables climbers to sample new challenges on a frequent basis.

Programming

When choosing an indoor climbing facility, you will likely consider the overall space, the atmosphere, the operation, and especially the services of the gym. A climbing gym's ability to retain customers depends on the consistency and quality of the services that it provides.

In addition to the regular rotation of climbing routes, it is often the combination of social and educational programming offered by a climbing gym that keeps climbers coming back again and again. The following sections focus on the general types of educational and social programming available at most climbing gyms.

Basic Skills Clinics

Most climbing gyms offer instruction for beginners. Basic skills clinics are regularly offered as a means of educating new climbers in the basic skills required to safely climb within the particular facility. These clinics are designed to educate new climbers and to encourage them to adopt climbing as a new sport. Basic skills clinics are often offered for a fee that covers the cost of the instruction and equipment rentals.

TYPICAL SKILLS TAUGHT AT A SKILLS CLINIC

Basic skills clinics will often teach the following skills:

- Putting on a climbing harness
- Tying a figure eight knot
- Tying into the climbing harness
- Setting up a belay system
- Using the belay technique approved by the facility
- Using the climbing commands approved by the facility ("on belay," "belay on," "climbing," "climb on," "slack," "take," "lower," "off belay," "belay off")
- Lowering another climber
- Spotting another climber who is bouldering

Belay Checks

Belay checks are a recognized means of assessing the skills and knowledge of climbers who have previous experience with either indoor or outdoor climbing activities. Climbers who have experience are often able to demonstrate the same skills taught in a basic skills clinic. Successful demonstration of the core competencies desired by the gym will allow the individual to be registered as a climber for that facility. Many gyms charge a small fee to take part in a belay check.

Instructional seminars that cover movement and technique can help both beginner and advanced climbers improve their balance and efficiency of movement. These seminars may teach climbers how to effectively use techniques such as edging, flagging, mantling, matching, smearing, and stemming. These classes are favorites at most climbing gyms because all climbers can improve some aspect of how they move across or up a rock surface. See chapter 9 for more information regarding climbing techniques.

Lead Climbing

Many indoor climbing facilities have lead climbing opportunities available for their climbers. To lead climb at most indoor gyms, a climber will be required to either demonstrate a baseline competency in lead climbing or take an instructional seminar. Lead climbing seminars will typically focus on the generally accepted techniques used for leading indoor and outdoor sport climbing routes. Topics covered in a lead climbing seminar may include body positioning for movement on the route, rope position in relation to the climber's body and route features, optimal body and hand positions for clipping lead anchors, rest techniques, lead belay techniques, and the clear communication required between leader and belayer.

So we climb... and in climbing there is more than a metaphor; there is a means of discovery.

Rob Parker

Rappelling

Rappelling seminars are taught at many climbing gyms as a unique activity. More important, these seminars help climbers safely make the transition to outdoor climbing. In outdoor climbing, many rock faces require the climber to descend down the rock face via rope rather than walk down from the top. Rappelling seminars often cover how to effectively set up rappel stations, establish personal rappel and backup systems, descend rappel lines, and retrieve the rope when done. Though the knowledge learned in the controlled environment of a climbing gym will not directly translate to all outdoor climbing environments, these seminars do help new climbers learn the skills in a familiar and structured learning environment.

Building Climbing Anchors

For climbers who plan to make (or have already made) the transition to outdoor climbing, many gyms offer seminars on building climbing anchors. While indoor climbing gyms have manufactured anchors that keep climbers safe, outdoor climbing sites often require climbers to establish their own anchors before top-rope or lead climbing. Concepts, principles, and techniques for building efficient and secure anchors can be taught in the controlled environment of a climbing gym. Seminars may focus on the use of quickdraws, carabiners, cordelettes, webbing ropes, knots, and hitches to construct anchors at both natural and bolted sites. Though anchor-building seminars are useful for helping climbers learn the concepts, these seminars cannot adequately prepare a climber to safely set anchors in all situations and conditions.

Self-Rescue

Climber self-rescue is another advanced yet useful seminar that is often taught in a climbing gym. Generally, these seminars focus on the basic equipment and knots required for rigging basic rescue and hauling systems. They also cover how to ascend and descend ropes and how to escape the belay system. Similar to anchor-building seminars, rescue seminars taught indoors cannot adequately prepare a climber for all situations and conditions that may be presented in a rescue situation.

Competition

Climbing competitions, both vertical and bouldering, serve as a forum for those climbers who are competitively inclined. Competitions also attract climbers who are eager to test their skills and strength on new and unseen routes. Most climbing competitions are set up to accommodate all ranges and skills of climbers. Competitions can offer something for everyone, from beginners to experts. Competition formats vary from gym to gym, but all competitions provide a unique social atmosphere for climbers to meet new people and interact with friends and fellow climbers. Some U.S. climbing competitions are sanctioned through the USA Climbing Association. For more information, visit usaclimbing.net for speed, boulder, and sport climbing competitions.

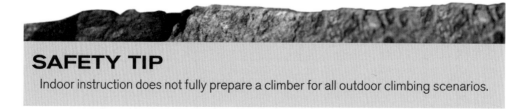

SAFETY TIP

Indoor instruction does not fully prepare a climber for all outdoor climbing scenarios.

Special Events

Special events are another key programming area for many climbing gyms. These events give the gym an opportunity to reach beyond its core constituents and attract the community at large to the facility. Special events are often paired with a peripheral event such as a climbing competition and can generate a lot of media attention for the lesser event. This exposure often helps draw large numbers of climbers and nonclimbers to the event. Special events often include speakers, films, slide shows, and conservation efforts such as the Access Fund's Adopt a Crag program.

Additional Services

Many climbing gyms also offer additional services such as yoga, Pilates, and personal training to help climbers become stronger and more limber through cross-training. These services are often available as a fee-for-service option, and they are usually limited to peak hours of use at the climbing gym.

Summary

Whether climbers are drawn to a climbing gym for the accessibility and convenience or the camaraderie they find in the familiar confines, indoor climbing provides a valuable experience for both beginner and experienced climbers. Some climbers use indoor climbing gyms because they prefer the feel of molded holds in the comfort of a climate-controlled environment under fluorescent lights. But most climbers use indoor climbing to improve their climbing skills in a more controlled environment so that they can attempt more challenging routes outdoors. Chapter 4, Know Before You Go, provides information on what you need to do as you prepare to rock climb in outdoor settings.

CHAPTER 4

Know Before You Go

Confidence and courage come through preparation and practice.

Unknown Author

Rock climbing has become a very popular recreational pastime. Rock climbing opens up a world of adventure where people take on mental and physical challenges in the midst of beautiful and wild places. Many types of rock climbing exist, and each type requires a specific set of skills and knowledge. You may be wondering how to begin acquiring the rock-climbing skills you need in order to be proficient and to have a safe and enjoyable experience. Doing so begins with your own acquisition and application of knowledge. Although there is something to be said for just getting out there and learning by doing (experiential learning), being prepared mentally and physically will only enhance your experience. Gaining a broad base of skill and knowledge will also help decrease your odds of having a preventable accident.

In addition to understanding *what* you should know before rock climbing, you also need to understand *why* certain knowledge is important. Personal safety and the responsibility that goes along with climbing—especially climbing with others—are important reasons for spending as much time as possible making sure you are prepared ahead of time. Being responsible for yourself and others is a matter of integrity. Most people consider it a privilege to get to spend time in the outdoors. You should value life (yours and that of others) and the environment that becomes your playground by treating rock climbing with a sense of responsibility. You must hold the inherent dangers, risks, and consequences in high regard. To do this, you need to realize that climbing can involve the best of times, but it can also involve the worst of times. You should be aware of the benefits of climbing but should also know the consequences of not being prepared. The best way to avoid negative situations (or surprises, regrets, and mishaps) is to arm yourself with a good foundation of knowledge and skills before you go. Whether you are planning to climb recreationally with your friends or you have aspirations of leading others, it is up to you to be well prepared with a solid base of knowledge before grabbing your harness and heading to the rock.

How much you need to learn before beginning a new activity should relate to the seriousness of the consequences if a mistake is made during the activity. Obviously, the stakes are high when you leave the ground with numerous variables at work, such as rope, anchors, equipment, and the human dimension. Therefore, you must be sure to (1) have a good grasp on the fundamentals, (2) work to perfect each skill, and (3) avoid being in a hurry and skipping steps. Acquiring knowledge and performing skills both require thorough preparation, but many aspiring climbers are tempted to skip ahead to the fun stuff—the climbing. If you do this, you will likely end up wishing you had been better informed before you started to climb. Your first step should be to assess your own abilities compared to what is required for successful and safe climbing. For example, you should determine your proficiency in the skills and knowledge identified in the following skills checklist. Second, you should make sure you know the basic terminology of the sport of rock climbing. The terms covered in this chapter deal specifically with the different types of climbing. In addition, you should know the fundamental skills that are foundational regardless of the level of climbing you choose to pursue.

Skills Checklist: Every Skill Is Important

The following is a list of skills or areas of knowledge you should be comfortable and proficient with before you go climbing. Some of these skills will be covered in this chapter, and the others will be addressed in other chapters.

- ☐ Climbing terminology
- ☐ Climbing rating system
- ☐ Route ratings and other guidebook symbols
- ☐ Site appropriateness
- ☐ Industry standards and ratings for all climbing equipment
- ☐ How to plan a rock-climbing trip
- ☐ Purchase, care, and handling of a rope
- ☐ How to belay
- ☐ How to properly wear and secure a harness
- ☐ Functions of the harness
- ☐ Knots used for rock climbing
- ☐ Climbing commands
- ☐ Climbing hardware and its uses
- ☐ How to build anchors appropriate for the terrain where you will be climbing
- ☐ Rappelling
- ☐ Ascending
- ☐ How to plan for and handle an emergency or self-rescue
- ☐ Rock-climbing etiquette and environmental responsibility (i.e., Leave No Trace principles)

Free-Climbing Rating Systems

Climbing classifications are used to rate the level of difficulty for rock-climbing routes. Many classification systems are used within the field of recreation. In fact, many different systems are used for the specific activity of rock climbing—including the Australian, Brazilian, British, French, and UIAA (Union Internationale des Associations d'Alpinisme) rating systems. The system used in the United States is called the Yosemite Decimal System (YDS). The YDS is a modified version of the German Welzenbach system. The YDS was first introduced to the United States in 1937 as the Sierra Club system, which was based on climbing being done in the Sierra Nevada range. In the 1950s, the system was modified again by adding the decimal point to the class 5 rating. This was done in order to more accurately describe rock climbing taking place in California at Tahquitz Rock. The decimal further breaks down roped free climbing based on the physical difficulty of a route and the techniques required to ascend. Here are the classifications used to describe movement over increasingly steep terrain:

Class 1: Simple hiking with no use of hands across even, straightforward terrain.

Class 2: Hiking across more varied or sloped terrain that might involve simple scrambling and the occasional use of hands for balance

Class 3: Scrambling, which involves climbing and frequent use of hands for balance and to pull body weight to negotiate terrain. A rope might be used but is generally not necessary.

Class 4: Climbing that is simple but exposed. The primary difference between class 3 and 4 is both the exposure and the consequences of a fall. Therefore, a rope is often used to protect against what could be a fatal fall. Class 4 terrain often has many natural features, but the stability and quality can be questionable at best and may provide a false sense of security.

Class 5: Climbing that should involve the use of a rope as protection against a fall.

Class 6: Climbing with a rope but with the additional use of pitons and etriers (equipment designed to wedge into very small features and allow the climber to weight these devices in order to ascend the rock face). This kind of climbing is called *aid climbing* and has its own rating system, which ranges from A.0 to A.5.

Rock climbing falls under the class 5 rating in the previous list. Class 5 climbing should involve the use of a rope, protection (fixed and artificial), and belaying. The YDS begins with 5.0 and currently ends at 5.15. The system is fine-tuned with the addition of plus (+) or minus (–) symbols as a suffix to indicate if a route is at the higher or lower range of a grade (e.g., 5.7+ or 5.8–). At most climbing sites, both indoors and outdoors, ratings for the climbs usually begin at a 5.5 or 5.6, and those climbs that range from 5.0 to 5.4 are noted as fifth-class scrambles. Of course, there are exceptions. The following ratings are general descriptions based on class 5 terrain. These ratings are subjective, and they are assigned to climbs based on region, the experience and opinion of the person giving the rating, and whether the rating is for indoor or outdoor climbing.

5.0–5.7 (easy). These climbs may be steep and exposed, but they typically have good hand- and footholds, and the holds tend to be straightforward. The climb may incorporate a variety of climbing moves—such as matching, flagging, mantling, liebacks, and so on—but it has positive holds. Generally, a variety of moves may be used to complete climbs at this grade.

5.8–5.9 (moderate). These climbs require more strength and balance, and they have fewer positive holds. The variety of hand- and footholds on these climbs may also be more limited.

5.10–5.11 (difficult). Most people have a difficult time making the jump from the intermediate to advanced level. However, with consistent weekly or weekend climbing, this can be done. Climbs in this range require significant balance, shifting of weight, and hand and finger strength. Additionally, a more distinct route or series of moves is required to complete these climbs, with fewer options to get to the top. Climbers need more endurance as well as perfected technical skills. At this range, climbs will also receive a plus (+) or minus (–) rating or will be further categorized as a, b, c, or d. Both of these methods communicate different levels of difficulty within the same rating. For instance, a climb that requires one 5.10 move might be called a 5.10–, and a climb where the 5.10 level is more sustained may be called a 5.10+. If there are four 5.11 climbs and they are ranked by difficulty, the 5.11d would be the most difficult, and the 5.11a would be the easiest.

5.12–5.15 (elite or expert). Climbs within this range are for climbers who are very naturally gifted, who can devote the time to training (including cross-training and proper diet), and who climb several times a week. These climbers have become experts and have usually acquired a high strength-to-weight ratio. They are typically very lean and have great endurance. These climbs are very difficult and sustained. In addition, very specific sequences and techniques are required for making each move. Climbing at this level requires significant commitment. The ratings of a, b, c, and d become most prominent in this range of climbing.

Bouldering Rating System

Bouldering is unique in that the moves are close to the ground and involve a much shorter sequence than typical rock climbing. Bouldering may also include dynamic moves that challenge the climber's skill. The current grading scale used by the bouldering community is the V-scale, which was created by John V. Sherman. John Sherman is an American climber known for being a pioneer of bouldering. The *V* in the V-scale comes from Sherman's nickname of "Vermin." The Sherman V-scale provides bouldering with its own unique rating system. As the popularity of bouldering increased, so did the need for a rating system that was comparable to the Yosemite Decimal System. Bouldering ratings range from V0 minus (–) to V15. See table 4.1 for a comparison of the YDS, the V-scale, and other rating systems. These ratings are based on the sequence of moves and how they would compare to moves on the YDS system.

Table 4.1 Rock-Climbing Rating Systems

YDS (USA)	British (UK) Tech/Adj		French	Bouldering	UIAA	Australia and New Zealand)	South African
5.2			1		I		8
5.3			2		II	11	10
5.4			3		III	12	11
5.5	4a	VD	4		IV	12	12
5.6		S	5a		V−	13	13
5.7	4b	HS	5b		V	14	14
	4c				V+	15	15
5.8		VS	5c		VI−	16	16
5.9	5a	HVS	6a		VI	17	17
5.10a		E1	6a+	V0	VI+	18	18
5.10b	5b					19	19
5.10c		E2	6b	V1	VII−	20	20
5.10d	5c		6b+		VII	21	21
5.11a		E3	6c	V2	VII+	22	22
5.11b			6c+			23	23
5.11c	6a	E4	7a	V3	VIII−	24	24
5.11d			7a+		VIII		25
5.12a		E5	7b	V4	VIII+	25	26
5.12b	6b		7b+			26	
5.12c		E6	7c	V5	IX−	27	27
5.12d	6c		7c+	V6	IX	28	28
5.13a		E7		V7	IX+	29	29
5.13b			8a	V8			30
5.13c	7a		8a+	V9	X−	30	31
5.13d		E8	8b	V10	X	31	32
5.14a			8b+	V11	X+	32	33
5.14b	7b		8c	V12		33	34
5.14c		E9	8c+	V13	XI−	34	35
5.14d	7c		9a	V14	XI	35	36
5.15a			9a+	V15	XI+		37

Selecting a Location

With a greater understanding of your abilities and the types of rock climbing, your next step in preparing for a climb is choosing the right spot. Selecting the right rock-climbing location and the appropriate routes is crucial to having a fun and safe experience. This section will examine criteria for selecting climbing routes and locations, along with a discussion of safe approaches to climbing sites (i.e., the nuts and bolts of actually getting to your chosen spot).

Criteria for Selecting Climbing Routes and Locations

Several factors should be considered when you are deciding where to go rock climbing. First, you must determine if your abilities and preferences will enable you to have an enjoyable experience

Scout the route before you begin your climb.

at a specific location. While some climbing locations offer various types of climbing, other locations are limited to just one. Choose a location based on your preferred type of climbing and your own climbing ability. If you are primarily a top-rope climber, you

Consult with a knowledgeable climber familiar with the area before climbing at a new location.

should determine if the rock-climbing location has suitable anchors at the top and is short enough for one rope to be used when halved in length. Remember, most climbing ropes are 60 meters (197 ft) in length, though some may be shorter. If you prefer to lead climb, you must ensure that the rock is suited to the protection you use and your skill level. When heading out to a new location to climb, you should always confirm the type of anchors at the top of a climb. You can do this by visual inspection, by asking experienced or knowledgeable climbers in the area, or by consulting a guidebook that covers that particular crag.

CRITICAL QUESTIONS TO ASK WHEN SELECTING A LOCATION

- Will your belayer have to follow you up the climb?
- Can you walk to the base of the climb from the top?
- Will it be easier and safer to rappel instead of walk from the top to the base of the climb?
- Will you need two ropes to safely descend?
- Are there anchors at the top of the climbs? If so, what kind? Does this location allow the use of trees as anchors? How will you protect the tree from being harmed by the rope?
- Will you be able to lower off a climb at any given point without running out of rope?

Being able to answer the questions in the sidebar before you go climbing is essential to your safety. Many of these questions will be answered in guidebooks written for your selected climbing area. A guidebook will also specify which style of climbing is available in a given area. Guidebooks are a vital tool in determining what type of rock and what type of climbing are present at various locations. Climbing guidebooks can be purchased at local outdoor retailers and online retailers (see the list of Web resources at the end of this chapter). Figure 4.1 identifies symbols often used in guidebooks to describe the important features of particular rock-climbing routes.

Another factor in determining where to climb relates back to your assessment of your abilities (see Skills Checklist on page 67). Say you feel confident lead climbing using traditional protection on 5.7 cracks at your local crag. Is the new location you are considering slabby rock with 40-foot (12.2 m) run-outs (sections of rock that are unprotectable and can result in very long falls)? At a new location, you should start out by climbing routes that are well below your ability level. This enables you to (a) build your confidence on the new type of rock, (b) determine the quality and frequency of protection and anchors, and (c) give yourself the opportunity to downclimb anything you feel uncomfortable on. Climbing below your ability level in a new location will also let you determine if the ratings coincide with the ratings on previous climbs. Rating a climb is a subjective judgment made by the first ascentionist; therefore, you can expect a 5.9 to mean different things at different locations. Guidebooks may note that a climbing area is easier or more difficult than the recorded ratings, but you should let your experience determine what grades you are able to climb at specific locations.

When selecting a location for rock climbing, you should also take into account the anticipated number of people in your group. Climbing with a party of more than six

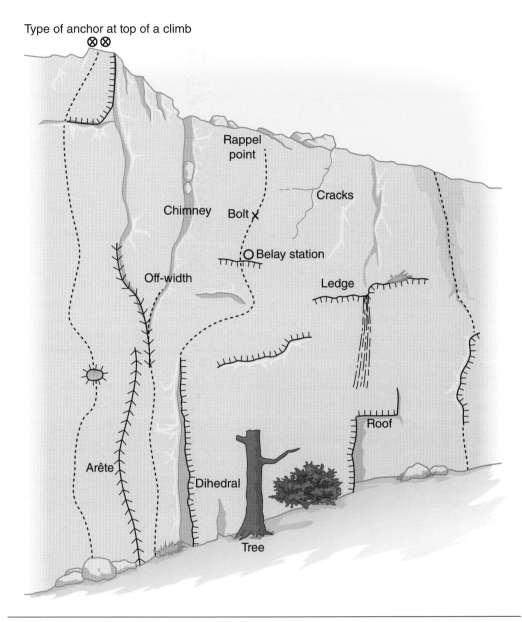

Type of anchor at top of a climb

Rappel point

Cracks

Chimney   Bolt

Belay station

Off-width

Ledge

Arête

Dihedral

Roof

Tree

Figure 4.1   Common symbols used to describe important features of a rock-climbing route.

people can have a negative impact on the generally positive vibe that exists at most climbing areas. Also, if you are climbing with an organization, your behavior with a group may affect your organization's reputation and future access to rock-climbing areas. When climbing in a large group, think about choosing a location that provides plenty of climbs for your party to spread out on. This will help ensure that your group doesn't inhibit the activities of other climbers. Climbing in a large group will be discussed in more detail later in this chapter (see Climbing Etiquette on page 92).

In summary, before you select a location, you should do the following:

- Define your style (i.e., top-rope climbing, sport climbing, or traditional climbing).
- Realistically assess your abilities.
- Locate an appropriate climbing area—that is, one that will accommodate your style and ability—based on information gathered from guidebooks or a knowledgeable salesperson from the local climbing shop.

Approaching the Climb

Approaching many climbing areas is a no-brainer, while other areas demand a level of gumption and sense of direction found only in legend. This section provides information to help the aspiring climber avoid the climbing epic that involves all approach and no climb.

Most rock-climbing guidebooks will give information on the approximate time and distance for approaching specific routes or specific areas within a greater climbing area. In fact, some guidebooks provide a grading system (I through V) for approaches that mimics the rock-climbing grading system. The grade levels for approaches are as follows: Grade I indicates an easy approach done within one or two hours; grade II approaches take no more than half a day; grade III approaches can take the better part of a day; grade IV approaches generally take one full day; and grade V indicates an approach that takes a minimum of one day. When heading out to a climbing location for the first time, keep in mind that the guidebook's estimations are simply that—an estimation. When estimating the time it will take you to reach your location, you should always take into account your aerobic fitness level, the number of people in your party (and their ability), the weather, the type of terrain, the number of hours of daylight, and how much gear you will be carrying.

Many climbing areas have approaches that are steep and exposed. Approaches described with class 3 or 4 terrain can often be more dangerous than your class 5 destination because of exposure, a lack of protection, and the perception that terrain rated below class 5 is safe. Take the time to set hand lines in areas that present the potential for a fall. This will help to protect climbers approaching and leaving the actual climbing area. Another safety consideration is to wear your helmet whenever you approach an area with the potential for rock fall, even if you are far from the actual rock-climbing location.

Don't forget to estimate the time it takes to reach your climbing location when planning a rock-climbing trip.

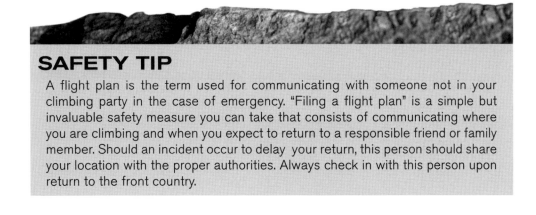

SAFETY TIP

A flight plan is the term used for communicating with someone not in your climbing party in the case of emergency. "Filing a flight plan" is a simple but invaluable safety measure you can take that consists of communicating where you are climbing and when you expect to return to a responsible friend or family member. Should an incident occur to delay your return, this person should share your location with the proper authorities. Always check in with this person upon return to the front country.

Understanding issues concerning private property, trespassing, and permits is also important when you are accessing many climbing areas; these topics are discussed in the following section.

Planning and Pretrip Logistics

In chapter 1, you were introduced to the Leave No Trace (LNT) principles. The first of the LNT principles, "plan ahead and prepare," is worth revisiting. This step is by far the most detail oriented, and for most people, it ranks low on the fun scale compared to actually going on a climbing trip. Yet this step can mean the difference between a stellar trip and a disappointing one.

There is no shortage of examples that demonstrate how avoidable situations can arise if proper preparation is not done. You have probably heard of Aron Ralston, the young man who went climbing alone only to have his arm crushed by a shifting boulder. After days of not being able to move the boulder to free himself or seeing another living soul, he had to cut off his arm in order to have any chance of survival. Had another person been aware of his location and his projected return, assistance might have been initiated resulting in a different outcome. How about the disappointment that follows after being asked by a land management representative to leave the climbing site you just spent five hours driving to because you don't have the needed permit? It is easy to be so excited about your upcoming climbing trip that you forget to take the necessary steps to be well informed about the area in which you wish to climb. Although it may seem cumbersome, taking the extra time to think through some of the details of your trip—including estimating your time of return and communicating this information to a trusted and responsible person who is not going on your trip—can make the difference between a rescue and a recovery.

The pretrip tasks discussed in this section are logistical in nature, but are just as much a part of the experience as the actual activity itself. In many cases, these tasks can be quite rewarding after you have had a successful trip.

The steps you should complete before any climbing trip include (1) researching the rules, requirements, and regulations of the areas you will be climbing; (2) creating a checklist and itinerary; and (3) creating a risk management plan.

Rules, Requirements, and Regulations

Each land management agency is different. Climbing areas may be managed by federal, county, state, or city governments. The rules may differ between the U.S. National Park Service, the National Forest Service, and the Parks Canada system. Furthermore, the rules can be different in various parks managed by the same agency. Climbing areas may also be managed by private landowners who allow climbing on their property. Therefore, you should not assume that rules, requirements, and regulations are the same across the board. Guidebooks and local climbing shops are a great resource, but these should supplement (not substitute for) the information you acquire on your own.

Review the rules of the climbing area at the trailhead before embarking on your climb.

Some of the rules, requirements, and regulations that might affect you or your group include the following: (1) group size, (2) scheduled and unscheduled closings, (3) permits and requirements, (4) Leave No Trace considerations, and (5) camping, parking, and fees.

Group Size

Group size should always be a consideration regardless of the policies at a climbing area. However, you must be aware of regulations regarding the number of climbers allowed in an area at one time. Many parks have a maximum capacity of climbers at given locations. Some climbing areas just don't accommodate large groups well, or the formation you wish to climb may accommodate only a couple of climbers safely. For all climbing trips, you should do your homework to avoid surprises so you can minimize your impact.

Scheduled and Unscheduled Closings

In some areas, federal and state parks will have scheduled closings during hunting season or during wildlife nesting or mating seasons. Uninformed climbers could be assessed large fines for not following the rules. Knowing the rules and adhering to them helps to keep climbing areas accessible. Climbers must be responsible and support the regulations that park officials make in regard to management. It is the land manager's job to protect the best interests of both the resource and the people who use it. Some climbing areas are fragile and may be closed during certain seasons. After a fire (scheduled or natural), some areas may be in a regrowth phase, and this may cause the access trail to be closed. For example, Mineral Wells State Park, a state park in Texas, closes after heavy rain in order to keep soil in this fragile environment from being transferred to the rock face by climbers.

Permits and Requirements

Unfortunately, there is no all-encompassing rule about when to expect permit requirements. This varies from agency to agency and can differ within states. However, requiring a permit is an acceptable practice all across the United States and internationally. You must be sure to either refer to a guidebook, check the applicable Web site, or contact the climbing area directly (i.e., make a phone call) to find out about the requirements. Permits are required in order to regulate use. Permits can also enable the land management agency or park to get valuable user information or to disseminate important information to the climber. Regardless of the circumstances, compliance is necessary. In addition, you should be aware that extra fees are sometimes involved with permits or insurance requirements.

At Enchanted Rock State Park in Texas, a new rule was passed requiring universities or companies to carry a specific amount of liability coverage in order to bring guided groups into the park. Most federal agencies require a special use permit for groups that fall under the category of "commercial." If you are accepting money for your services, you fall under this category. In certain parks, such as Rocky Mountain National Park, only one guiding company or outfitter (Colorado Mountain School) has a permit to take clients climbing. At Joshua Tree National Park, a classic climbing location, the rules have recently changed so that anyone leading a group must have (at a minimum) the climbing certification provided by the American Mountain Guide Association (www.amga.com) or the Professional Climbing Guides Institute (www.climbingguidesinstitute.org).

Leave No Trace Principles

It is important to remind ourselves once again of the Leave No Trace principles. Even if your favorite crag is a three-minute walk from the road and hardly qualifies as a "wilderness experience," the Leave No Trace principles help ensure that you prepare and use the area in a way that protects resources for the next generation of climbers. You should also make sure to familiarize yourself with the Leave No Trace principles specific to the type of terrain or area of the country you are climbing in. For instance, the Leave No Trace practices that are accepted in the Rocky Mountains may differ from those applied in a desert terrain.

The more the climbing community can do to promote and advocate responsible use in the outdoors, the more climbers will be respected and accepted by others.

Camping, Parking, and Fees

Lastly, you need to be aware that fees are often associated with overnight camping and parking. Some locations also charge a climbing fee. At many locations, the fees are not collected by a ranger or park attendant. In these cases, you might be asked to place your money in an envelope on which you would note your name, the date, and the number in your party. You then drop this envelope into a box provided at the location. For climbers, having cash on hand is important.

If you are organizing the trip and your friends are spending money and time to drive to a new climbing site, you do not want to let your friends down by failing to prepare. You may have some disgruntled friends if you are unaware of some rules or if you don't have the necessary fees or paperwork required to climb, preventing your group from being able to climb. The objective is to avoid surprises and to protect yourself and the climbing resources. It is also your responsibility to know the rules and to follow them. Trying to bypass the rules is never worth it, and adherence to good ethics is a matter of integrity. In some areas, rock climbing has fallen under scrutiny because of overcrowding, misunderstood risk, and damages to the environment. Every climber has a duty to support the sport of climbing as a whole by being responsible both to land management providers and to the environment. This helps ensure that access and opportunity are not limited in any way.

What's in an Itinerary?

Once you are clear on what rules and regulations might affect your trip, it is time to begin thinking about logistics. Spontaneity is a much treasured characteristic of being outdoors—and understandably so. Any outdoor endeavor is a chance to get away from the routine, the deadlines, and the set daily schedules. Seldom do you stick to a strict schedule when on an outdoor trip, and you will often lose track of time when you become engrossed in the activity at hand. However, having a rough idea of what a day of climbing might look like can be beneficial, especially when it comes to time management considerations (such as travel to and from the climbing location). Furthermore, if you or members of your party are new to climbing or new to a given location, a schedule provides a mental picture of what you are about to do. This can ease a troubled mind, decrease anxiety, and help you feel more in control. You should consider several items when you are creating your itinerary: (1) what time to leave based on how long it takes to get there, (2) estimated time that it will take to set up the climbs, (3) any time that must be allotted for on-site education or review that needs to occur before climbing (often called ground school), (4) time set aside for actual climbing and meals, and (5) estimated departure time from the site, as well as the estimated arrival time back home.

A sample itinerary might look something like this:

7:00 a.m.	Meet at rendezvous point and depart (eat breakfast before you come or bring it with you)
7:00 to 8:00 a.m.	Travel time
8:00 a.m.	Arrive at trail head and begin hike
9:00 a.m.	Arrive at climbing site
9:00 a.m. to 12:00 noon	Climbing
12:00 noon to 1:00 p.m.	Lunch break (bring your own)
1:00 to 3:30 p.m.	Climb at site 2
3:30 to 5:00 p.m.	Tear down, sweep area for trash, and hike out
5:00 p.m.	Depart
5:30 p.m.	Dinner
7:30 p.m.	Arrive home

Another aspect of good logistical planning is a checklist. A checklist can include anything you need to remember, from group gear to individual gear, paperwork, and vehicle details. (A sample checklist is provided at the end of the chapter.)

Your checklist should also have a section for standard equipment items needed for personal and group gear. In addition, you should include a section where you can note things specific to your trip. The importance of a checklist cannot be emphasized enough. Besides being useful, a checklist can help ease pretrip stress and lead to a calm and enjoyable departure.

General Risk Management Considerations

Formal risk management plans are usually associated with institutional climbing; however, understanding the general concepts behind risk management can benefit any climber, regardless of whether the climber is a beginner or an expert. This section addresses some of these concepts, including the scope of risk, physical risk, the dynamic aspects of risk management and personal evaluation. Many resources on risk management can be used to supplement your learning. Some excellent resources include *Lessons Learned: A Guide to Accident Prevention and Crisis Response, Adventure Risk Management in Adventure Programming,* and *Outdoor Leadership.*

No one likes to think about risk and accidents, but thinking through the "what ifs" is the best way to avoid regrets (or the lament of "if I had only . . ."). Formally, such a preventive step is known as a risk management plan. One aspect of a risk management plan is documenting important information about your trip and bringing that information with you. This information should also be included in a "flight plan" to be discussed at the end of this section. Another copy should be left with a trusted person who will be responsible for monitoring your return—this person will also be responsible for contacting the appropriate authorities if you have not returned by the time indicated in your plan. Part of the risk management plan should include the following:

1. Where and how you will be going
   a. This information will allow others to be able to find you in case of an emergency or if you fail to arrive back at your scheduled return time.
   b. Documenting your travel directions will allow others to retrace your steps.
2. Arrival time and departure time
   a. This gives others a clue that something has gone wrong if you do not arrive back when you indicated you would.
   b. You may also indicate in your risk management plan when family, friends, or your employer should begin to worry. (Climbers will often give themselves a cushion for unexpected delays such as a flat tire.)
3. Names of those attending
   a. You should create a simple list that identifies each individual on the trip, along with emergency contact information.
   b. Although you may not need to use a formal medical form with a group of friends, it is helpful for everyone to be aware of any pertinent medical conditions.

4. Name of the area or areas in which you will be climbing
   a. This should indicate trail head information along with estimated mileage and any distinguishing information about the areas you will be climbing.
   b. You should also provide a detailed description of how other people could find you if they needed to.

5. Emergency numbers
   a. Provide the contact number for you or whoever is in charge.
   b. Numbers that could be used in case of an emergency should also be included, such as the local police or sheriff, any park or land management agency emergency number, local search and rescue, and the nearest hospital.
   c. You should also include information on whom to call if someone were to find you unconscious. If you are guiding a trip and need to call back to your office or to your boss, you should include these numbers as well. You do not want to realize that you don't know how to get in touch with anyone at your workplace while in the middle of an emergency.

Another aspect of the risk management plan is anticipating scenarios or situations before they occur. For the individual climber, risk management is nothing more than a mental exercise of thinking through possible risks, potential accidents, the consequences of potential accidents, and the steps needed to avoid these risks (or at least minimize them). In addition, some preplanning should be done regarding what steps will be taken in the event of an accident. Risk management requires critical thinking but is a worthwhile exercise for anyone. It can involve simple things such as the person doing the driving for the trip making a point of telling everyone else where he is putting his car keys. If something were to happen to this person, precious time is not wasted looking for the car keys. Thinking ahead about potential scenarios results in you being more prepared and ready to respond when a real situation arises.

Scope of Risk

In the context of rock climbing, risk is often perceived to mean physical injury. However, risk is not limited to just physical injury or death. Risk is defined as the potential to lose something of value and can include emotional, physical, psychological, financial, or property loss. For example, when expectations are not met, disappointment follows. If you are led to believe that you will have a certain type of experience for a certain amount of money, but then you receive less than you were promised, you have experienced some financial loss—the product you received was not worth the value of your money. When you think about the risks of any rock-climbing trip, do not limit your considerations to just physical injury. On a recent trip where mules were used as transport, a group was informed of the possible risk that bags could take a permanent trip down the river. With this information, group members could make informed decisions about what they allowed to be transported by mule and what they opted to carry on their back.

Physical Risk

Certainly, there is a difference between the risks associated with disappointment or some financial loss and the risk of physical injury. Also, a minor injury (such as a scrape or strain) and a major injury (such as a broken bone) are not as severe as an accident that leads to permanent disability or death. As a responsible climber, you must assume that every decision has an outcome as well as consequences that go along with that

> Consider what you want to do in relation to what you are capable of doing. Climbing is, above all, a matter of integrity.
>
> *Gaston Rébuffat*

outcome. You cannot know every outcome with certainty, and it is impossible to foresee everything. However, in climbing, you will be faced with judgment calls based on your experience and your ability to anticipate potential consequences. Therefore, when faced with scenarios that expose you or others to risk, you should ask yourself what the worst-case scenario would be. Consider the likelihood that things could go wrong, and then make your decision.

Dynamic Aspects of Risk Management

In rock climbing, the dynamic aspect of risk management must be taken into account because conditions in the outdoors can change so quickly. A storm can appear in an instant, or an illness or injury can strike suddenly. You might find yourself in a new climbing area that is very exposed to rock fall, or the actions of someone in an outside party might pose a threat to your group. Whatever the circumstances, you must evaluate the potential for risk and make decisions appropriately. This ongoing process makes risk management dynamic because there is not an obvious beginning and end until the trip is completely over. With this being said, you can deal with the dynamic aspects of risk management by continually asking yourself the following two questions: "What is the nature of the risk?" and "What level of risk is acceptable?"

Personal Evaluation

In summary, whether you are climbing individually or taking a group of friends on a climbing trip, you must evaluate each situation, identify the risk involved, and determine what consequences you can accept. Another way to approach risk management is to consider if the benefits of a particular action outweigh the risks. This is often referred to as the risk management equation.

Risk Management Scenarios

The following list highlights some of the common mistakes that all climbers can make; however, beginners are most susceptible to these errors. These scenarios should be seen as examples. As a climber, your challenge is to think through the other possible scenarios that could arise, identify the reason they might occur, and determine how you could prevent them.

1. Injuries occurring when climbers hit the ground at the beginning of a climb

   Why: Elongation of the rope while the climber is close to the ground

   Prevention: Keep a tight belay or use spotters until climbers are at a distance where they are safe from a ground fall caused by the stretch in the rope.

2. Belayers being pulled off the ground when a climber falls

   Why: Inexperience and a disparity in weight between the climber and the belayer

   Prevention: Use a person as a backup anchor, or use a ground anchor to secure the belayer.

3. Forgetting to lock a carabiner, double-back the harness, or wear a helmet

   Why: Too many new skills to remember; lack of habit

   Prevention: Use commands and follow a systematic checklist.

   Reminder: "On belay" is the first command and should cue the belayer to check to make sure (1) all slack is removed from the rope, (2) helmet is on properly (covers forehead with snug fit), (3) harness is backed up, (4) carabiners are locked, (5) knots are tied correctly, and (6) both climber and belayer are ready and focused. The "five Hs" is a common phrase used to describe the belayer's responsibilities (see table 4.2).

Table 4.2   The Five Hs

Harness	The harness is doubled back on the belayer as well as the climber.
Helmet	The helmet is on and secured tightly.
Hardware	The knot is tied correctly. The knot is secured to the harness according to the manufacturer's recommendations. The carabiner is locked, and the belay device is rigged correctly.
Hair	Hair is pulled back and away from hardware. In addition, the belayer should check to make sure that jewelry or anything else (rings, clothing) that could get caught while climbing is removed.
Human	The belayer ensures that the climber is mentally and physically ready to climb.

4. Unclipping and becoming unprotected at a ledge

Why: Sensory overload, being in a hurry, and possible anxiety

Prevention: Use a buddy system on the ground. Have someone watching you to make sure you are always clipped in. Communicate each move with your climbing partner.

5. Belaying errors

Why: Lack of experience performing a new skill

Prevention: Practice with your belayer and observe his skill before you climb. Select a self-locking belay device that your belayer is proficient in using. Have someone with more experience observe. Use a backup belayer.

6. Lowering errors

Why: Poor communication

Prevention: (1) Practice good and consistent communication, and (2) create a closed belay system by ensuring both ends of the rope are secured (one end fastened to climber, the other with a knot tied in the rope). These are simple steps that can prevent common lowering errors—such as climbers leaning back and falling because they mistakenly believe they are on belay (and about to be lowered) or belayers who simply allow the end of the rope to feed out of the belay devise resulting in a fall by the climber.

Although these scenarios are just a few examples, they demonstrate that with each action or component of any climbing trip, the potential exists for things to go wrong. If you take the time to think through each of them and establish an action plan to address each one, you will decrease the likelihood of their occurrence. Risk management is like preventative medicine. We take intentional measures to decrease the likelihood of accidents happening.

Bringing It All Together

When you have completed all the planning steps covered in this section, you should put it all together to create a "flight plan." A copy of your flight plans should be left with someone not going on the trip or with your employer. You should also carry one set with you. As a review, your flight plan should include the following components:

1. Date of trip
2. Location of trip
3. Names and phone numbers of those attending
4. Directions and planned route for travel, which may include a map
5. Estimated departure time and return
6. Location of where you will be and what trail head you will use to access the climbing area
7. Any alternative locations if you are not at the initially planned location
8. Emergency numbers (including local police or sheriff, land management emergency numbers, nearest hospital, and whom to contact in case of an emergency)

and the location of the nearest telephone (land line) in case cell service is not available (e.g., a gas station)

9. Itinerary of the climbing trip
10. Checklist for personal and group gear
11. Potential hazards and risks and how these will be addressed or minimized
12. Plan of action in the event of an accident

To prepare yourself, think of some potential risk management scenarios that you might encounter on a rock-climbing trip. Come up with solutions or preventions for the scenarios you have been faced with.

What to Bring

As you have seen throughout this chapter, the various styles and types of rock climbing can affect how you prepare for your climb. This section provides information that will assist you in selecting gear for almost any rock-climbing outing, regardless of the type of climbing you will be engaging in. The end of this section provides a list of ten essential systems that rock climbers should consider employing in order to survive emergencies and stay comfortable when things don't go according to plan.

Soft goods include ropes, slings, and shoes.

Soft Goods

Soft goods refer to rock-climbing gear that is composed of fabric material, including harnesses, ropes, slings (runners), and shoes. Soft goods needed for most climbing outings include the following: one dynamic rope; one harness for the climber and one for the belayer; and enough slings (approximately six) to anchor the belayer, climber, and rope according to the standard practices noted in chapter 5. As noted earlier in this chapter, you should ensure that your rope is sufficiently long enough for your chosen route. Many guidebooks provide recommendations for the length of rope in a particular area. Climbers who rappel often should invest in a static or nonstretching rope.

Hard Goods

Belay and rappel devices, carabiners, and artificial protection are considered to be the hard goods necessary for most rock-climbing activities. Most belay devices are designed to handle a broad range of rope diameters, and most are adequate for rappelling (see chapters 5 and 10 for more information). If you will be rappelling often or if your belay device kinks the rope when rappelling, consider purchasing a device such as a figure eight descender or rack-style device that is designed specifically for rappelling. If you will just be top-rope climbing, then only the belayer will need a belay device. The type and amount of carabiners you bring should be determined by the type of climbing and the location you choose. Because the number of carabiners needed on any given climb can vary a great deal, you should always have more on hand than you think you may need. You will need one locking carabiner for attaching your

Hard goods include belay and rappel devices, carabiners, artificial protection, and your helmet.

belay device to the belay loop on your harness. The belay carabiner is often used only for this purpose. Locking carabiners are usually used to attach the rope to anchor slings in a top-rope or rappelling system. Nonlocking carabiners are used to attach anchor slings to each other, attach quickdraws to bolt anchors and the rope while sport climbing (at least 30 nonlocking carabiners or 15 quickdraws are needed for a sport climb with 15 bolts), and attach protection pieces to the climbing rope while traditional climbing. See the information on sport climbing in chapter 11 for more details. The final piece of essential equipment for outdoor climbing outings is a helmet for both the climber and the belayer.

CONSUMER TIP

"Quick links" found in hardware stores are a cheap alternative to "leaver biners" on climbs that may have bolt hangers at the top but no chains or means to attach your rope to the bolt hangers.

Some nonessential but helpful rock-climbing gear includes chalk and a chalk bag, a bag to transport all your gear, and a rope bag to store your climbing rope and protect it from ground debris while climbing. If you will be traditional climbing, you should bring a device (often referred to as a nut tool) for dislodging stuck protection gear from the rock. Some people prefer to wear leather gloves while belaying and rappelling; if you choose to wear gloves, make sure they don't interfere with your ability to grip and handle the rope. Athletic tape is often used to protect hands from abrasive rock while climbing cracks. A foldable pocket knife can be helpful in emergency situations (make sure the knife cannot open unintentionally). Additional items are identified as part of the ten essential systems (see sidebar on this page).

TEN ESSENTIAL SYSTEMS

The list of systems has been adapted from the traditional list of ten essentials in order to encompass new technology and allow for ingenuity on the part of the climber.

1. Navigation
2. Sun protection
3. Insulation
4. Illumination
5. First aid supplies
6. Fire
7. Repair kit and tools
8. Nutrition
9. Hydration
10. Emergency shelter

Source: Cox, S., & Fulsaas, K. (Eds.). (2003). *Mountaineering: The freedom of the hills* (7th ed.). Seattle, WA: Mountaineers Books.

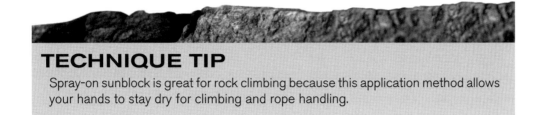

TECHNIQUE TIP
Spray-on sunblock is great for rock climbing because this application method allows your hands to stay dry for climbing and rope handling.

Essential Systems

The ten essential systems are described as follows:

1. **Navigation.** Climbers should be able to reach their destination and return safely. Mistakes in route finding are often a climber's first steps toward putting themselves in dangerous situations. You should carry and know how to read topographical maps. Knowing how to use a compass and GPS unit is also helpful.

2. **Sun protection.** Sunburn and sunstroke are common ailments for rock climbers who do not use sun protection. Sunglasses, a hat, and sunscreen (minimum of SPF 15) are small items that should always be included in your climbing pack. When possible, you should coordinate your climbing to take advantage of the shade provided by rock walls.

3. **Insulation.** Besides the clothing you would use for a normal rock-climbing outing, you should have insulating layers that would enable you to survive an unplanned night out. This is especially important for remote climbs.

4. **Illumination.** Will you be able to continue on a climb or be able to hike from a climb once darkness has set in? Keep a small headlamp with a set of extra batteries in your pack for those climbs that take longer than you expected.

5. **Medical supplies.** Keep a small first aid kit in your pack. You may need to add or remove items from your kit based on the length and remoteness of your trips. More important, you must know how to use your first aid kit. Certification in Wilderness First Aid (WFA) or Wilderness First Responder (WFR) is priceless.

6. **Fire.** The ability to start a fire when you are cold and wet can be very important. Butane lighters, waterproof matches, manual spark makers, and fire-starting material should be considered when heading into the backcountry. Keep your fire-starting material in a waterproof container.

7. **Repair kit and tools.** Critical gear carried into the backcountry should be reparable or replaceable with tools and equipment found in this kit. Research the best ways to fix the gear you carry, and design your repair kit accordingly. Duct tape and a multitool with knife and pliers are two of the most important items found in such a kit.

8. **Nutrition.** As in the case of insulation, nutrition refers to carrying an amount of extra food that is dependent on the remoteness of your rock-climbing location and the length of your trip. Carry food that will withstand being knocked about in your pack, doesn't need to be cooked, and will stay fresh.

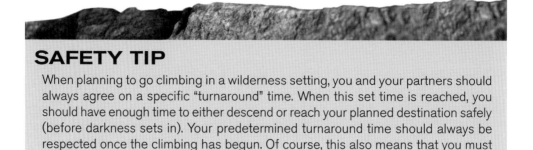

SAFETY TIP

When planning to go climbing in a wilderness setting, you and your partners should always agree on a specific "turnaround" time. When this set time is reached, you should have enough time to either descend or reach your planned destination safely (before darkness sets in). Your predetermined turnaround time should always be respected once the climbing has begun. Of course, this also means that you must bring a watch.

9. **Hydration.** As with nutrition, hydration refers to carrying extra water in addition to what you would already be carrying. The ability to purify water through mechanical purifiers, boiling, or chemical tablets is equally important, because your extra water may not see you through an unexpected ordeal. Adding electrolyte powder to your water can be an easy and lightweight way of maintaining your energy.

10. **Emergency shelter.** When you are on a day outing in a remote area, you should carry an emergency shelter in case your climb takes longer than you anticipated, you get lost, or unexpected weather forces you to stop. An emergency shelter can be a trash bag, a tarp, a waterproof house sheathing, a tent fly, a small tent, a bivy sack, or even a backpack designed as a backup emergency bivy sack. The options are numerous; you just need to make sure your shelter is water- and windproof and will hold up to a night on the rock. If you do have an unplanned night out (bivouac), you should use your rope or backpack as insulation between the ground and your body, cover yourself in your emergency bivy, and remove any wet layers of clothing.

There is a fine line between carrying all the gear you need to be safe and carrying so much gear that you are slowed down, thus adversely affecting your safety. You should experiment with different equipment and be creative with your gear. For climbing in the backcountry, a general rule is that each piece of equipment you carry should be useful for at least two purposes. Avoid bringing gear that duplicates the purpose that another piece accomplishes. At the same time, you should never sacrifice essential gear that is related to your physical well-being. When preparing for a climb, having a list of what gear to bring is very helpful; however, understanding the limitations of gear and the risks you face while rock climbing—even when carrying the best gear—is still more important. The following section discusses rock-climbing safety and the dangers that climbers encounter.

Personal Climbing Safety

Consideration for your personal well-being should permeate all other considerations as you prepare to go rock climbing. Though you may not have known it, you are already off to a good start for climbing safely. Previous topics in this chapter have prompted you to make realistic assessments of your own abilities, to select a proper location, and to decide on the proper climbing gear. These are some of the most important decisions that will affect your safety while rock climbing. The old adage "an ounce of prevention is worth a pound of cure" is wisdom that all rock climbers should hold close. In this section, we discuss the types of dangers you may encounter while rock climbing and how you can reduce the risk they pose to you and those you climb with.

Objective Danger

To better understand the hazards that accompany rock climbing, you need to make a distinction between naturally occurring (objective) dangers and human-initiated (subjective) dangers. Objective dangers refer to naturally occurring phenomena that can be present in any natural environment. Such natural events and conditions occur regularly, without human initiation, and they only become risks when humans are present. Objective dangers in a rock-climbing setting can include falling rock, rain, sun, extreme temperatures, lightning, and, of course, gravity. The possibility and number of objective dangers generally increase as the remoteness of the climbing area increases.

Good judgment comes from experience. Experience comes from bad judgment.

Evan Hardin

Objective dangers are a constant in rock climbing. To be removed from these dangers entirely, you will need to climb in a gym or not climb at all. However, it is possible to mitigate the risk of objective dangers you may encounter while rock climbing. Having knowledge of weather patterns, using caution when climbing on new terrain, testing holds, and being familiar with the topics covered in this book are all positive steps toward reducing the risk that objective dangers pose. Obtaining first aid training is another step you can take to increase your chances (and those of your climbing partners) of surviving an encounter with objective dangers.

Subjective Danger

As previously mentioned, subjective dangers refer to human-based dangers that can cause harm to the climber or to others climbing with or around the climber. Common subjective dangers include overconfidence in abilities, ignorance, being ill-equipped, being out of shape, and misuse of gear. A majority of rock-climbing accidents that involve injury or death are related to dangers that are subjective in nature—in other words, they are preventable. Frequently, accidents occur when objective dangers are encountered (unintentionally or otherwise) by a rock climber who then introduces subjective dangers by responding to the objective danger with faulty reasoning and poor decision making.

Because you have more control over yourself than over the natural environment, addressing any subjective dangers you may exhibit is one of the best ways to promote safety while rock climbing. Several psychological influences affect a person's propensities for certain subjective dangers.

Perhaps the most obvious psychological factor that affects climbing safety is fear. *Excessive* fear can paralyze your motion and conjure thoughts that destroy your confidence to move up the rock or perform necessary actions (such as tying knots or clipping the rope to carabiners). Of course, when realistic and controlled, fear is healthy and important because it reminds you of the consequences of mistakes. The trick is to be able to assess and distinguish actual risks from falsely perceived risks. Such realistic assessments of risk will enable you to have confidence in your physical abilities, your climbing systems, and your climbing equipment, which allow you to avoid actual risks.

Climbing within your ability is also affected by several psychological factors. People often have a desire to perform or compete that can lead them to attempt climbing routes that put them in danger (routes that are beyond their physical capabilities). The related concepts of confirmation bias and nonevent feedback also play a psychological role in influencing how people stay safe while rock climbing. Confirmation bias suggests that humans prefer to confirm rather than disprove their hypotheses. Once a climber has started a route, the climber has adopted the hypothesis that the climb is doable; when faced with contradictory evidence, such as poor weather or loose rock, the climber will unrealistically hold to the original hypothesis (that the climb is doable) and will continue on. Nonevent feedback occurs when a rock climber experiences a dangerous situation without any harmful outcomes (Atkins, 2003). It is easy to see how situations involving nonevent feedback can influence a rock climber's decisions made with confirmation-biased hypotheses. For example, a climber may tell himself the following: "I have climbed a route similar to this before without any problems (nonevent feedback). In addition, the guidebook says it is an easy 5.6, and I can climb 5.9 (confirmation bias). Therefore, the loose rock I am encountering and the setting sun shouldn't be a problem." Addressing subjective dangers involves realistic self-assessment of your mental and physical abilities. It also involves an awareness of the psychological factors influencing your decisions. Simply being aware of these dynamics is often impetus enough to allow you to mentally step back from situations and make decisions rationally and objectively.

PRACTICAL SAFETY STEPS

In addition to understanding the dangers you face while climbing, you can take a number of practical steps to reduce your chances of harm in the event of a rock-climbing accident:

- Always wear a helmet to protect your head from falling rocks or gear and from collisions with the rock face.
- Regularly check the condition of all your climbing gear, and store it properly when not in use (see chapter 5).
- Discard any climbing gear that is worn or abraded, has been exposed to chemicals, or is past its manufacturer's suggested life expectancy.
- Stay up-to-date on the best practices for anchor systems by reading relevant literature (see chapter 8).
- Know your knots and anchor systems inside and out. You should be able to spot an improperly tied knot from 20 feet (6.1 m) away.
- Always give a copy of your itinerary to someone who is not going with you on the climbing trip.
- Always carry a fully charged cell phone in case of an emergency. Identify spots where you have the best chance to establish reception, but be aware that many places don't get cell reception.
- Always be prepared to rescue yourself and your climbing partners. Don't assume that carrying a cell phone nulls your responsibility to be able to rescue yourself.
- Read the annually published *Accidents in North American Mountaineering* by the American Alpine Club to gain awareness about how accidents occur and how to avoid accidents.

Overcoming subjective dangers and learning to exist among objective dangers are an important part of becoming a proficient rock climber—just as important as training your muscles to move you up the rock. Self-awareness, training, keeping current with best practices, learning from others, and personal experience are all contributing factors toward your safety while rock climbing.

Lionel Terray, the famous and historic mountaineer, summarized the nature of objective and subjective dangers as follows:

> Whatever his skill and natural aptitude, the climber who abandons the beaten track for the profounder and more austere joys of the great alpine walls, or the highest summits in the world, will always have to undergo serious risks. The mineral world into which he forces his way was not made for man, and all its forces seem to unite to reject him. Anyone who dares seek the beauty

and sublime grandeur of such places must accept the gage. But as far as the man himself is concerned, careful physical and technical training in the complex arts of surmounting rock and ice can eliminate almost all subjective risk.

Dangers stemming from the forces of nature, called objective dangers, are very much harder to avoid. In doing big climbs on high mountains it is impossible never to pass under a tottering serac, never to go in places where a stone could fall, or never to set out in any but perfect conditions. He who respects all the wise rules found in the climbing manuals virtually condemns himself to inaction (Terray, 1963, p. 74).

Climbing Etiquette

In previous sections, we touched on some issues related to interacting conscientiously with the environment and those around you while rock climbing. The following are some additional guidelines for basic etiquette that you should keep in mind when you go rock climbing.

- Avoid walking between the belay and the rock, especially when the climber is low enough that he could hit you if he fell. If you must walk under a rope, ask the belayer for permission first.
- Be aware of pathways along the base of climbing areas. Keep your gear in a bag and off the trails. As a belayer, you should stand on either side (preferably on the side closest to the rock) to allow access for others to freely come and go.
- If you drop anything from a climb, yell "Rock!"
- Do not throw your rope down from the top of a climb without first making sure it will not land on anyone. When you do toss your rope, yell "Rope." Once you have yelled "Rope," listen for a "Clear" from those on the ground before you toss the rope.
- Don't camp out on a climb that others want to use. Share.
- Don't leave your rope set up on a climb unattended.
- While on multipitch climbs, allow faster parties to pass when it is safe to do so.
- Do not alter a climb by removing bolts, attaching holds, or chipping the rock.
- Keep dogs on a leash. Believe it or not, not everyone loves Fido as much as you do.
- Don't be too loud. Although climbing areas certainly are not libraries, loud and obnoxious behavior is generally not appreciated. You may even want to consider keeping your *Masters of Stone II* soundtrack at home.
- Practice Leave No Trace principles.

If you will be climbing in a large group, try to avoid climbing at popular (i.e., overcrowded) locations and on weekends. Indeed, finding a parking spot on a sunny Saturday may be the most dangerous aspect of a day of climbing at a popular crag. This same location can be vacant during the week. If you will be climbing in a large group, remember to spread out along the rock, be prepared to share your top-roped routes, and respect the experiences other climbers will be having.

Climbers assume responsibility for their safety, the safety of those around them, and the general well-being of the area they are climbing in. Many climbing areas are on privately owned land or are used based on special agreements with state and federal agencies. Landowners are known to protect their property by restricting or shutting down climbing areas that have been misused by climbers who fail to act courteously and reflect the etiquette practices just described. Climbing etiquette is not only important for you and those you are climbing around, but also for everyone who enjoys these areas. Several other etiquette issues are covered in other chapters.

Beyond the acquisition of skills and climbing etiquette, you also need to consider the role you will play in climbing trips. When people take up a new recreational hobby, especially one as exciting as rock climbing, they often want to introduce others to it as well. You may want to introduce your friends to rock climbing, and they may bring along their friends—and before you know it, you are "in charge." The lines can become blurred between what constitutes just a group of friends out climbing and when you are formally or informally leading others. You need to be aware of the expectations of others. If you are the expert, your friends may think that you are "leading" them, whether or not you are accepting money. Although it may not be necessary to have your friends sign a release form, it is a good idea to let them know of the inherent risks of the trip. If you are indeed leading others (even informally) in a rock-climbing experience, you need to feel comfortable with your abilities. Guided climbing, by definition, infers that you are accepting payment for taking others climbing, and it suggests a high level of skill and responsibility. Individuals who are professional guides are prepared to accept legal and moral responsibility for leading others. The purpose of this book is to teach fundamental rock-climbing skills and to prepare you for leadership of top-rope climbing. Guiding is not within the context of this book, and the climber who wishes to consider guiding should pursue professional training. Beginning climbers should also be encouraged to seek training from professionals—through a clinic, course, guide, academic class, climbing school, and so on.

Summary

In summary, being prepared is the first step in obtaining a good foundation for rock climbing. To be a responsible climber, you need to understand all aspects of the level of climbing in which you want to participate. There is no substitute for sound skills and good training. Understanding terminology, good practices, and the scope of climbing will make you better informed, safer, and prepared to make good decisions. Reading about accidents is a great way to learn, to evaluate your own understanding, and to grasp all that you still have to learn. An excellent resource for this is the yearly publication of *Accidents in North American Mountaineering*. While sobering, this book is a great tool. Your greatest resource is your commitment to learning and to climb safely from trained, experienced climbers. In many ways, gaining experience is like putting together a puzzle. Once all of the pieces are put together, you have a complete and accurate picture; thus, you are then prepared to venture into the activity of choice. When one piece is missing, there may be problems—problems you might not have anticipated. The purpose of this book is to help provide you with knowledge in all the areas necessary to give you sound foundational skills. The next important piece of the climbing puzzle is gaining knowledge about selecting the proper clothing and the appropriate equipment.

Group Equipment

- ☐ Tents
- ☐ Water bag
- ☐ Potable water
- ☐ First aid kit
- ☐ Compass
- ☐ Rope for bear bag
- ☐ Stuff sacks for food
- ☐ Stoves
- ☐ Fuel bottles
- ☐ Spatula
- ☐ Ladle
- ☐ Spoon
- ☐ Pots and lids
- ☐ Fry pan
- ☐ Soap
- ☐ Matches or lighter
- ☐ Extra zip-top bags
- ☐ Toilet paper
- ☐ Trowel

Logistics

Automobile

- ☐ Oil checked
- ☐ Gas checked
- ☐ Lights and signals checked
- ☐ Spare tire and jack

- ☐ Fire extinguisher
- ☐ Walkie-talkies

Important Phone Numbers
- ☐ Emergency dispatch: 911
- ☐ Park rangers: _____
- ☐ Sheriff: _____
- ☐ Hospitals: _____

Climbing Equipment

- ☐ Helmets (Providing head protection for climber and belayer)
- ☐ Harnesses
- ☐ Carabiners (Attaching the rope, harness, and protection gear to each other)
- ☐ Belay or rappel devices (Controlling the rope on ascent and descent of the rock)
- ☐ Protection and trad gear
- ☐ Climbing Shoes (Ascending grade 5 rock)
- ☐ Sit harness (Linking you to your rope, the rock, and your partner)
- ☐ Dynamic climbing rope (Protecting you from dangerous falls and allowing you to descend the rock)
- ☐ Slings, runners, and webbing or cordelette (Building anchors and attaching yourself and your gear to the rock)
- ☐ Quickdraws (Attaching two carabiners to bolt hangers for sport climbing)
- ☐ Artificial protection (Building anchors and traditional lead climbing)

Your Own Miscellaneous Items
- ☐
- ☐
- ☐

CHAPTER 5

Gearing Up for Rock Climbing

With the best
equipment in the
world the man with
poor judgment is
in mortal danger.

Royal Robbins

Proper equipment is an essential part of the rock-climbing experience; however, the knowledge of how to use gear properly and care for it is equally important. Many climbers have gotten hurt or even killed from the improper use of their climbing gear. This chapter covers basic equipment used in rock climbing. For each type of equipment, information is provided about its function and use, proper care, proper fitting, cleaning, storage, and approximate cost (U.S. dollars). (Instructions for using the equipment are not provided in this chapter but are discussed throughout the book.) Approximate prices are not included for all equipment items because the prices will vary from year to year. See the table at the end of the chapter for recommended equipment for various types of climbing.

Climbing Ropes

The climbing rope is the most essential piece of equipment that a climber uses. It is the lifeline of the climber, connecting him to a safety net that can arrest his fall and save his life. Modern climbing ropes are very dependable. This is largely because of the international standards placed on the climbing rope industry.

Figure 5.1 Kernmantle rope with core exposed and sheath around it.

Climbing ropes typically consist of a core of long twisted fibers known as the kern and an outer sheath of woven colored fibers known as the mantle. Hence, these ropes are referred to as kernmantle ropes (see figure 5.1). The core provides most of the tensile strength, while the sheath is a durable layer that protects the core and gives the rope desirable handling characteristics. The cost of a climbing rope can vary. Factors such as diameter, treatment, length, and number of falls a rope will sustain play a role in the suggested retail price of a climbing rope. Ropes can range in price from $130 to $200.

Rope Types

The ropes used for climbing can be divided into two classes: dynamic ropes and static ropes. Dynamic ropes have a certain amount of elasticity and are usually used as belay ropes for top-rope climbing or lead climbing (see chapter 7 for more information on belaying). The elasticity reduces the maximum force experienced by both a climber and her equipment should she fall. The forces generated in a fall can be extreme; a climber's body and equipment could not sustain these forces without the elasticity of the dynamic rope.

Static ropes are less elastic than dynamic ropes, and they are usually used for carrying or attaching equipment. They are also used for rappelling because they make for an easier descent. Static ropes cannot be used for lead climbing because too much force will be generated in a fall, causing damage to the climber and breaking equipment.

Strength

The only ropes approved for climbing come with endorsement from the Union Internationale des Associations d'Alpinisme, or UIAA (www.uiaa.ch/index.aspx). The UIAA is an international organization that sets minimum standards for all commercially available rope as well as other climbing equipment. The UIAA tests ropes to make sure they are able to hold falls of the most extreme kind. In a single-rope test, an 80-kilogram (176 lb) weight is attached to a 2.5-meter (8.2 ft) rope, and the weight is dropped 5.0 meters (16.4

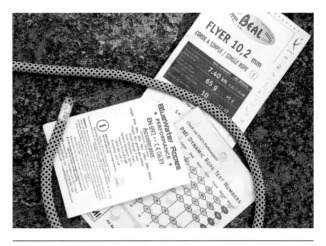

Figure 5.2 Rope tag showing UIAA numbers and information.

ft). A half-rope test is made by attaching a 55-kilogram (121 lb) weight to a 2.5-meter rope, and the weight is dropped 4.8 meters (15.7 ft) (see the UIAA Web site for more details of the rope tests). Climbers should not buy a rope that is not UIAA approved. Rope manufacturers provide the findings from tests performed by the UIAA on the rope tag found on the end of the rope (see figure 5.2).

The first number on the rope tag will be either a 1 or 1/2. A rope with a 1 is a single rope and is considered safe for use by itself; a rope with 1/2 is a double rope and must be used in conjunction with another similar rope. Single ropes are the most common type of ropes used in the United States; however, double rope systems are used more extensively in Europe and other countries, and they can be used in most conditions. The main advantage of using this type of rope is the simple rope handling. The standard single rope is 10.5 or 11.0 millimeters in diameter and 60 meters (197 ft) long. Twin ropes (two separate thin ropes of the same size used primarily in ultralong rock and ice routes) must only be used in pairs and are clipped together into each piece of protection, as with single-rope technique. The two ropes offer redundancy and thus increased safety in the case of shock loading (when slack occurs in the rope while climbing and a fall can generate up to four times more force than falls that occur without slack) over a sharp edge, which may result in cutting of one of the ropes. Twin ropes are especially suited for alpine climbing or on routes where retreat may be necessary. They offer the highest safety margin and allow full-length rappels. Another two-rope setup is referred to as half or double ropes. This setup uses two separate ropes of the same size, and each rope is clipped separately into pieces of protection or gear. This differs from twin ropes in that a larger diameter of rope is used (usually 8.8 millimeters) and the ropes clip into the gear or protection devices independently, instead of together. The major advantage of double ropes over single or twin ropes is that they place less force on gear in the event of a fall. See chapter 10 for information on rope techniques.

Elongation

The strength of a rope is measured by the rating of static elongation and maximum impact force. The elongation measures the amount a rope stretches when weighted with a standard load (80 kilograms [176 lb]). Ropes with low static elongation stretch less; therefore, higher static elongation means ropes have more stretch, which will cushion the impact of a fall. Maximum impact force refers to the amount of force transmitted to a climber during a fall. Low maximum impact force means the rope, not the climber or the protection, absorbs more of the energy generated in a fall. However, such ropes stretch more, increasing a climber's chance of hitting the ground or a ledge.

Diameter

Rope diameters range from 7.5 to 11.0 millimeters. A thicker diameter rope means a stronger and more durable rope, but it is also heavier. Historically, a rope diameter between 10 and 11 millimeters is appropriate for travel on rock, ice, and glaciers. However, newer ropes such as the 9.1-millimeter Beal Joker are available for single-roped rock climbing. Ropes with a diameter less than 10 millimeters can also be used in pairs and clipped to separate protection pieces (using the double-rope technique) to reduce rope drag.

Length

Rope length should be chosen based on the types of routes you typically climb. Longer ropes allow for longer pitches and rappels; however, shorter ropes weigh less and take up less space. Although the standard rope length has been 50 meters (164 ft) and is still adequate for many climbing areas, most modern climbs are longer and require a 60-meter (200 ft) rope. Having a 200-foot rope allows the sport climber to lead to the top, clip the top anchors, and lower back to the ground. When top-roping with groups, these longer ropes are advantageous because you can set up a slingshot belay with a top-rope anchor, allowing both ends of the rope to touch the ground.

Rope Treatments

When shopping for a climbing rope, you might want to consider buying a treated rope. Manufacturers provide ropes treated with a waterproof compound called dry treatment. This consists of silicone or other fluorochemicals that provide some water resistance, protection against ultraviolet rays, and increased resistance to abrasion. No treatment can completely waterproof a rope, but dry treatment can make a rope much more resistant to water than an untreated rope. Dry treatment does however dramatically reduce the effect of ultraviolet rays that can damage the rope and cause it to become weak. Additionally, this dry treatment has been shown to increase the abrasion resistance of rope by approximately 33 percent when compared to nontreated ropes. The extent of this treatment can influence the rope's handling ability by making it stiffer. A double dry treatment is also available on climbing ropes. This involves treating the core fibers as well as the outer sheath with dry treatment. Dry-treated ropes are recommended for use in longer climbs where the rope could get soaked or freeze, such as in alpine rock climbing.

Climbing Rope Care

A rope may appear to be in good condition, not having any signs of wear and tear, but it still may have questionable usability. The amount that the rope has been used—the total number of climbs as well as the number of falls—will determine a rope's usability.

TECHNIQUE TIP
Marking the Center of Your Rope

You will often need to know where the center of your rope is—for example, when rappelling down (you need half your rope on either side of the anchor) or while belaying (you need to know how much rope is left for the leader). An easy way to do this is to tie a whip knot around the center (www.inquiry.net/images/whip.jpg) with dental floss or thin cotton thread. Bicolor ropes that change colors or patterns at the center of the rope are also available. Standard markers or paint should not be used for this because they can reduce rope strength by 50 percent. However, there are special marking pens available that won't compromise the strength of the rope.

The more a rope is used, the more it will stretch and the less it will return to its original length. As a result, the rope will be less likely to stretch and elongate in order to absorb the energy generated in a fall. The UIAA suggests replacing rope after 10 years if it is rarely used; however, you may need to replace rope after 3 months of daily use or a year of regular weekend climbing. Certainly, the type of use will determine the life expectancy of the rope. For example, when a rope is used for sport climbing, which requires more hanging on the rope, replacement may be needed more often. Regardless of the application, remember that a long fall or abrasion may require that the rope be retired immediately. Another thing to keep in mind regarding rope care and replacement is sheath slippage. All kernmantle ropes have a distinct core and sheath. With use, it is inevitable that the sheath of a rope will, to some extent, slip over the internal core. This is accentuated by the use of descenders and belay devices. Sheath slippage ultimately reduces the life of a rope because it causes wear points. More significantly, it makes a rope much more difficult to handle and manage.

Here is a list of things that should be done to take care of climbing ropes:

- Check the rope regularly. As with all other rock-climbing gear, visual inspection is very important. Check the rope for signs of wear and tear—such as damaged sheath, fraying, flat spots, and abrasion—before and after each climb. Do this by folding the rope carefully between your fingers and working it from one end to the other.

- Use the rope only for what it is designed for. In other words, climbing ropes should be used for climbing purposes only (do not tow your truck with it).

- Make sure that the rope is always clean. This does not mean that you need to wash your rope every time it is used. You just need to clean it when it gets dirty after many uses. The rope should be machine washed (without an agitator) using cold or warm water and nondetergent soap. Use the delicate fabric setting, and rinse twice. Do not use bleach or other chemicals that can weaken the nylon rope. Air-dry the rope away from direct sunlight by spreading it out on the floor, letting the water evaporate until the rope is dry.

- Do not step on the rope. Doing so can cause dirt particles to go deeper and damage rope fibers. Since glass is made out of sand, if you grind sand into the rope, it is essentially the same as grinding in small particles of glass that can cut the fibers.

- Store the climbing rope in a rope bag if it is not being used. This will keep it clean and out of direct sunlight. Direct sunlight, acids, and oxidizing agents can weaken the rope and shorten its life.

BUYING NEW VERSUS USED EQUIPMENT

Climbers are often tempted to buy used equipment to save a few bucks. This can be a dilemma when the budget is tight and a climber is just getting started. Generally, used equipment should never be purchased because the climber does not know its history (e.g., how many times a rope has taken a fall, or whether it has been exposed to lots of rain or UV light). Additionally, carabiners could have been dropped or been used for purposes other than climbing, or protection devices could have been found at the bottom of the crag. The exception might be if the individual selling the equipment is a close, trustworthy friend who will acknowledge the accurate history of the gear. Another exception is equipment that is not essential for safety, such as climbing shoes, chalk bags, and rope bags.

Webbing and Accessory Cord

Webbing and accessory cord have many uses in rock climbing, such as connecting the rope system to natural or artificial protection. These connections do not need to act as shock absorbers because the rope does this; therefore, webbing and accessory cord are static. They stretch a relatively small amount and are very strong. Kevlar and Spectra have become two of the favorite materials for these applications because their strength allows for smaller diameters and widths to be used compared to the traditional nylon. Specifically, Kevlar is more resistant to heat, and Spectra is more resistant to abrasion and holds up well to bending and abuse. Because anchor systems receive a lot of abrasion against the rock, webbing and accessory cord are often used, providing good abrasion resistance. You should care for and store all webbing and accessory cord the same way you would for rope.

Figure 5.3 Various webbing.

Webbing

Webbing is a versatile piece of climbing equipment mainly used for building anchors (see figure 5.3). It is essentially a flat rope that is tubular or hollow inside and comes in many widths. Modern webbing is often made from exceptionally high-strength material and is usually tied or sewn into a loop, which is then known as a runner, sling, or quickdraw.

Runners and Quickdraws

Runners are used to extend the clip-in point of a piece of protection so that the rope can follow a better line. They are also used to connect several points of protection into an anchor point to build an anchor for the belay (see figure 5.4a). Runners may also be used as makeshift harnesses (for carrying equipment) and as a component of quickdraws. Quickdraws are used by climbers to attach ropes to bolt anchors in sport climbing or for protection in traditional lead climbing (see figure 5.4b). They allow the rope to run through them with minimal friction by keeping the rope in a straight line. Quickdraws usually consist of two nonlocking carabiners connected by a short, presewn loop of webbing. They come in varying lengths, and some even come as extendable slings.

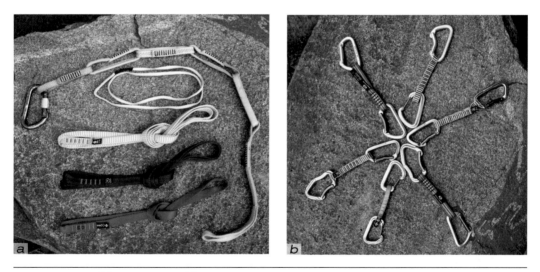

Figure 5.4 *(a)* Runners and *(b)* quickdraws.

Accessory Cord

The main use of accessory cord is to make a cordelette. A cordelette is primarily used for equalization of an anchor system and for rescue techniques (see page 202). It is a 16- to 25-foot (4.9 to 7.6 m) piece of small-diameter cord (a diameter of 7 millimeters for a nylon cordelette and 5.5 millimeters for the high-strength cord fibers such as Spectra, Tecnora, and Dyneema) that is tied into a loop. Accessory cord has also been used for sling protection with stoppers and hexes; however, most protection now comes from the manufacturer slung with steel wire or a presewn runner. Additionally, the Prusik can be tied with accessory cord. The Prusik is a knot commonly used to ascend a rope

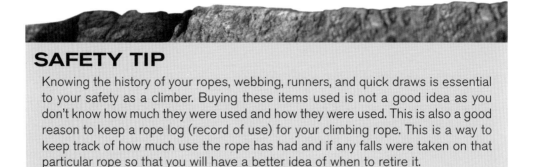

SAFETY TIP

Knowing the history of your ropes, webbing, runners, and quick draws is essential to your safety as a climber. Buying these items used is not a good idea as you don't know how much they were used and how they were used. This is also a good reason to keep a rope log (record of use) for your climbing rope. This is a way to keep track of how much use the rope has had and if any falls were taken on that particular rope so that you will have a better idea of when to retire it.

without using a mechanical device; this knot is also necessary for many rescue situations (see page 153). Accessory cord usually comes in diameters ranging from 5 to 8 millimeters; different sizes and materials have different strength ratings from the UIAA. Cords smaller than 5 millimeters in diameter should not be used for climbing. Webbing and accessory cord can range in price depending on material, diameter, length, and manufacturer. Generally, these items are sold by the foot, and the price is based on the diameter and the length purchased.

Hardware

Rock-climbing hardware is the indispensable equipment used to attach the climber to the rock face through the rope system. Hardware makes it possible for the climber to complete the anchor system in a way that is safe and practical for the applicable style of climbing. The rope is the lifeline, but without proper climbing hardware, it is nearly impossible to do any type of rock climbing. Whether you're running the top rope through locking carabiners, clipping a quickdraw on a sport route, or placing a camming device into the rock on the route you're leading, you will be relying on essential rock-climbing hardware.

Carabiners

A carabiner, also called a biner, is a metal loop with a spring-loaded or screwed gate usually made of aluminum alloy. Carabiners are an important piece of climbing hardware designed to connect things together. For example, biners can connect a climber to his rope, connect the rope to an anchor, or connect gear together. Different kinds of carabiners are used in many different situations, from securing items to rescue work. This section focuses on carabiners specifically designed for climbing, which can typically be categorized by their shape, gate type, strength, weight, and size.

Shape

Carabiners come in four basic shapes: oval, D, asymmetrical D, and pear (see figure 5.5). Oval biners have a uniform top and bottom curve, which helps to control load shifting and distribute the pressure on both sides. In general, oval carabiners are less expensive

Figure 5.5 *(a)* Oval, *(b)* D-, and *(c)* pear carabiners.

but weaker compared to D-carabiners. D-carabiners are designed to shift weight loads toward the spine—the strongest part of the biner—and away from the gate, which is the weakest part. D-carabiners can be symmetrical or asymmetrical. Symmetrical carabiners are easy to clip into protection pieces, are used in lead and top-rope climbing, offer more room for the rope, and can take more pressure compared to ovals. Asymmetrical Ds work like regular Ds, but they are slightly smaller at one end to further reduce weight. Compared to similar-sized regular Ds or ovals, asymmetrical Ds have larger gate openings but not as much room inside.

Gate Types

A locking-gate carabiner has a locking mechanism that provides extra protection against accidental gate openings. These carabiners can be oval, D-shaped, or asymmetrical, and they are most often used in belaying or rappelling. Locking carabiners should be used any time a climber depends on a single carabiner for safety, such as at the top of a top-roped climb or while belaying. The locking devices are usually either simple threaded collars that screw down over the gate or spring-loaded, "automatic" mechanisms (see figure 5.6).

Carabiners with straight gates are the most common type and can be used for many situations. They open easily when pushed because of the spring, and they close automatically when released. Bent-gate carabiners have concave gates designed to make clipping into protection easier. A wire gate carabiner uses a loop of stainless steel wire for a gate, which allows for a larger opening. This wire loop creates its own spring mechanism as it pivots. Also, because of the lower mass in the gate, this type of carabiner is less likely to vibrate open during a fall. Wire gate carabiners also weigh less and allow climbers to carry a lighter gear rack. Figure 5.7 shows the various gate types of carabiners.

Figure 5.6 Locking carabiners (auto and screw gate).

Figure 5.7 Carabiners with various gate styles: *(a)* straight, *(b)* bent, and *(c)* wire.

Strength and Performance

The UIAA tests the breaking strength of carabiners. The strength of a carabiner is marked on the gate or the spine in kilonewtons (kN). One kilonewton is roughly 220 pounds. With the gate closed, most biners are rated at a strength of 20 kilonewtons, or 4,400 pounds. With the gate open, most biners are only rated at 7 kilonewtons, or 1,540 pounds, which can easily be generated in a typical fall. Therefore, carabiners are designed to be loaded along their long axis with their gates closed. If used incorrectly (e.g., loaded with the gates open or cross loaded), any carabiner can fail at loads below its rated strength. Try to avoid placing carabiners near rock edges that might open gates when the rope comes taut. Carabiners can vary greatly in price depending on the type that is purchased. A basic oval or D-shaped carabiner will cost from $6 to $10. Locking-gate biners and auto-lock biners will cost from $10 to $20 depending on the brand and model.

Carabiner Care

Always keep your carabiners free from dirt. Clean them after any exposure to salt air or saltwater. An air compressor can be used to blow sand and dust from gates and gate openings. Carabiners can also be washed with warm soapy water, rinsed thoroughly, and then wiped dry. Inspect carabiners for burrs that could damage the rope. Sand down burrs with high-grit sandpaper (220-400 grade), but do not file them for any reason. Check carabiners regularly for cracks or corrosion. Make sure that the gate opens and

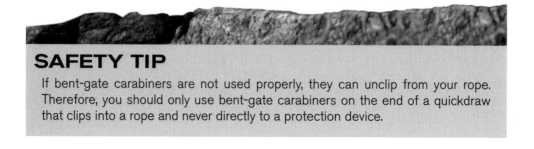

SAFETY TIP

If bent-gate carabiners are not used properly, they can unclip from your rope. Therefore, you should only use bent-gate carabiners on the end of a quickdraw that clips into a rope and never directly to a protection device.

closes smoothly and is properly aligned. The gate should open without catching or having to be closed by hand. Apply a small amount of dry silicone at the gate hinge to keep the gate functioning smoothly. Keep all carabiners stored away from humid or salty air, damp equipment and clothing, and corrosive chemicals.

DROPPING GEAR

Dropped equipment can be a frequent problem when rock climbing. If a climber drops a piece of gear, that climber should shout out the command "Rock" so that the belayer and others below can take appropriate precautions. The dropped equipment should be retired because there is no way to tell if there is any structural damage that would compromise its strength. Carabiners that have been dropped while on the climb or are damaged should also be retired. Remember, "when in doubt throw it out"—it is better to throw away a $10 carabiner than risk a life using it.

Belay Devices

A belayer controls the movement of the rope to protect the climber at the other end. A belay device acts as a brake on the climbing rope by applying friction. The device—plus the belayer's quick "braking hand" (which locks off the free end of the rope)—stops the climber's fall (see chapter 7 for more information on belaying techniques). The following are various types of belay devices and their specific applications.

Slotted Belay Devices

Slotted belay devices are the most widely used belay devices (see figure 5.8). They are commonly referred to as an ATC, which stands for air traffic controller and is made by Black Diamond. Their shape is best described as an oversized thimble with twin holes in the bottom. A bight (bend) of the rope is folded and pushed through the device and is clipped with a locking carabiner to the belayer or directly to the anchor. The bend in the rope and its contact with the device put friction on the rope to slow it down. These devices are suitable for any kind of climbing. Tube or cone devices are compact, light, and easy to use. They work with many rope diameters, can accommodate single or double ropes, and can be used for rappelling as well as belaying. However, some people, especially lighter-weight climbers, find slotted belay devices slow for rappelling because they create a lot of friction on the rope. Generally, devices have a plastic-coated steel cable loop on one end to keep the device attached to the carabiner when inserting or removing the rope. This loop also keeps the device from climbing up the rope, out of reach of the belayer. A basic

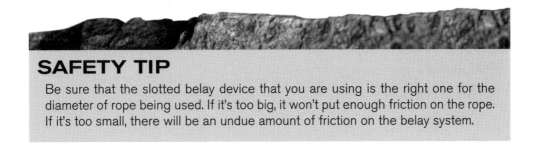

SAFETY TIP

Be sure that the slotted belay device that you are using is the right one for the diameter of rope being used. If it's too big, it won't put enough friction on the rope. If it's too small, there will be an undue amount of friction on the belay system.

Figure 5.8 Slotted belay device (ATC).

slotted belay device will range in price from $18 to $20 depending on the brand or model.

Another slotted belay device that is gaining popularity is the Reverso ATC. Developed and patented by Petzl, the Reverso is a belay device that can be used to belay the leader or a descender during rappelling. It can also be used in self-braking mode if attached directly to the belay. When belaying a lead climber from below, this belay device is similar to the devices mentioned previously. However, when belaying a climber from the top, the Reverso differs from the traditional ATC because it is self-locking. This is accomplished by attaching the Reverso to a carabiner through its extra loop.

Auto-Locking Belay Devices

Auto-locking belay devices have a mechanism that locks down on the rope when a sudden force is applied, operating similar to a car's seatbelt. The rope is threaded through the inside of the device, which is clipped to the anchor or the belayer. These devices are used mainly for sport climbing, either at gyms or climbing areas.

Figure 5.9 Auto-locking belay device (Grigri).

Since these devices automatically lock when the climber falls, they do not require any stopping force from the belayer's hand. They feed rope smoothly and are easy to operate for lowering the climber. However, auto-locking devices can put high shock loads on the rope during a fall. Additionally, they should only be used with supple, 10- or 11-millimeter ropes; they do not function with wet or icy ropes. Though the device is termed automatic, proper training is a must to ensure safety on behalf of the belayer and climber team. The Petzl Grigri is a very popular auto-locking device used in many indoor climbing gyms and by many sport climbers (see figure 5.9). An auto-locking belay device will range in price from $80 to $90.

Figure Eight Belay Devices

Figure 5.10 Figure eight device.

As the name implies, figure eight devices are shaped like the number eight, with one hole larger than the other (see figure 5.10). A bight of rope is fed through the large hole and looped around the outside of the small hole until it rests on the "neck" of the figure eight. The small hole is clipped to the climber or the anchor. Figure eights are frequently used as rappel devices in traditional climbing, search and rescue, and caving. As belay devices, they should be used like a belay plate with rope going only through the small hole. Figure eights are very efficient and smooth for rappelling, they dissipate heat efficiently, and they can be used with just about any rope diameter. Figure eights require more attention and force from the belayer's hand than other devices, and they put a twist in the climbing rope, which can make rope handling difficult. Figure eight devices will range in price from $15 to $25 depending on the features they have.

Protection Devices

Two types of protection devices are typically used as anchors during rock climbing: active and passive protection devices. Active protection devices have moving parts and spring-loaded features, and they expand to fit into cracks. Passive protection devices have no moving parts and are usually connected to a cable, cord, or sling. All protection devices come in a range of various sizes. They can be purchased individually but most climbers buy them in sets so that they have the entire range of sizes to fit a variety of climbing applications.

Active Protection

Active camming devices have larger expansion ranges than tapers or hexes do; therefore, you can get one camming device to fit where you may have tried several different sizes of tapers or hexes before finding the correct size. Active climbing protection features spring-loaded parts that are retracted and then expanded to fit the crack. These devices can be divided into spring-loaded camming devices (SLCDs) and spring-loaded tube chocks. SLCDs can be used in wide or parallel cracks where passive chocks and tapers often do not hold. Spring-loaded tube chocks are typically reserved for cracks measuring more than 6 inches (15.2 cm) wide, often referred to as off-width cracks.

Spring-loaded camming devices (SLCDs) feature three or four teardrop-shaped lobes of aluminum alloy; these lobes are called cams. When the spring-loaded trigger wire is pulled, these metal lobes retract and make the device narrower. This allows a climber to slide the unit inside a crack. When the trigger is released, the cams expand to fit the rock. Each unit has a minimum and maximum degree of latitude, and each is adjustable within those parameters. SLCDs also have different stem options. Rigid stems offer more durability, but they can be problematic with horizontal crack placement, where a fall could break the stem (see figure 5.11*a*). Flexible single-cable stems are a better choice for horizontal placements, and although not as durable as rigid stems, they fit narrow and odd-shaped cracks well (see figure 5.11*b*). Flexible U-stems work equally as well as the flexible single-cable stems; in addition, the U-stems offer the advantage of allowing you to operate them with only your forefinger and thumb (see figure 5.11*c*). Because

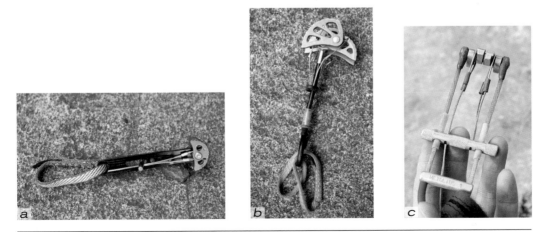

Figure 5.11 *(a)* Rigid stem, *(b)* flexible single-cable stem, and *(c)* U-stem (double) camming devices.

Figure 5.12 Tube chock (Trango Big Bro).

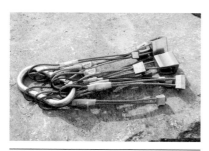

Figure 5.13 Various sizes of stoppers.

of their ability to mechanically move, SLCDs are probably the most functional, adaptive, and easy-to-use piece of protection for the climber. SLCDs vary in price depending on size, manufacturer, and materials they are made from. Smaller cams (1/2 to 3 inches [1.3 to 7.6 cm]) cost from $40 to $70, and larger cams range from $70 to $110.

Spring-loaded tube chock devices consist of a spring-loaded telescoping aluminum tube. A button is depressed to allow the tube to expand to the width of a crack. The devices have a lock-off screw collar that is twisted once the tube has been placed. Expandable tube chocks are typically used in uniform cracks or pockets that are more than 6 inches (15.2 cm) wide. The Trango Big Bro Tube Chock (see figure 5.12) is a very popular spring-loaded tube chock on the market today. Spring-loaded tube chocks range in price from $70 to $100.

Passive Protection

As the name implies, passive protection has no moving parts. This type of protection includes tapers and chocks. Tapers are commonly referred to as nuts or stoppers. Chocks are referred to as hexentrics or hexes.

Stoppers consist of aluminum pieces that are larger at one end and become smaller at the other (see figure 5.13). They are designed to slide into tapering cracks and wedge into the narrowest part of the rock. Stoppers typically work the best in narrow to medium-width cracks. The best placement occurs when the majority of the surface area of the stopper is in contact with the rock; however, because of their wedge shape, stoppers are not as well suited to parallel-sided cracks. Stoppers can also have slightly curved faces or cutout areas for better fit in uneven rock surfaces. Stoppers with curved faces have one side that is convex, and the opposite side is concave. The convex side locks against the two contact points of the concave side, creating a stable triangulation of forces.

TECHNIQUE TIP

Many climbers place their stoppers in the cracks of the rock and tug them to "set" them. This can present a problem to the climber who follows the lead climber in that they can't get the stopper out by hand. In these cases it's nice to have a nut extraction tool to help remove the stopper or any other protection device that may get stuck in the rock. These can be purchased for $7 and up to $30.

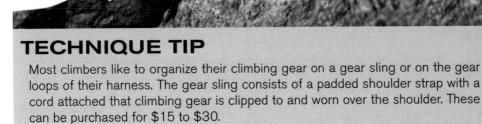

TECHNIQUE TIP

Most climbers like to organize their climbing gear on a gear sling or on the gear loops of their harness. The gear sling consists of a padded shoulder strap with a cord attached that climbing gear is clipped to and worn over the shoulder. These can be purchased for $15 to $30.

Micronuts are a smaller type of stopper. They are reserved for thin cracks or old piton scars when no other protection will fit. They are as much as 75 percent smaller than most standard stoppers. Micronuts have a very small tolerance—a fraction of an inch can make the difference between having a poor placement and a great one. Because of this, micronuts should only be used by experienced climbers who have a lot of practice placing the larger stoppers.

Tri-cams are unique protection pieces that are rounded on one side and come to a point on the other (see figure 5.14). They look like a triangle on top of the rockers of a rocking chair. Tri-cams can be placed directly into cracks (like stoppers) or can be placed with the sling running alongside the curved edge. When force is applied to the sling, it rocks the curved edge up and forces the point into the rock. Tri-cams work well in horizontal cracks and pockets.

Figure 5.14 A tri-cam.

Hexentrics (or hexes) are asymmetrical, six-sided tubes or chocks (see figure 5.15). Like stoppers, they can be placed directly into narrowing cracks. In parallel cracks, they can also be rotated into place. A downward force on the wire or sling rotates the hex and wedges it tightly in the crack.

Care of Protection Devices

The following are some points to remember regarding the proper care of protection devices:

Figure 5.15 Various sizes of hexentrics.

- Check your climbing gear regularly, especially before and after using it. Inspect it for deformation, cracks, chips, or rust.
- Store the protection devices properly. Keep them in a clean and dry place that is out of direct sunlight. Also, the devices should not be in direct contact with any corrosives.
- For active protection devices, such as spring-loaded cams, clean out all debris and use a dry lubricant such as graphite.
- When in doubt, replace the gear immediately.

Personal Gear and Clothing

Most climbing gear is universal and has many applications to meet the desired need. However, when it comes to personal gear and clothing for rock climbing, fit and comfort become subjective to each and every climber. The harness, helmet, climbing shoes, and clothing that a climber chooses need to fit properly in order to function correctly. A poorly fitting harness or helmet could have severe consequences involving injury to the climber. This section covers various types of harnesses, helmets, climbing shoes, clothing, crash pads, and chalk and chalk bags. Information is also provided on how to properly fit these items and how to care for them.

Harnesses

A harness links the climber to the climbing rope, so having a harness that fits properly is very important. A harness should be fit for comfort and safety, and it should be designed to meet the requirements of the specific climbing style. Harnesses are available that are designed for alpine, big wall, and competition climbing as well as general-purpose crag climbing.

Types of Harnesses

The following are the common types of harnesses:

• **Multipurpose** (see figure 5.16). These are also known as all-around, crag, or sport harnesses. This type of harness is ideal for beginners because the harness is designed to function well in a number of climbing applications, such as top-rope, sport, and gym climbing. Most have padded leg loops and waist belts for maximum comfort when working a route or taking a fall. Detachable leg loops let a climber answer calls of nature without untying from the rope. Most models also feature convenient gear-racking loops for easy access to hardware or a chalk bag without the need for a shoulder sling. These harnesses typically feature a dedicated front loop or belay loop so a climber can easily attach a belay or rappel device.

Figure 5.16 Various styles of harnesses.

• **Alpine** (see figure 5.16). Designed for long mountain trips, these harnesses typically have minimal padding and features in order to save weight and bulk. Nonabsorbent materials are used to withstand the rough weather often encountered in glacier and alpine climbing. The highly adjustable waist belt and leg loops allow for clothing changes between predawn chill and afternoon sunshine.

• **Competition** (see figure 5.16). These streamlined harnesses are the best choice for climbing competitions such as on-sight difficulty or speed events. Their slim design and narrow webbing allow a full range of motion. These harnesses typically have little padding and few, if any, frills or extras.

Styles of Harnesses

The different styles of harnesses include the following:

- **Leg loop and waist belt.** This popular style of harness consists of a padded waist (or "swami") belt and a pair of leg loops joined together in front with a belay loop. The waist belt buckles in front or off to the side, and the leg loops are typically held up in back with elastic straps. These straps are often detachable, making it easy for the climber to change clothes. Leg loop size may either be fixed or adjustable. Some manufacturers sell swami belts and leg loops separately to offer a truly customized fit.

- **Full body.** Full-body harnesses are designed for children or adults with narrow waists and hips. The harness holds the climber's shoulders as well as the legs, preventing the climber from slipping out if she rotates upside down during a fall. Since full-body harnesses have a higher tie-in point than seat harnesses, they reduce the chance of flipping over backward. Despite this, many climbers prefer separate seat and chest harnesses because of comfort and versatility.

- **Chest harnesses.** Chest harnesses are typically worn only on climbs where a climber could easily turn upside down. Falling into a crevasse during a glacier climb or rappelling with a heavy pack are examples of such situations. The chest harness is really a component part. It must be worn in conjunction with a seat harness. The resulting combination is the same as the full-body harness, but the climber has the versatility of being able to add or remove the chest portion as needed.

Fitting the Harness

Finding a harness that fits well is essential. Too tight and it will pinch and will restrict the climber's movement. Too loose and it will slip and chafe. Also, during an inverted fall, a harness that is too loose could allow the climber to fall out of the harness. Just like clothing, different brands of harnesses fit different body shapes better than others. The harness waist belt should be snug, but not uncomfortably so. It should ride just above the hipbones, but it should not interfere with breathing. The harness should not be able to be pulled down over the hips. Also, make sure that there is at least 3 inches (7.6 cm) of webbing extending out of the buckle of the waist belt once the belt has been properly secured and doubled back. The harness leg loops should also be snug but not uncomfortable. If they are an adjustable design, their webbing straps should be long enough to double them back through their buckles with at least 2 inches (5.1 cm) left over.

Buckling Up and Tying In

Most harnesses use full-strength buckles to join the waist belt. Read the manufacturer's instructions carefully and learn how to use the harness and buckle correctly. If the harness and buckle are not secured properly, climbers risk injury and possibly even death.

Most harness buckles must be buckled a specific way to be secure; however, as an extra precaution, you should always double-back all webbing straps through the harness buckles (see figure 5.17). Under the impact force of a fall, webbing straps that are not doubled back can pull through buckles, causing climbers to fall out of the harness altogether. Be careful not to be distracted while putting on the harness; once you start

Figure 5.17 Harness with the waist belt doubled back through the buckle.

the process of putting on the harness, you should finish it before doing anything else. Also, remember that the harness is only as reliable as the knot used to tie a climber into it. You must read, understand, and follow the manufacturer's instructions that come with the harness.

Harness Care and Cleaning

Protect the harness as much as possible from direct sunlight and heat (both of which can break down nylon). Also keep it away from nylon-damaging substances such as acids, alkalis, oxidizing agents, and bleach. Keep the harness clean, and store it in a dry spot out of the sun. When the harness gets dirty, try rinsing it first. If this doesn't remove the dirt particles, you should hand-wash the harness in cool water with mild soap. Then rinse it and allow it to dry in a shaded area. After each cleaning, check the harness carefully to make sure the stitching is intact. Inspect the climbing harness regularly for signs of wear. Pay special attention to the harness stitching and the tie-in points. Retire the harness when it shows visible signs of wear, such as fading or abrasion, or after it has held a severe fall. Over time, the harness webbing may get slightly fuzzy at the tie-in points. Although this is okay, significant wear to the stitching or excessive wear to the tie-in points is not. A harness should last about two years under normal weekend use. You can extend the life of the harness by working the rope back through the tie-in points gently when untying. Forceful pulling of the rope through the tie-in points causes these points to abrade quickly.

Helmets

Helmets are made to protect a climber's head from injury while rock climbing. Falling rocks are the number one reason to wear a helmet; however, a fall into the rock face or an unexpected bash into a low roof can also potentially ruin the day if a climber's head is unprotected. A helmet will also protect you from unexpected obstacles such as a dropped carabiner or piece of protection when you are standing directly below a climb.

Types of Helmets

Two basic types of climbing helmets are available: plastic shells with internal webbing suspension and plastic shells with polystyrene foam liners (see figure 5.18). Although both are designed to absorb impact, the internal strapping systems stretch, while polystyrene liners deform and become compacted. Webbing suspension has been standard for many years. In addition to dissipating impact force, this design offers the advantages of being adjustable to variable head sizes and allowing good ventilation between the plastic shell and the climber's head. Polystyrene foam construction is newer in climbing helmets but has been standard in cycling helmets for some time. These helmets are usually available in different shell sizes, and the fit is fine-tuned by adding pads to the inside. These helmets are also very lightweight and comfortable.

Fitting and Choosing the Helmet

Make sure the helmet fits properly. If your helmet is too tight or too large, it will become a nuisance, and you will be

Figure 5.18 Climbing helmets with and without foam liners.

tempted not to wear it. Make sure the helmet fits straight down on top of the crown of your head. The front brim should remain straight across your forehead so if your head is tilted backward, the helmet will not leave your forehead unprotected. The buckles and straps should be adjusted properly. This will keep the helmet from tilting back or shifting forward and obstructing your view. Most climbing helmets are offered in one size that can be adjusted to fit anyone. This flexibility can be an asset if the helmet is shared or if it is worn with a hat on colder days. You should also consider the environmental conditions that are most common when you are climbing. If you climb in areas that are typically hot, you should look for a light-colored helmet with a generous number of air vents. For colder climates or alpine climbs, consider wearing a hat that will fit comfortably underneath the helmet. For example, a balaclava, which is typically thinner than a hat, makes a good layering piece underneath a helmet. Look for a helmet with clips or straps for attaching your headlamp. This will be helpful if you do all-day alpine climbs with predawn starts. However, sport climbers might choose a helmet that is lightweight and simple.

SAFETY TIP

Do not substitute other helmets, such as paddling or bike helmets, for a climbing helmet because they are not rated for the same types of impacts. Climbing helmets all meet standards set by the CEN (European Committee for Standardization; www.cenorm.be/cenorm/index.htm) and the UIAA (Union Internationale des Associations d'Alpinisme; www.uiaa.ch/index.aspx). Rock-climbing helmets are tested for shock and energy absorption, conical impact, security of retention straps, and ventilation. The CEN ensures that these products go through quality control testing as well.

Helmet Care

As with all climbing gear, helmets have a limited lifespan. Helmets should be retired

- if they have been dented, cracked, or damaged in any way, including the straps;
- after a serious impact, even if they don't show outward signs of damage; or
- after five years, mainly because UV radiation from sunlight weakens the materials.

Climbing Shoes

Pierre Allain revolutionized rock climbing with his soft-soled shoe in 1934. Modern climbing shoes, with their sticky rubber soles, continue to help climbers advance this sport by allowing them to test the limits of their skills. Climbing shoes are arguably the first piece of equipment that a beginner should invest in. The shoes a climber wears when rock climbing do more than simply protect the feet. They also help grab, hold, and interact with the rock. Different climbing shoes are designed to perform best in different situations. You need to find a pair that matches your foot shape and your particular style of climbing. Beginners who enjoy climbing different kinds of rock should stick with an all-purpose shoe that can handle a variety of different climbing situations. A more experienced climber should consider choosing a more specialized rock shoe to enhance his performance in specific climbing conditions.

Climbing shoes come in many styles and designs, and several factors contribute to the shoes' performance. One factor to consider is the shoe height. Ankle-high shoes provide extra support for the ankles and foot muscles. They also help protect the ankles from scrapes and scratches. Low-cut shoes provide less ankle support, but they allow more freedom of movement for high-angle smearing and other advanced climbing techniques. Shoe stiffness is another factor that influences performance. Shoes with stiff, supportive soles protect the feet, make things easier on foot muscles, and make it easier for the climber to stand on thin edges and holds. Stiff midsoles also limit shoe flex when jamming feet into cracks and pockets, making things easier to climb. Flexible midsoles allow the feet to "feel" the rock better and take advantage of small footholds. More flexible soles also allow as much rubber as possible on the rock, making steep-angle smearing easier. Finally, shoes also come in slipper style or lace-up styles. Slippers and shoes with hook-and-loop closures are easy to get on and off, which makes them perfect for bouldering and gym climbing. Lace-up rock shoes provide a more snug and adjustable fit; they can be cinched up tight even after the shoes stretch (most rock shoes stretch slightly over time as a result of normal use).

Types of Rock-Climbing Shoes

Organizing rock shoes into distinct categories is difficult because most can be used in a wide variety of situations. However, there are basically three types of rock-climbing shoes on the market today:

- **High-performance shoes** (see figure 5.19). High-performance rock shoes are built for the high-intensity climbing of competitions or difficult sport climbing routes. These shoes provide reliable, high-end performance in those situations when proper technique is crucial. High-performance shoes are cut low for added flexibility and lighter weight. They're also designed to fit tight for maximum rock sensitivity and control.

• **Slippers** (see figure 5.19). Slippers are as close as one can get to climbing barefoot. They have extremely thin soles for maximum sensitivity, and they hug the foot like a second skin. Slippers make it easier to grab small, difficult footholds. They also have a trim toe profile for jamming in thin cracks. Slippers are ideal for training, gym climbing, and bouldering. They're lighter than regular rock shoes, and they're much easier to get in and out of. Keep in mind, however, that slippers provide very little support, so they don't edge well. They can also be tough on the foot muscles. Slippers wear down more quickly than other shoe styles, and they are more prone to stretching.

• **All-purpose shoes** (see figure 5.19). All-purpose shoes are workhorses; they're designed to handle a wide variety of rock-climbing situations and to perform respectably in all

Figure 5.19 Three types of climbing shoes: (from top to bottom) high-performance shoes, slippers, and all-purpose shoes.

of them. All-purpose shoes can be used to climb cracks, to edge, and to smear. They are popular with beginners who want the freedom to try out a wide variety of techniques. They are also often used by general rock climbers who enjoy climbing many different types of rock and by climbers who perform multipitch climbs. Typically, all-purpose shoes are the lace-up style and are cut high to protect the ankles. These shoes are designed to be comfortable as well as protective.

Fitting Climbing Shoes

A beginning climber should look for a durable, comfortable rock shoe that fits well. Finding a good fit is especially important, because rock climbing will be tough on the feet at first. Look for stiff and supportive soles, a substantial rubber rand (the strip of rubber that encircles the shoe above the sole) around the outside, and high-grade leather uppers. Buy high-cut shoes to protect and support the ankles. Make sure the shoes keep the foot flat and the toes straight. Also look for a semi-rigid sole, one that bends with about as much resistance as a tennis shoe. The stiffness will help when standing on edges and when developing footwork.

The most important factor to consider when choosing any rock shoes is finding a pair that fits well. When testing different models, wear a thin pair of liner socks (this will make it easier for you to get in and out of them all) and try on a number of styles before making the final decision. Feet tend to swell in the afternoons, or after standing on them

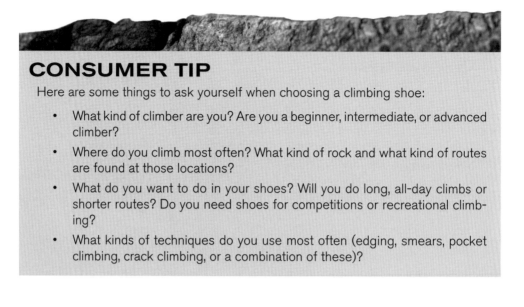

CONSUMER TIP

Here are some things to ask yourself when choosing a climbing shoe:

- What kind of climber are you? Are you a beginner, intermediate, or advanced climber?
- Where do you climb most often? What kind of rock and what kind of routes are found at those locations?
- What do you want to do in your shoes? Will you do long, all-day climbs or shorter routes? Do you need shoes for competitions or recreational climbing?
- What kinds of techniques do you use most often (edging, smears, pocket climbing, crack climbing, or a combination of these)?

for a while, so try on climbing shoes late in the day to make sure the shoes are not too snug. Keep the following tips in mind when trying on climbing shoes:

- If the rock shoe has laces, loosen them all the way to the toe of the shoe.
- Make sure your socks aren't bunched, then lace the shoes up tight.
- Look for a fit that is snug but not painful. You want to eliminate foot slippage as much as possible, but there's no need to climb in pain.
- When testing lace-up shoes, make sure the eyelets run parallel to one another after you've laced up tight.
- If you plan on climbing short, difficult routes, opt for a slightly tighter shoe for optimal control. For long, all-day routes or for general climbing, choose shoes that are tight but comfortable.

Rock shoes come in U.S., European, and U.K. sizes, which can make finding the right size difficult. Most climbing shoe companies will provide a comparison chart to help make conversions. But remember—every shoe is different, so knowing that one men's size 9 (or 42) fit previously does not mean others will as well. The only way to know for sure if a rock shoe fits well is to try it on. Opinions vary on whether or not it's beneficial to wear socks with rock shoes. Some people feel more comfortable with socks. But climbing without socks often gives climbers a better "feel" for the rock.

Climbing Shoe Care, Cleaning, and Resoling

The average active climber can wear out two pairs of rock shoes in a year. Some climbers, especially those who climb indoors, tend to eat them up at an even faster rate. A person's climbing style can affect the durability of rock shoes. The cleaner a climber's footwork, the less the climber will wear out the rubber by dragging shoes across rough surfaces. Beginners will tend to wear out shoes quickly while they are learning their footwork. To help extend the life of the shoes, you should only use them for climbing. Walking in climbing shoes allows dirt and gravel to grind into the rubber and wear down its surface prematurely. Dirty soles also have less grip when you get on the rock.

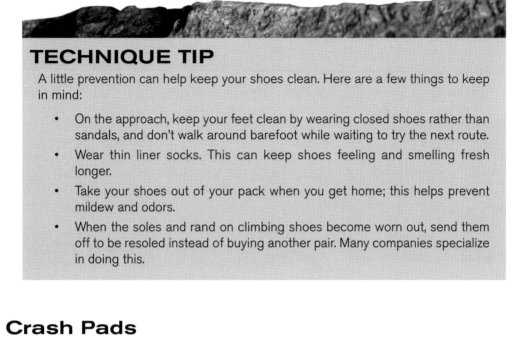

TECHNIQUE TIP

A little prevention can help keep your shoes clean. Here are a few things to keep in mind:

- On the approach, keep your feet clean by wearing closed shoes rather than sandals, and don't walk around barefoot while waiting to try the next route.
- Wear thin liner socks. This can keep shoes feeling and smelling fresh longer.
- Take your shoes out of your pack when you get home; this helps prevent mildew and odors.
- When the soles and rand on climbing shoes become worn out, send them off to be resoled instead of buying another pair. Many companies specialize in doing this.

Crash Pads

Bouldering is climbing in its simplest form. In bouldering, the climber can practice a series of moves just a few feet off the ground, and a rope is unnecessary. Many people get introduced to the sport of climbing by bouldering first. The only equipment needed for bouldering is climbing shoes and a chalk bag. However, some climbers prefer to also have a crash pad. The crash pad is essentially a large pad or mat covered with a durable material. A crash pad has shoulder straps sewn to it in order to carry it to the bouldering site. The pad is placed under the climber to keep her from landing directly on the ground or the rocks below. Crash pads range in price from $130 to $300 depending on the size and quality.

Chalk and Chalk Bags

Gymnastics chalk or carbonate of magnesium is often used by climbers to soak up sweat from fingers and hands. Chalk has become standard equipment for most climbers, and some are even "addicted" to dipping their hands in as they look at the next series of moves. The great thing about chalk is that it does provide the climber with dry hands to better grip the rock with. However, there has always been controversy over the use of chalk because it leaves marks on the rock face showing where people have climbed. Though not permanent, excessive chalk buildup can be an eyesore.

Chalk comes in a variety of styles. It can be purchased in block form, in powder form, or in a mesh bag that is placed in the chalk bag. Several companies have developed various colored chalk that blends in with the rock better, but this chalk needs to be matched up with the rock color that is being climbed on. Additionally, Metolius markets the Eco Ball, which is a colorless chalk that leaves no marks. All chalk can be carried in a chalk bag that is tied around the climber's waist and usually hangs in the back. The climber can then access the chalk by reaching behind and dipping into the bag (see figure 5.20).

Figure 5.20   A climber chalking up.

Clothing for Climbing

When choosing clothing for climbing, you need to take a few things into consideration. The first thing to think about is what type of weather conditions you will be climbing in. If conditions are cold, insulation and warmth should be considered. As with any outdoor pursuit, layers are important. Layering clothing makes it easier to adjust your body temperature to the activity level and outside conditions. This is known as thermoregulation. One way to consider this is to use the WISE acronym (Drury & Bonney, 1992):

W—Wicking layer. This is the layer closest to the skin and should be a material that will wick moisture away from the body. It is usually a base layer consisting of polyester, which won't hold moisture close to the skin. Capilene, Thermax, and microfleece are good choices for this layer.

I—Insulating layer. This layer provides insulation from colder outside temperatures. Good materials for this are wool, fleece, or down.

S—Shell layer. This layer provides the protection from outside moisture and wind. A shell can consist of nylon or a jacket. Gore-Tex is a good choice for this because it allows moisture from the body to escape in vapor form while keeping water from the outside from coming in.

E—Extra layers or articles of clothing to keep the climber warm. A fleece hat and gloves are good things to have because much of a person's body heat escapes from the head, neck, and hands.

Clothing for climbing should be functional for climbing. For example, you should consider your ability to move freely while climbing. Pants should be loose fitting and stretchy to allow for this. Many climbing pants come with a gusseted crotch (for expanded range of motion) and articulated knees that follow the contour of a slightly bent knee (for more efficient movement). Upper body layers should also be comfortable and relaxed fitting to allow for a free range of motion. These layers should also be made of a quick-drying fabric that dissipates moisture during sweat-producing activity. Many clothing manufacturers can be found that make clothing specifically for rock climbers.

CONSUMER TIP
Go to www.bouldering.com/cart.php for a full line of bouldering products.

Summary

Having the right equipment is an essential aspect of rock climbing. In this chapter, we covered all the standard gear used in rock climbing. We also discussed how to care for that gear as well as its approximate cost. Part II of this book will cover the basic skills needed to rock climb. A good climber should always know how to use his gear and should have a working knowledge of what equipment to use and when. This can only come from experience, and it is an important part of being a safe climber. As Paul Petzolt, the founder of the National Outdoor Leadership School (NOLS) and the Wilderness Education Association (WEA), once said, "Knowledge without judgment is useless, and we gain judgment through experience." What you learn from this book is no substitute for actual climbing instruction from a knowledgeable and experienced climber.

Recommended Equipment for Various Types of Rock Climbing

	Bouldering	Top-rope	Sport	Trad
Climbing shoes	X	X	X	X
Climbing helmet		X	X	X
Climbing harness		X	X	X
Chalk bag with chalk	X	X	X	X
Rope		X	X	X
Belay or rappel device		X	X	X
Locking carabiner		X	X	X
Quickdraws (8-10)			X	X
Oval carabiners (8-10)				X
Nuts and stoppers (set)				X
Hexentrics (set)				X
Tri-cams (set)				X
SLCDs (set)				X
Shoulder-length runners (6-8)				X
Extra webbing (25-30 ft or 7.6-9.1 m)		X		X
Nut extraction tool				X
Gear Sling (optional)				X
Crash Pad (optional)	X			

Note: This table is a sample and is not an all-inclusive list. Skill level, terrain, rescue systems, and group size are not factored in.

PART II

On the Rock

CHAPTER 6

Knots for Climbing

A knot not neat is
a knot not needed.

Unknown Author

For some people, knot tying is an enjoyable hobby, while for others it is a limitless source of frustration. Whatever your perspective, you need to understand two inescapable facts about knots: They take hard work to master, and they are a necessity in rock climbing. In rock climbing, our lives rely on the knots we tie. Therefore, climbers must focus on producing good knots, and they must put in the time and energy required to master the systems that are the foundations of knots. This chapter focuses not only on providing you with a repertoire of knots, but also on helping you develop the ability to tie the knots safely, consistently, and efficiently. Note that this chapter is designed to be a resource rather than a "straight-through read." The structure of the chapter allows you to pick and choose which knots you want to work on and refer to just those sections.

Basic Terms and Concepts in Knot Tying

As you begin to develop your understanding of knots, you must be familiar with a few basic terms and concepts. These basic concepts provide the foundation that can help ensure that you are enjoying your day of climbing instead of wasting your time being frustrated with tying knots. Many climbers learn knots by repeating them in a given scenario (such as when the knot is facing toward the body), but they have not taken the time to observe the general construction and system of the knot. When the climber is required to tie the knot in a different situation (such as when the knot is facing away from the body), the knot seems backward and can be confusing. To tie knots efficiently, you must understand the systems behind the knots. You cannot understand the systems without understanding the basic concepts.

The first step toward mastering knot systems is to understand some basic terms. To tie any knot, you will need to move the rope around itself. Being able to describe which end to move is critical. The system used to tie every knot relies on distinguishing between the standing end and the working end. As the names imply, the *standing end* is the end that does nothing, while the *working end* is the end that moves in relation to the standing end. Another important basic concept is to differentiate between a loop and a bight. *Loops* occur any time the working end passes over the standing end. *Bights* are simple bends in the rope where the working end and standing end touch each other but do not cross.

Dressing and *setting* are other terms you will hear on a regular basis regarding knots. Although these terms aren't directly related to how you tie a knot, they are related to the quality of the final result; therefore, you need to understand these terms as you learn to tie each knot.

Dressing a knot is getting the knot in a condition in which the strands of the rope cross (or don't cross) each other in a specific way that (1) maintains the maximum amount of strength in the knot and (2) allows for ease of untying after the knot has been weighted. Every time you tie a knot, the strength of the rope is reduced. In addition, every knot has a "release" that lets you untie it more easily. It is possible (and common) to tie knots so that they look correct but have incorrect crossings of the rope that either weaken the knot or cause it to be difficult to untie. A knot that is not dressed correctly would be called "undressed." You shouldn't settle for an undressed knot.

Dressing knots can be very confusing when you are learning knots, but if you learn correct systems, dressing can be simple and quick. Thankfully, there are systems of tying that incorporate simple methods of not only tying the knot, but dressing it as well. Because your safety depends on the strength of the knot—and because you would probably rather spend time climbing than dressing or untying jammed knots—learning simple dressing systems is well worth your time.

Setting a knot is simply tightening the knot. Although this might seem insignificant, some knots do not tighten in an intuitive manner, and if the knot is not tightened properly, it will not function at its best.

In addition to understanding terms, you must pay attention to "orientation." Many knots can be tied in a left and right as well as an overhand and underhand orientation. In other words, a knot may be tied in any of four possible orientations. If you have ever been frustrated while learning a knot, it is likely that your knot was oriented differently than the example you were following and that you didn't even realize it. For example, one of the most common knots, the bowline, is often taught with this story: "The rabbit (the working end) comes out of the hole (a loop in the standing end), runs around the tree (the standing end), and runs back into his hole." The problem is that the "hole" can be oriented in each of the four ways mentioned (see figure 6.1). If you don't take the time to observe the orientation in which you construct the knot, you will undoubtedly, at some point, find yourself unable to produce the knot even though you could just moments before.

Every knot may be tied using a variety of systems. When you begin to learn a knot, you should pick one system and memorize it, paying careful attention to details such as orientation (underhand, overhand, right, or left). Try to learn knot-tying systems that incorporate tricks for dressing the knot as well. As your skill develops or if you find yourself in a position of teaching others frequently, you should memorize a few different systems for each knot. Different systems seem to work better for different people, and some systems work better in different scenarios.

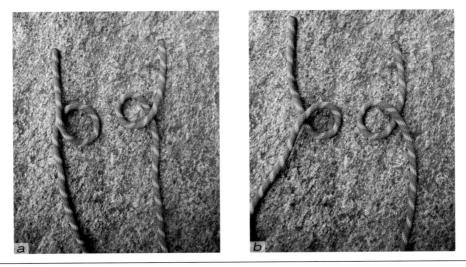

Figure 6.1 Possible orientations of a knot: (a) right and left overhand loops and (b) right and left underhand loops.

You should also be aware that there are a variety of opinions in the climbing community regarding methods of tying knots. Don't get stuck thinking that only one system is effective for tying a knot, and don't criticize others if their knot looks slightly different than yours. Instead, pay attention to the components of knots that are critical for safety, and focus on understanding *why* you tie the knot the way you do. Learn to critique knots based on what is safe and efficient, not on method or style.

The following sections present a variety of systems for tying the knots that are most commonly used in rock climbing. The knots are divided into four categories based on their use in rock climbing: (1) knots for attaching the rope to your harness, (2) knots for attaching yourself to an anchor or for building anchors, (3) knots for creating loops or tying two ropes together, and (4) safety and rescue knots. As you learn the knots, try to avoid just making the knot happen through repetition. Instead, pay attention to the system and construction (right-handed, left-handed, overhand, underhand). If you already know a knot by a different system than is presented here, you should try a new system in order to develop a deeper mastery of knot tying. The systems presented here were chosen because they not only produce a knot, but also simplify dressing and allow for application in a variety of scenarios. If you take the time to learn and practice these methods, you will soon find that you are producing safe knots consistently and quickly.

Attaching the Rope to Your Harness

A variety of methods can be used to attach the rope to your harness. Each method has pros and cons—usually related to the balance between speed, simplicity, and security. All the attachment methods mentioned here are acceptable in all circumstances, but in certain situations, you should definitely lean toward using one over the other. In addition to learning the various methods of tying in to your harness, you should also learn the scenarios in which one method might make sense over another.

Figure Eight Follow-Through

By far, the most common method of tying in to a harness is the figure eight follow-through. This knot offers a good balance of security and simplicity—especially after you examine and memorize the system by which you tie the knot. Because this knot is so familiar, climbers tend to gloss over the intricate details of its construction. Since you will be tying this knot frequently, you should take the time to pay careful attention to the details. The system presented here might seem to include more steps than you need; however, each step is included to help you focus on the small details that will allow you to master the knot and therefore produce it more effectively. As you develop mastery, you will begin to notice that some steps can be shortened or even omitted.

A figure eight follow-through is essentially two figure eight knots tied inside of each other. The first step in mastering the knot is learning where the first figure eight needs to be tied. If the first figure eight is tied in a random location, the final result will be inconsistent, and you will end up spending a lot of time adjusting the final knot. To ensure consistency, always start by focusing on where—that is, how far down the working end—to tie the first figure eight. A simple way to do this is to grasp the working end in your right hand and the standing end in your left hand. Raise the working end (think *Saturday Night Fever*), allowing the standing end to slide through your left hand until your left hand is holding the rope approximately an arm's length away from the tip of the rope (see figure 6.2). Pinch the rope with your left hand and drop the working end to create a bight in the rope.

Don't let go of the bight in your left hand until the first figure eight is complete. The location of this bight determines how long the tail of your knot will be when you have completed the figure eight follow-through. The tail is the length of the working end sticking out of the knot when the knot is completed. If the tail is too short, safety is compromised. If it is too long, the excess rope can get in your way. If you consistently end up with a tail that is too long, you should shorten the distance you extend your arm when finding this initial bight. If you consistently run out of rope before the follow-through is complete, stretch your arm a little farther.

Continuing to pinch the bight in your left hand with the working end to your right, pass your right hand and the working end behind the standing end (move your right hand away from you). Continue passing the working end around the standing end until it has made a complete revolution around the standing end, creating an overhand loop (see figure 6.3).

Figure 6.2 Measuring how far from the end of the rope you should tie the first figure eight.

Figure 6.3 First figure eight with bight pinched and working end getting ready to finish.

Figure 6.4   Last pass on first figure eight.

Figure 6.5   Finished initial figure eight showing length of tail and approximate tightness.

Pass the standing end through the loop, making sure to start passing the tip of the rope through the side of the loop that is farthest away from you. Pull it through as if it were aiming directly at you (see figure 6.4). Continue holding the original bight in your left hand until you have slightly tightened the first figure eight. To do this, pull the working end upward until the figure eight knot is approximately the length of your extended hand. It is now okay to let go with your left hand (see figure 6.5).

The completed initial figure eight should now have a tail that extends about 2 feet (61 cm) out of the knot. Remember, paying attention to the length of this tail and practicing getting a consistent length are important to your ability to tie this knot efficiently. Practice achieving consistency through standardizing your "Travolta" move, not by having to adjust the knot after it is completed.

To complete the figure eight follow-through, all you have to do is pass the tail of the first knot through your harness and then retrace the initial figure eight. Unfortunately, to make sure you achieve a well-dressed knot in a consistent fashion, you need to focus on a few additional details. These next few steps are commonly overlooked, but they are perhaps the most important details to examine if you want to tie this knot efficiently.

Begin the second phase of the figure eight follow-through by paying attention to the orientation of the first knot (see figure 6.6a). In the system presented here, the working end should exit the initial figure eight on the bottom right side (viewed from the perspective of the one tying the knot). If the tail is exiting the top left side of the knot (see figure 6.6b), simply flip it over. If you did not follow the previous diagrams, you could also end up with an initial figure eight that is tied in the opposite orientation so that the tail exits on the top right rather than the bottom right. The opposite orientation is not wrong; however, it can hinder your efforts toward developing efficiency (unless you learn the entire system in the "top right" orientation). Subtle differences will appear in the final phase—the actual follow-through phase—if you have a "top right" orientation in your first figure eight instead of a "bottom right" orientation. Either system will work, but you should make sure you know which one you use and stick with it. The procedure that follows assumes you are working with the system in which your first figure eight has a tail that exits on the bottom right of the knot as it points at you.

As you begin the follow-through, first pass the working end through the tie-in point (or points) of your harness according to manufacturer's instructions. After passing the working end through your harness, pull the working end so that the first figure eight is relatively close to your harness; the working end is now lying parallel and to the right of where it exited the first figure eight. Separate the two strands of the first figure eight that are closest to you (the left strand will be the working end itself), and insert the working end in this gap (see figure 6.7a). Pull the working end until all of the slack has been pulled through the gap and the first figure eight is quite snug against your harness.

At this point, all you need to do is continue laying the working end alongside and parallel to the first figure eight. Be very careful to avoid any crossing. Don't hurry this step, especially as you are learning. This is the point at which many people develop problems that lead to poorly dressed knots. If you take the time to lay the strands flat and parallel to each other in this step, you will not have any problems later on. Your goal is to create a double figure eight knot with two flat and parallel strands that resemble a two-lane racetrack (see figure 6.7b). If you follow along each lane of the racetrack with your fingers, the "cars" would never switch lanes.

Figure 6.6 *(a)* Proper orientation for the first figure eight in the system presented here. *(b)* Reverse orientation.

Figure 6.7 *(a)* Insertion point of working end. *(b)* Racetrack Danish.

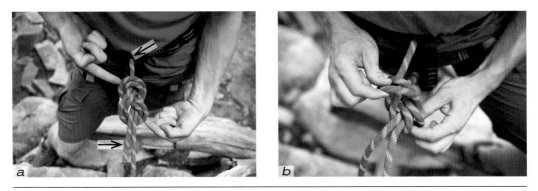

Figure 6.8 The climber is pointing at the "outer loops" while the arrows designate the parallel strands.

To complete and dress the knot, identify the bends in the "racetrack" that are closest to you and farthest from you. Also identify the two sets of parallel strands that are made up of the loop attached to your harness and the standing end and working end of the rope lying flat against each other (see figure 6.8a). The outer bends of the knots will always flip away from the parallel strands coming out of the knots. In the example shown in the photo, the loop farthest from you will flip down, while the loop closest to you will flip up (see figure 6.8b).

To set the knot, identify the parallel strands that are opposite each other. You should see two sets of parallel strands; if you use a little imagination, these sets of strands will make an X. In the example shown in figure 6.9, the standing end (labeled 1) and the right side of the loop attached to your harness (labeled 2) make one side of the X. The working end (labeled 3) and the left side of the loop attached to your harness (labeled 4) make the other side of the X. Grab opposite sides of the X and pull them away from each other.

At this point, almost everyone's knot needs minor adjustments. The benefit of obsessing over rights and lefts and tops and bottoms in every step to this point is that the adjustments you need will be predictable. If you tie the knot differently every time, you will have to spend additional time trying to figure out what adjustments you need. For instance, if you regularly fail to pull the initial figure eight close enough to your harness, you can count on needing to grab the right strand of the loop attached to your harness (labeled 2 in figure 6.9) and pushing this end into the final knot. Continuing to push this strand through the entire knot will result in lengthening the tail of the knot while at the same time shrinking the loop attached to your harness. If you do not follow a system, you will find yourself having to lengthen or shorten the tail by trial and error. Trial and error takes away from the time you should be climbing.

Figure 6.9 The parallel strands forming an X.

Figure 6.10 "Clenched fist" loop and "hang loose" tail.

The goal is to end up with a loop attached to your harness that is about the size of your clenched fist. You also want your knot to end up with a tail that is about the length of the distance from your thumb to pinky while flashing the "hang loose" sign (see figure 6.10).

Figure Eight Backup

There is great debate about whether the knot is finished at this point. Some people think stopping at this point is sufficient; others believe that since your life depends on this knot, you should back it up. The backup knot is one option. The other option is the extra pass (discussed in the following section). Logic says that the knot shouldn't come untied because it is designed to tighten when weighted. Testing also seems to indicate that the manner in which this knot tightens makes it impossible for the tail to pull through and untie the entire knot. Although backup knots can give a climber more confidence, they do take more time to tie and make inspection of the main knot a little more confusing. Whether or not a backup is used, everyone agrees that the tail needs to be sufficiently long so that it is nowhere near the main body of the parallel eights. The hang loose sign (see figure 6.10) is a safe bet on how long the tail should be.

The most common backup knot is a double overhand. You may find this knot useful if you regularly climb with groups that use a backup knot, or if you simply feel safer with a backup knot. The first step in adding a double overhand to the figure eight follow-through is going all the way back to step 1. Your *"Saturday Night Fever* move" (see figure 6.2 on page 129) needs to add approximately 12 more inches (30.5 cm) to the tail that comes out of the figure eight (shown in figure 6.10). This tail is the working end to the backup knot.

Take the working end and cross it over the top of the standing end. Continue to pass the working end around the standing end, wrapping toward the main figure eight until there is an X on top of the standing end (see figure 6.11) and a loop behind the standing end.

Figure 6.11 Backup knot X.

Figure 6.12 Figure eight backup finished.

To finish the backup knot, pass the working end under the X created by the wraps. Pull the tail away from the figure eight while at the same time snugging the X up against the figure eight. A well-dressed and well-set backup knot will be touching the main figure eight follow-through, and the tail will again be about the length of the hang loose sign (see figure 6.12).

Figure Eight With Extra Pass

Another option for finishing the figure eight follow-through is taking the tail of the knot and passing it back into the main body of the figure eight. Ending the figure eight follow-through with an extra pass is a new development that is getting mixed reviews. Although it is gaining in popularity, this option is still controversial. Make sure you understand this variation well before hanging your life on it. You can judge whether the pros outweigh the cons. Passing the tail into the main body of the knot may increase your confidence that the tail will not slip and become untied. More important, this option provides the advantage of making the knot easier to untie after it has been weighted. In addition, the extra pass concentrates the bulk of the knot closer to your harness, which reduces the likelihood that the knot will get in your way while climbing—no more being whacked in the face by a bulky knot when you fall. The extra pass is simple enough that it doesn't take much additional time. In fact, it is quicker than adding the double overhand knot.

When you have finished the figure eight follow-through, simply pass the tail back under the two strands of the figure eight that are closest to your harness (see figure 6.13). Leaving the extra pass slightly slack allows for easier untying.

Figure 6.13 Extra pass.

Bowline Tie-Ins

Bowlines are popular among sport climbers because they can be tied extremely fast and they untie with phenomenal ease—even after hanging for great amounts of time while working the most challenging routes. The benefit of ease in untying is also the greatest drawback of this family of knots. Unlike the figure eight follow-through, there is no debate regarding whether or not to back up a bowline. If you are hanging your life on it, you must back it up.

Bowlines can be extremely simple to tie, but a few of the steps can be confusing when you are learning the knot. Although the steps provided here may be different to you, they eliminate the difficulties encountered by most beginners.

As mentioned earlier in this chapter, when teaching the bowline knot, people often refer to the working end as "the rabbit." This knot is as simple as having the rabbit come out of his hole, run around a tree, and go back into his hole. However, creating the hole that the rabbit comes out of is the first confusing step. To make it simple, hold the standing end in your left hand, and extend your index finger as if you were making a gun that is shooting to the right. Drape the working end over the back of your hand and lift it back up, wrapping it around the "gun barrel" in the process (see figure 6.14). The "rabbit hole" should be about an arm's length away from the end of the working end. You can easily adjust the length of the working end. To do this, simply touch your index finger to your thumb so the loop in the rope doesn't come undone, and then slide your index finger up or down the rope until the length of the working end is where you like it.

Remove your index finger, but don't let go of the loop completely. Pinch it at the point where the ropes cross over each other. As you hold this loop, it should be facing to the right, and the standing end should be underneath the working end. To tie in to your harness, reorient the rope so that it is facing you, but be careful not to flip the loop over. The working end must stay on top of the standing end. Note: This knot can also be used to attach the rope to an anchor point. If you are using this knot as part of an anchor system, simply pass the working end around whatever you are using as an anchor point.

Pull the working end to the point at which the rabbit hole loop is fairly close to your harness. Pass the working end through the loop, making sure you pass from bottom to top (see figure 6.15).

Figure 6.14 Gun barrel bowline rabbit hole.

Figure 6.15 Rabbit passing up through the hole.

Figure 6.16 Rabbit passing back through the hole to finish.

Figure 6.17 Bowline release point.

Figure 6.18 Bowline backed up with a double overhand knot.

Figure 6.19 Yosemite finish.

Pass the working end underneath the standing end. Then pass it back through the rabbit hole loop, this time making sure you pass it from the top to the bottom (see figure 6.16). To set the knot, pull the standing end and working end in opposite directions.

No matter how hard you pull to tighten this knot, it is always easy to untie it by simply pulling on the loop that is wrapped around the standing end—the release point (see figure 6.17). Because this knot unties so easily, sometimes even by simply rubbing against your body, you should be precise with the final product. Always make sure the tail ends up inside the loop, and always back this knot up.

You can use the double overhand knot to back up the bowline in the same way you use it to back up the figure eight follow-through (see figure 6.18). Be careful to tie the double overhand around the side of the main loop that the working end would naturally lie against if you didn't tie the backup. Don't tie the backup across the loop.

Yosemite Bowline

A more graceful way to finish the knot is to create a Yosemite finish. To do this, pass the working end back outside the main loop, wrap it parallel to the rabbit hole, and pass it back through the release point (see figure 6.19). The Yosemite finish allows you to tie your backup knot outside the main loop for easier inspection. It also creates a "double rabbit hole," which increases friction on the working end and increases the distance the working end would need to travel to come untied.

Double Bowline

Another simple way to add a little security to the bowline is to start with a double rabbit hole. A double bowline is created by wrapping the working end twice around the gun barrel (see figure 6.20). This extra step adds security with almost no extra time commitment. All other steps are the same as with the simple bowline. Figure 6.21 shows the finished knot.

Figure 6.20 Double gun barrel wrap.

Bowline on a Bight

The bowline on a bight is commonly used at climbing towers and ropes courses. The knot is attached to the harness with carabiners (preferably either two carabiners placed in an "opposite and opposed" placement or one "triple-lock" carabiner; see chapter 8, page 183). This knot allows rapid changes between climbers. As with standard bowlines, it is extremely easy to untie even after being weighted all day by many climbers.

Start by tying a double overhand backup knot onto the standing end of a bight. (Make sure the tail is about the length of your thumb-to-pinky extension.) This will create a loop similar to a slip knot. Slide the double overhand up or down the standing end until you have a loop about the length of your arm (see figure 6.22).

Using the same "gun barrel" method as with the simple bowline, create a right facing overhand loop with both strands of the bight. Make sure this loop is as close to the double overhand knot as possible (see figure 6.23).

As with the simple bowline, pass the end of the bight through the overhand loop, making sure to pass from

Figure 6.21 Finished double bowlines: standard backup and with a Yosemite finish.

Figure 6.22 Bowline on a bight backup knot on a simple loop (arm-length loop).

Figure 6.23 Rabbit hole on a bight (close to the backup knot).

Figure 6.24 Bowline on a bight: "rabbit" pulled halfway through the rabbit hole.

Figure 6.25 Rabbit "engulfing the world."

Figure 6.26 Setting the bowline on a bight.

the bottom to the top (see figure 6.24). Stop pulling when the "working-end" bight (on the right) is about the same length as the double loops on the left.

Carefully flip the single loop completely over the double "rabbit hole" and double "attachment point" loops until it is touching the double overhand backup knot (see figure 6.25).

Set the knot by holding the "rabbit hole" and single loop stationary and pulling the attachment loops away from the main knot (see figure 6.26). A finished, well-dressed knot will have attachment point loops that are equal in length; the rabbit hole loops will be parallel with no crossed strands.

Knots for Attaching Yourself to an Anchor and Knots for Building Anchors

Invariably, you will find yourself in the position of needing to attach yourself, the rope, or some equipment to an anchor at the top of a cliff. All of the following knots work well for these applications. Learning all of them will enable you to have a "bag of tricks" to pull from. With a little experience, you will soon discover the benefits and drawbacks of

SAFETY TIP

Harness Tie-In Nonnegotiables

Certain details should never be overlooked when it comes to attaching the rope to your harness. Although there might be a debate about whether to back up the figure eight, everyone should agree on a few simple rules. The tail length needs to be perfect. It must be long enough to not slip through the main body of the knot as it cinches down on itself. At the same time, the tail should not be so long that it dangles in the way of your climbing or that it could be confused with other strands of rope. The main knot needs to be close enough to your harness so that the knot doesn't hit you in the face as you weight the rope. The knot also needs to be close enough so that the loop attached to your harness isn't large enough to allow your head to go through. Make sure that the rope is attached to the designated tie-in point or points on your harness. If you are not sure whether your harness is designed with a single or double tie-in point, check with the manufacturer. Manufacturers often attach diagrams showing this type of information on the inside of the leg loops. If the manufacturer indicates that you should attach a certain way, don't debate.

each. For example, the clove hitch offers great adjustability for anchoring yourself in a multipitch setting; however, this high level of adjustability may be a cause for concern when you want a secure knot for a top-rope anchor that you will not be able to monitor on a constant basis. All of these knots are quick and easy to tie. The most important variable to understand is the balance that each offers between ease of adjustment and security.

Clove Hitch

In recent years, the clove hitch has become one of the most popular knots for attaching oneself to an anchor. It is popular because it is quick, secure, and easily adjusted—with a little bit of practice. If you are attaching yourself to the anchor with the clove hitch, we will assume you have already attached the rope to your harness using one of the methods described earlier in this chapter. The construction of the clove hitch knot is a bit unusual in that it doesn't have a working end. The knot is tied into the middle of the rope.

To tie the clove hitch, simply make two identical loops and lay one over the top of the other. Common mistakes that make the clove hitch fail include (1) making mirror image loops rather than identical loops, (2) folding the loops onto each other rather than overlaying them on each other, and (3) putting the wrong loop on top.

To ensure that your loops are identical, make them both following this method: Pinch the rope with your right hand about as far away from your harness as you would like to make the knot. Your palm should be facing down, and your thumb should be to the left. Next, while maintaining your grip, simply flip your hand over so your palm is up.

You will find that your thumb will automatically point first toward you and then to the right. It is very awkward to flip your hand the other way, so your loops will be created correctly every time.

Grasp this first loop in your left hand and then make one more loop—to the right of the first loop—following the same method as described (see figure 6.27).

Now lay the loop in your right hand on top of the loop in your left hand. Don't flip the right loop over. Simply lift and slide it over the left loop (see figure 6.28).

To attach to the anchor, clip both loops into a carabiner, making sure to align the strand that will be weighted along the spine of the carabiner (see figure 6.29).

Figure 6.27 Loop construction for the clove hitch.

Figure 6.28 Clove loop: laying the right loop over the left loop.

Figure 6.29 Weighted strand on spine of biner.

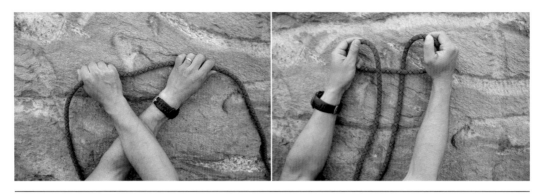

Figure 6.30 Alternate method for making clove hitch loops (hands crossed).

An alternate method for making the loops is to cross your right hand over your left and grab the rope so that both thumbs are facing outward. Keep your hands about 10 inches (25.4 cm) apart (see figure 6.30). Uncross your arms, being careful to keep both palms facing down. Proceed as previously described, lifting the loop and laying it above the loop in the left hand.

A major benefit of this knot is that you can adjust the distance between yourself and the anchor without completely untying yourself. All you have to do is loosen the loops around the carabiner and slide whichever strand you need shortened through the knots. The fact that this knot will slide makes some people uneasy about using it in an anchoring system. The knot will slip at different rates depending on the rope it is tied on, but you can count on it holding at least 1,000 pounds on most climbing ropes. This is more than sufficient for body weight and for most top-belay systems, but lead climbing falls can easily generate more than 1,000 pounds. Use this knot appropriately.

Figure Eight on a Bight

The figure eight on a bight, or figure eight loop, is quick to tie and extremely secure. This is a good knot for attaching yourself to an anchor if you are uncomfortable with the clove hitch, or if you need something more secure. You can tie this knot anywhere in the length of rope, so the working end is actually a bight, not the end of the rope itself. If you do tie this knot near the end of the rope, follow the same guidelines for tail length and backups that were discussed for the figure eight follow-through.

Many people tie this knot without supporting the rope against anything; they simply let the rope dangle in the air. In the system presented here, you will use your hand as a guide. Wrapping the rope around your hand might seem awkward at first, but it provides insurance that the knot will be dressed properly every time, thus saving you time in the long run. The automatic dressing property is so effective that before long you will be able to tie this knot perfectly every time—with your eyes closed, behind your back, while having a conversation. The trick is to make sure the strands stay parallel as you wrap them around your hand. Also, be careful not to wrap your hand too tightly.

Figure 6.31 Double-barrel pistol with first drape of figure eight on a bight.

Figure 6.32 Figure eight on a bight: step 2.

Figure 6.33 Figure eight on a bight: step 3.

Figure 6.34 Predictably undressed strand on the figure eight on a bight.

To begin, grasp a bight of rope—about the length of your arm—in your right hand. Control the standing-end strands of the bight with your bottom two fingers, and drape the working-end bight over your top two fingers (see figure 6.31).

Pull the working-end bight gently toward you and drape it over the back of your hand to the right. The bight should now be wrapped *loosely* one full wrap around your hand (see figure 6.32).

Grab the dangling working end, being careful to grab it from underneath the standing-end strands. Fold your index and middle fingers toward your wrist to create a gap above these fingers. Tuck the working end into this gap (see figure 6.33). Don't pull the knot tight yet.

After you remove your right hand, you will have a perfect figure eight with one predictably undressed portion. To dress it, grab the loop of the double figure eight closest to the single loop, and flip it away from the single loop (see figure 6.34). This one crossed strand will always be there and is always fixed with this simple flip. With practice you can remove your right hand and flip the undressed strand in one motion. Set the knot in the same way as the figure eight follow-through.

Overhand on a Bight

The overhand on a bight, or overhand loop, has become very popular with guides as a quick and secure method of attaching a rope to an anchor point or incorporating a loop into an anchor system. Although it does have a tendency to weaken the rope more than a figure eight loop, this knot is still strong enough to meet a climber's most rigorous demands.

Simplicity is the real beauty of this knot. You simply make a loop and pass the bight through the loop (see figure 6.35). If you tie this knot at the end of the rope, follow the same guidelines for backing up as used with the figure eight follow-through.

Water Knot

The water knot, also called the ring bend (*bend* is the technical term for a knot that joins two ends of rope together), is the most common way to join two ends of one piece of webbing or to join two pieces of webbing together. Many times, you will need to attach webbing, rather than rope, to anchor points. The simplest way to do this is to tie a water knot to create a loop with your anchor point inside the loop.

The water knot begins with an overhand knot about 8 inches (20.3 cm) from the end of the webbing. The length of a generously extended "hang loose" sign is appropriate for the distance from the end (see figure 6.36). Keep this first overhand slightly loose.

To finish the water knot, trace the other end of webbing through the first overhand knot. Insert the second piece of webbing into the first overhand knot at the point where the tail extends out of the first overhand knot. After inserting the second tail into the first knot, pull about 12 inches (30.5 cm) of slack through in order to make sure you have enough to complete the knot and still have an appropriate tail length (see figure 6.37). It is possible to insert the second end of webbing into the first knot on either side of the tail; however, with careful examination, you will notice that insertion on one side causes you to "dead end" more quickly. Always insert the second end into the first knot on the side of the tail that allows it to trace freely all the way through the first knot.

The completed water knot will be two interlocking, overlaid, and parallel overhand knots. There should be no twists inside the overhand knots, and the webbing should lie completely flat against itself

Figure 6.35 Overhand on a bight.

Figure 6.36 First overhand on webbing for a water knot.

Figure 6.37 Second tail inserted in first overhand and pulled to about 12 inches (30.5 cm).

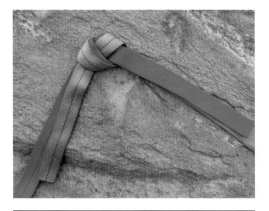

Figure 6.38 Finished water knot.

(see figure 6.38). The tails of the overhand knots should be pointing in opposite directions and should both be around 8 inches (20.3 cm) long. Testing has shown that the water knot actually allows the ends to pull through after weighting and unweighting. Although it takes many cycles of weighting and releasing for this to happen, you should allow long tail lengths or even back up this knot by tying overhand knots in the tails. If you use tied webbing as runners, you should untie and retie these runners on a regular basis to avoid the ends getting dangerously short.

Basket Hitch

If you need to attach sewn runners (see chapter 5, page 103) or loops of webbing to trees, the basket hitch is not only the simplest, but also one of the strongest methods. To "tie" a basket hitch, all you do is wrap the webbing around the tree as if the webbing were a taco shell. Attach a carabiner to the two bights extending away from the tree (see figure 6.39).

A few words of caution on the basket hitch: You cannot use it if the webbing is too short. Ideally, the angle created by the bights attached to the carabiner should not exceed 90 degrees (see figure 6.40). An angle much greater than 90 degrees can cause dangerous stresses to the carabiner. Also, if you are using tied webbing to construct a basket hitch, make sure the water knot is nowhere near the point at which you attach the carabiner.

Figure 6.39 Good basket hitch with biner.

Girth Hitch

The girth hitch is a very common method of attaching webbing to trees. Its popularity is deserved, but you need to be aware of a few points. The girth hitch is quick, but it

Figure 6.40 Bad basket hitch: overextended angle.

is weaker than the basket hitch and significantly so if not used properly. In essence, the girth hitch is a basket hitch in which one of the bights is passed through the other (see figure 6.41). One of the benefits of the girth hitch is that you can use it anytime your webbing is too short to make a good angle on the basket hitch, but it is still long enough to pass one bight through the other.

As with the basket hitch, you should never attach a carabiner at the point where the water knot is located.

A common practice you should avoid is using the girth hitch in a cinching fashion (see figure 6.42). Since rope and webbing are weakened by tight bends, doubling the girth hitch back on itself can weaken the webbing significantly. If the girth hitch is tied in this manner with webbing in good condition, it will usually be strong enough to handle just about any typical force generated by a fall. However, since fixing this issue is so simple, why not do it? If possible, always tie the girth hitch so that the attachment bight extends in a straight line out of the bight at the anchor point.

If you are attaching webbing around an object and there is a possibility that the hitch could slip off, tying in cinching mode makes sense. Just try not to rely on one cinched girth hitch that is not part of a redundant anchor system.

Figure 6.41 Good girth hitch.

Figure 6.42 Cinched girth hitch.

Knots for Creating Loops or Tying Two Ropes Together

Technically speaking, any time two ends of rope are joined together, they are joined by a bend, not by a knot. Many different bends can be tied, but in climbing, you need to rely on bends that are not only very secure, but also have a low profile so they won't get snagged on you or on the rocks you are climbing. In climbing, the most common uses for bends are (1) to make loops that are used in anchor building and rescue situations and (2) to join ropes together for rappelling. Previously, you learned a common bend used for webbing, the water knot. In this section, we'll focus on bends tied in cord or the climbing rope itself.

Double Fisherman's

The most common bend in rock climbing is the double fisherman's. This bend fully meets the criteria of being secure, and it is relatively low profile. The only significant drawback is that it can be difficult to untie after it has been weighted significantly. This knot is often used for making loops and for joining rappel ropes, so it is a good all-purpose bend to know.

The double fisherman's is nothing more than two double overhand backup knots tied onto two opposite facing ropes (see figure 6.43). For this bend, it is possible to use the instructions included previously for the figure eight follow-through backup knot, but beginners often end up with an improperly dressed knot and are not sure what went wrong. A properly dressed knot, shown in figure 6.43, will consist of two interlocking Xs on one side and four parallel strands on the other side. An improper double fisherman's will have two strands and one X on both sides, or two Xs that don't interlock (see figure 6.44).

Figure 6.43 Finished double fisherman's.

Figure 6.44 Improperly dressed double fisherman's bends.

Figure 6.45 "Right over the top."

Figure 6.46 X of the double overhand.

One simple trick for making sure the knot is always dressed is to practice the mantra "right over the top." You should orient the two ends vertically so that the end you are about to use as a working end is on the right (see figure 6.45). If you do this, you will always begin by passing this strand over the top of the other and then wrapping toward the tip of the opposite rope until you have the same X as with the double overhand backup knot (see figure 6.46). Again, make sure the tail is long enough to match an extended "hang loose" sign (thumb to pinky).

For the second knot, flip the two ropes so that, again, the end that is serving as your working end is on the right (see figure 6.47). Notice that your new working end slides through the first knot. Pull a short arm's length of slack through the first knot to allow plenty of rope to complete the second knot. Pass this tail over the top of the standing end of the first knot, wrap it down toward the first knot two full wraps, and pass the tail under the X. You can adjust the length of the tail as you set the knot by pulling on either the tail end or the standing end while holding the wraps.

Figure 6.47 Free working end flipped to the right of the first barrel.

Experiment with this a little until you can get a consistent tail length as you tighten. Once the second double overhand is tight, make the two double overhands snug against each other by pulling the standing ends opposite each other.

Figure 6.48   Three-wrap barrel for the triple fisherman's.

A *triple fisherman's* is a variant of the double fisherman's that is used when tying loops in cord that has high tensile strength, such as Spectra, Dyneema, or Gemini. The material used in these cords is slippery enough that there is an increased chance of the ends pulling through the knots when weighted. You can significantly increase the holding power of the knots by simply adding one more wrap, creating a triple overhand rather than a double.

The principles of construction are identical for the double and triple fisherman's. Align the strands vertically and with the working end on the right, and always pass the working end over the top of the strand to the left. Instead of wrapping down two full turns, wrap three times before passing the tail up through the "barrel" created by the wraps (see figure 6.48).

Flat Overhand Bend

The flat overhand is a specialized option used for joining two ropes together for rappelling. This bend can be tied extremely fast, and it provides the benefit of being almost impervious to snagging on the rock when pulling the ropes after the rappel. The downside with this bend is its potential to untie. Some people actually know this knot as the "European Death Knot" because of the tendency for the two ropes to separate. However, there are ways to increase safety, and the ease of pulling combined with the simplicity of tying makes this a great knot to include in your bag of tricks.

To tie the knot, all you have to do is hold the two ends of rope parallel to each other and facing the same direction. Then, make a loop in the ends and pass the tails through the loop (see figure 6.49).

To increase the safety of this knot, you must make sure the tails of the completed knot are fairly long—approximately 12 to 14 inches (30.5 to 35.6 cm). You must also set the knot by pulling the overhands tight and then also

Figure 6.49   Flat overhand.

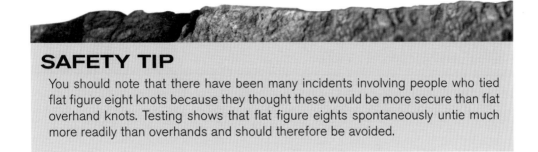

SAFETY TIP

You should note that there have been many incidents involving people who tied flat figure eight knots because they thought these would be more secure than flat overhand knots. Testing shows that flat figure eights spontaneously untie much more readily than overhands and should therefore be avoided.

pulling the tails apart firmly. Using good judgment is another way to increase the safety. This knot may not be the best choice if it will be used repeatedly and won't be monitored for a long period of time, as in the case of many rappellers following after each other. If you are worried about this knot and the rock face is not likely to snag your rope when you attempt to pull it down, you should use the double fisherman's.

Safety and Rescue Knots

Being able to improvise and having a well-developed repertoire of options are two traits that will keep you safe when unexpected things happen on a climbing trip. Some of the most important improvisational tricks include being able to operate without metal hardware (such as when you drop your belay device) and being able to attach hardware or other ropes to the main climbing rope (such as when you need to construct a hauling system for a fallen climber). The following knots introduce you to the basic concepts, but you need to realize that these are just the beginning. The possibilities for using these knots are too numerous to be covered entirely in this text. Have fun experimenting.

Munter Hitch

The Munter hitch, also known as the Italian hitch, is an unbelievably useful knot because it can be used as a belay device, as a rappel method, and for many rescue situations. After a little practice, you will find that this knot is easy to master and can be tied quickly.

The Munter hitch is a very close cousin of the clove hitch. To begin, form two identical loops using the same method as used for the clove hitch (see figures 6.27 and 6.30). After forming the loops, fold the right one over the top rather than lifting the right one and laying it flat on top of the left one (see figure 6.50).

Figure 6.50 Folding loops to make a Munter hitch.

TECHNIQUE TIP

Using the Munter hitch as a rappel method works best if you use it on a doubled rope when free hanging or when lowering heavy loads.

After folding the loops onto each other, clip a carabiner through both loops. You will notice that you can pull on either strand and the rope slides easily around your carabiner. One strand will always serve as the brake strand in the same way you always keep one hand on a rope running through a belay device. Figure 6.51 shows which strand is the brake strand and which strand is the strand that should be attached to a climber or rappeller (the weighted strand). Practice quickly identifying by sight which is the brake and which is the weighted strand.

When operating the Munter, you will notice that it produces low friction when the weighted and brake strands enter and exit opposite sides of the carabiner. When the two strands are parallel, friction is extremely high. One other function of the Munter that can be a little unnerving at first is that the Munter "flips" around the carabiner when it switches from letting out to taking in slack (see figure 6.52). This is normal; no need to worry.

Figure 6.51 The belayer is holding the brake strand.

Figure 6.52 This photo shows the Munter letting out rope. Compare this to figure 6.51 which shows the Munter taking in rope.

TECHNIQUE TIP

Always clip the carabiner into the Munter hitch so that the weighted strand is on the spine (as opposed to the gate side) of the carabiner. A Munter hitch works best on pear or HMS biners. A Munter hitch works poorly on an oval or D carabiner.

Munter Mule

The Munter mule is a fast and effective way to completely lock off a Munter hitch—this is a useful quality for rescues. If a victim is being belayed on a Munter hitch, the rescuer can tie off the Munter with a mule, thus freeing the hands of the belayer. The real beauty of the Munter mule is that it can also be released *while* it is still weighted.

You might find yourself needing to tie off a Munter in a variety of circumstances. You might be using it to belay directly off your harness, to belay directly off the anchor, or while rappelling (although tying and releasing a Munter mule while rappelling is an advanced skill that should be done with caution). The diagrams here illustrate the example of using the Munter to belay directly off the anchor. This is the most common way to use the Munter and also the easiest to learn. You should familiarize yourself with the mule in this context and then adapt the techniques to the other scenarios.

To begin, notice that in the example shown here, the brake strand is on the right, and the weighted strand is on the left—the perspective is that you are facing the Munter. (You will need to slightly adapt the techniques shown here if your brake strand is on the left or if you are oriented behind the Munter.) Pinch the brake strand between your index finger and thumb with your palm facing up toward the Munter and your thumb away from you (see figure 6.53). While pinching, rotate your hand until your thumb is

Figure 6.53 Munter mule: first pinch.

facing toward you and your palm is facing down. This should create a loop that causes the brake strand to exit underneath the loop and the weighted strand of the Munter (see figure 6.54). Make a bight in the end of the brake strand, which is now on the left side of the weighted strand; pass this bight over the weighted strand and back through the loop you created above. Pull this bight through about 12 inches (30.5 cm) (see figure 6.55). You should notice that this leaves you with a slip knot in the brake strand that is wrapped around the weighted strand.

Because the Munter mule is a slip knot, it is easy to unlock the mule when you are ready to release the weighted strand; however, this easy release is also a potential danger. You should always tie off the slipped bight with an overhand knot. Simply wrap the bight around the weighted strand, making a loop that completely encircles the weighted strand. To finish, pass the tip of the bight through this loop (see figure 6.56).

Figure 6.54 First loop in the Munter mule.

Figure 6.55 Munter mule just before backing up with the overhand.

Figure 6.56 Overhand backup on Munter mule.

To release the Munter mule, carefully undo the overhand backup and pull on the brake strand until the slip knot is released. Be very careful to make sure you are pulling the brake strand if a live person is attached to the weighted strand. When you release the slip knot, the entire Munter is in "active mode" again, and your hand should never be removed from the brake strand.

Prusik

The Prusik is the grandfather of a class of knots called "slide ascension knots" or "friction hitches." These knots have the wonderfully useful property of grabbing the rope securely when they are weighted—but also sliding easily along the length of the rope when you need to move them. The Prusik is the most well known of all slide ascension knots and is useful for a variety of purposes, such as ascending fixed ropes, building haul systems, and creating belay or rappel backups.

The first step in tying a Prusik is to create a "Prusik loop" in a short length of cord. The most commonly accepted cord for Prusik loops is either 7-millimeter nylon or 5.5-millimeter high-strength cord such as Spectra. The pros and cons of nylon versus Spectra are discussed on page 102. Whatever cord you use, you will need a length of 3 to 3.5 feet (91 to 107 cm). You should join the ends together using a double fisherman's for nylon or a triple fisherman's for Spectra.

Once you have a Prusik loop, lay it over your climbing rope with the fisherman's knot in your right hand. To begin, pass the fisherman's knot under the climbing rope and back through the bight in your left hand (see figure 6.57). (If you were to pull the fisherman's tight at this point, you would have a girth hitch.) Continue to pass the fisherman's knot around the climbing rope two more times. After the third pass, grab a strand of the cord to the side of the fisherman's knot and pull that one strand to tighten the knot (see figure 6.58). You must avoid clipping a carabiner directly onto your fisherman's knot. As you dress and set the Prusik, make sure you offset the fisherman's knot by pulling on one of the strands to the side of the fisherman's knot rather than by pulling on the fisherman's knot itself.

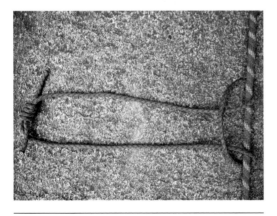

Figure 6.57 First "girth hitch" of the Prusik.

Figure 6.58 Getting ready to tighten by pulling a strand to the side of the fisherman's.

Figure 6.59 Completed Prusik.

To dress the Prusik, be careful to work out any crosses in the strands of cord. The finished Prusik should have three very neatly oriented parallel coils on either side of the bight that extends out of the knot (see figure 6.59). This bight is the attachment point for a carabiner. You should be able to pull very firmly (many hundreds of pounds firm!) on this bight without it slipping. In addition, if you need to relocate the Prusik on your climbing rope, you should be able to easily slide it by letting go of the attachment bight and pushing on the coils that are wrapped around the main rope. If the Prusik seems to slip too easily, simply add another coil as you are tying the knot.

Klemheist

The klemheist is a variation of the Prusik. It accomplishes the same purpose, but many people find that the klemheist can be tied more quickly than the Prusik. In addition, if you are using a sewn runner instead of a Prusik loop, the klemheist tends to operate more easily than a Prusik. The diagrams here will show the klemheist in a Prusik cord, but it is perfectly fine to tie this knot with a sewn runner. If you do tie the klemheist with a sewn runner, be cautious when using Spectra weave runners. Spectra is more slippery than nylon, and it also has a lower melting point. If you are using the klemheist in an application where it will be sliding on the climbing rope for long distances at relatively quick speeds, such as when backing up a rappel, you should steer clear of Spectra runners.

Figure 6.60 First bight of the klemheist.

To tie the klemheist, orient the knot of a Prusik loop (or the stitching of a sewn runner) about 3 inches (7.6 cm) from one end of the loop. Place the end of the loop without the knot (or stitching) over your climbing rope, leaving a bight of about 1 inch (2.5 cm) (see figure 6.60). Wrap the end with the knot toward the direction you intend to pull. After three complete wraps, pass the stitching of the runner through the 1-inch bight at the top of the wraps. Tighten it by pulling the end with the stitches toward your intended direction of pull (see figure 6.61).

Many people think of the klemheist as a one-way Prusik. The klemheist *will* hold in both directions, but the ease of operation and the holding strength are much greater in the direction the tail is facing when the knot is completed. As with the Prusik, if you need more friction, you should add more wraps. You should also avoid clipping a carabiner directly onto the stitching of the webbing or onto the fisherman's knot of your Prusik loop.

Alpine Butterfly

From time to time, you might find that you need to tie a loop in the middle of the climbing rope. The alpine butterfly is a wonderful knot to use because it is relatively easy to tie and because it is strong no matter what direction you weight the loop in.

To tie the butterfly, hold the rope in your right hand. (There won't be a working end since you are tying this knot in the middle of the rope.) Hold your left hand wide open in front of you, with your palm facing up. Lay the rope directly over your palm just to the right of your extended thumb (see figure 6.62). Next, very loosely wrap the rope around the back

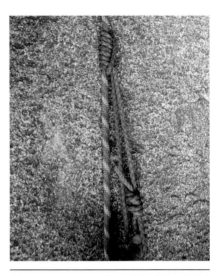

Figure 6.61   Completed klemheist.

of your hand and lay it over your fingers as close to your fingertips as possible (see figure 6.63). Wrap the rope one more time around the back of your hand and lay it between the thumb and fingertip strands (see figure 6.64). Finally, grab the strand lying over your fingertips. Lift it over the other two strands and then tuck it underneath until it exits as a

Figure 6.62   Butterfly: first lay.

Figure 6.63   Butterfly: second lay.

Figure 6.64   Butterfly: third lay.

bight at the fingertip end of your palm (see figure 6.65). Remove your hand, being very careful to leave the bight extending.

You should now have a jumble of rope that has a bight exiting out one end and has two parallel strands exiting out the other. To set and dress the knot, grab the bight in one hand and grab the parallel strands in the other. Pull in opposite directions. Then divide the parallel strands so that you are holding one in each hand, and pull these strands in opposite directions. This will give you a finished butterfly (see figure 6.66).

Figure 6.65 Butterfly: pulling the bight.

Figure 6.66 Finished butterfly.

Summary

Don't expect instant mastery with these knots. As with any skill worth having, knot tying takes patience and practice. Memorize the knots using the systems presented here, but then move on to develop mastery of the knots by trying other systems. Learn to tie these knots facing toward you and away from you, right side up, and upside down. Challenge yourself to tie them with your eyes closed and within time limits that you set for yourself.

In addition to mastering the systems that go into producing these knots, make sure you understand the systems for dressing them. You also need to understand the variety of situations in which various knots can be used. Don't be afraid to experiment, but never lose sight of the safety concerns—such as backing up knots that untie autonomously and leaving appropriate tail lengths in others.

CHAPTER 7

Managing Friction: The Skill of Belaying

> The mountains will always be there, the trick is to make sure you and your partners are too.
>
> *Hervey Voge*

Belaying is the essential interface between the technical climbing skills and human interaction skills that a person needs in order to safely climb with a partner. Because of the potential for human error, belaying is regarded as one of the most important skills in partnered climbing. Thus, a positive and constructive relationship between climber and belayer provides the foundation for safe climbing. The belayer needs to learn the requisite belay techniques and associated applications. Yet, equally important is effective and concise communication between the climber and the belayer. During periods of stress, the communication skills can be far more challenging than the technical belay skills. You should learn belaying from a qualified instructor—many times, this is not an acquaintance or your boyfriend or girlfriend.

Communication minimizes friction between partners, and effective rope management maximizes friction in the technical realm. Therefore, the role of the belayer is managing friction. This helps provide the climber with a safe and enjoyable experience as he moves on the rock. Climbing partners should work fluidly and effectively. Clear and concise communication techniques are essential to minimizing friction between the climber and the belayer. But if a fall occurs, the belayer must maximize the friction within the technical belay system in order to keep the falling climber safe.

Judgment is essential to determining what belay technique to employ during a climb. Judgment is gained through experience, knowledge, and training. This chapter provides information on belay equipment, various belay techniques and the associated applications, common communication techniques, and special considerations.

Belay Equipment

Depending on the type of climbing being done, all or just some of the equipment introduced in this section may be used during a belay. You may choose one tool over another for a variety of reasons. However, for the most part, choosing equipment is a balancing act between speed and safety. Throughout the chapter, we have highlighted the strengths and weaknesses of each device as it relates to the entire belay system. A belay system also includes the rope, an anchor, and the harnesses. Therefore, to understand the entire belay system, you also need to have detailed knowledge of this equipment (refer to chapters 5 and 8 for information on equipment and anchors).

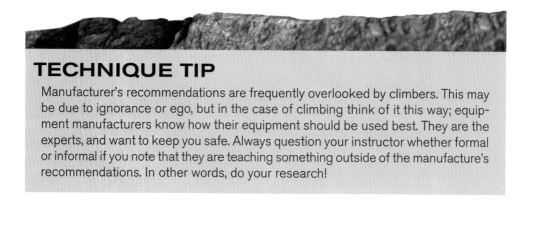

TECHNIQUE TIP

Manufacturer's recommendations are frequently overlooked by climbers. This may be due to ignorance or ego, but in the case of climbing think of it this way; equipment manufacturers know how their equipment should be used best. They are the experts, and want to keep you safe. Always question your instructor whether formal or informal if you note that they are teaching something outside of the manufacture's recommendations. In other words, do your research!

Locking Carabiners

Generally, a pear-shaped carabiner is recommended for belaying. These carabiners have a wide gate opening, and they handle rope very smoothly. They are also large enough to fit on a harness and to incorporate the belay device and the associated rope. Examples include the Petzl Attache, Black Diamond Rock-Lock, and Kong HMS Classic (see figure 7.1).

Figure 7.1 Examples of belay equipment (from left to right): Petzl Reverso, Petzl Grigri, Kong HMS, Petzl Attache, Black Diamond ATC.

Belay Devices

Many belay devices are on the market, and each device has its positives and negatives. When making a purchase, you should consider the type of climbing you will be doing and whom you will be climbing with. The most common and affordable type of belay device is the slotted or conical device—for example, the Black Diamond ATC (see figure 7.1), Trango Jaws, and ABC Arc.

Auto-locking devices are a slight variation of the slotted device. In addition to the benefits of a slotted device, these devices provide more options for the belayer. Examples include the Petzl Reverso, Black Diamond ATC Guide, and Trango B-52.

Mechanical auto-locking devices are becoming more prevalent, because when used correctly, they minimize the opportunity for belayer error. These devices are a bit heavy and relatively expensive, but they are extremely effective at aiding the belayer in the quest to keep the climber safe. Examples of this type of device include the Petzl Grigri and Trango Cinch.

Lastly, figure eight devices are metal devices that work similar to the slotted devices. In general, figure eight devices have become an archaic reminder of the past, and they are no longer used much in rock climbing. These devices are bulky, and they have a tendency to twist the rope. However, they are mentioned here because they are still around and can be used very effectively on frozen or extremely large ropes.

CONSUMER TIP

When considering which belay device to purchase, remember that a pear-shaped or HMS carabiner with a large gate opening is a very viable tool for belaying.

Maximizing Friction:
The Technical Skill of Belaying

"The process is fundamental and the technique is simple . . . still, 40 percent of all fatal climbing accidents in Yosemite were due to mistakes and failures in the belay" (Long, 1989). Belaying relies on friction to arrest the climber during a fall, to hold the climber in a fixed position when the rope is weighted, or to safely lower the climber to the ground. The belayer should always be attentive to his climber and should always practice safe belaying. Belays take place at a *belay station*, which is the location of the belayer. This could be on the ground, at the top of the cliff, or in the middle of a huge face. Four types of belays are discussed in this chapter: the hip belay, the slingshot top-rope belay, the lead climbing belay, and the top belay (see figure 7.2).

The hip belay was the earliest form of belaying; however, with modern techniques and tools, the hip belay has become obsolete in fifth-class climbing. The hip belay is discussed in this chapter because it is the backbone of modern belay techniques. The slingshot top-rope belay is commonly used on short climbs and allows both the climber and belayer to start and finish on the ground. The climber ascends the rock to the anchor and is lowered back down to the ground by the belayer. The belayer removes the slack created by the climber as the climber climbs

Figure 7.2   Examples of belays: *(a)* slingshot belay, *(b)* lead belay, *(c)* and top belay.

up the route. The belayer keeps the rope relatively taut in order to minimize falls. In lead belaying, the belayer provides slack to the lead climber as she moves up the rock. Lead belaying can be the most challenging and dangerous belay because the lead climber can fall great distances and generate significant forces. Lastly, a top belay occurs when the belayer is above the climber and is pulling up the extra rope as the climber moves up to the belay station.

As previously mentioned, a belay station incorporates the equipment, the climber, the belayer, and an anchor. You must use good judgment when considering how to use the anchor as part of the system. In many cases (lead, slingshot, or top belays), the belayer should be attached to the anchor.

Origins of Modern Belaying: Hip Belay

As mentioned, the hip belay has become obsolete in fifth-class climbing. However, on fourth-class terrain, hip belays are used periodically to quickly belay a person up low-angle terrain where a significant fall is unlikely. In this situation, the belayer is more likely to catch a "slip." In most climbing situations (lead or slingshot), this technique is not used. It is generally applied on low-angle fourth-class terrain as a top belay.

The live end of the rope is wrapped around the body of the belayer. The rope should be around the waist belt of the belayer. If the rope is higher on the belayer's body, it can slip up and over the belayer, causing the system to fail. Additionally, the belayer should be in a seated position with at least one leg in a well-braced location. A standing hip belay is hazardous and not recommended because the center of gravity is too high on the belayer, which may cause the belayer to get pulled off his feet.

Once belaying has started, the climber ascends the rock up to the belayer, and friction from the rope wrapping around the belayer is what holds the slip. The brake hand takes in the rope as it curves around the body, while the guide hand pulls the rope up from the climber. If a slip occurs, the brake hand wraps the rope tightly around the body, increasing the friction and the holding strength. This belay should not be used frivolously, and the belayer needs to have sufficient judgment to determine the validity of its use in a given situation. The speed it affords may not be worth the lack of security that it may offer. Consequently, using a more secure technique such as those described in the following sections might be a better option.

Slingshot Belay

The slingshot belay is typically used at climbing gyms and outdoor climbing crags that are half the length of a climbing rope or less. The belayer and climber start on the ground. They can set up next to each other, and they are able to double-check each other's systems using communication. Before the climber leaves the ground, any slack is removed from the system. Slack is also removed as the climber ascends the rock. The belayer removes slack by pulling rope through the belay system. A routine slingshot belay has three steps: setting up, belaying the climber to the anchor, and safely lowering the climber back to the ground. At times, a climber will need to hang on the rope to figure out a move or to rest. When this occurs, the belayer simply maintains friction on keeping the climber from being lowered. In this case, a belay anchor may be able to keep the belayer in

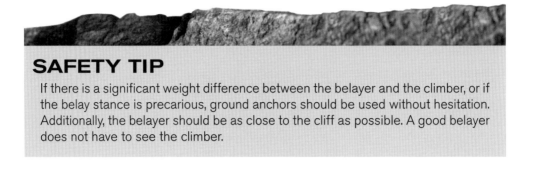

SAFETY TIP

If there is a significant weight difference between the belayer and the climber, or if the belay stance is precarious, ground anchors should be used without hesitation. Additionally, the belayer should be as close to the cliff as possible. A good belayer does not have to see the climber.

one spot. If the climber is larger than the belayer, the belayer should be clipped into an anchor before the climber leaves the ground. Ground anchors can be as simple as a sling around a large rock or tree or as complex as a traditionally placed anchor accounting for upward pull. It is not always essential to be anchored during slingshot belaying because the rope is generally tight between the belayer and climber—as a result, minimal forces should be generated within the system.

Slingshot Setup

Regardless of the type of belay being used, you must ensure that the rope system is "closed." This is commonly achieved when both the belayer and climber tie into the rope using a figure eight follow-through. It can also be done by placing a stopper knot, which is usually a fisherman's knot, in the end of the rope to ensure that it does not slip through the belay device.

The rope has a live end, which is the end of the rope leaving the belayer, going up to the anchor, and then going back down to the climber. The live end will bear the weight of the climber in the event of a fall. The other end of the rope is known as the brake line. The brake line is managed by the brake hand, which is the most important human factor in the technical system. Most belayers prefer to use the hand they write with as the brake hand, but many eventually become ambidextrous at belaying. The brake hand controls how much friction is applied to stop the rope from slipping through the belay device. Before starting to belay a climber, you must make sure that the belay device is arranged properly. If you are using a slotted device, you should set up the gear as follows:

1. Ensure that the rope system is closed—either by tying into the rope or by placing a knot in the end of the rope.
2. Consider using a ground anchor to ensure the safety of the climbing team (based on the belay stance and any disparity in the sizes of the climber and belayer).
3. Make a bight in the rope and pass it through one of the two slots in the belay device (see figure 7.3a). The rope should run parallel with the attachment cable of the belay device.
4. With the brake end of the rope on bottom, clip the bight and the belay device into a locking carabiner (see figure 7.3b).
5. Clip the locking carabiner onto the belay loop of your harness (see figure 7.3c). Lock the carabiner (see figure 7.3d).

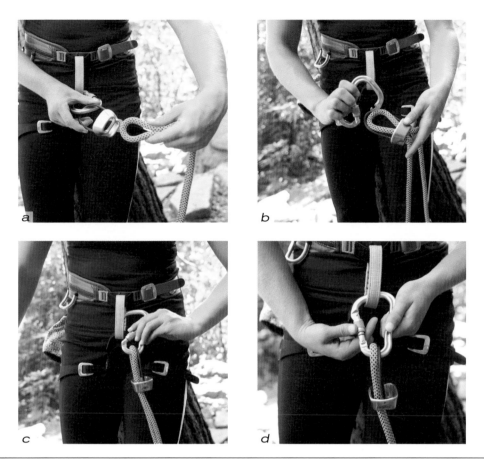

Figure 7.3 Demonstrating how to set up a belay using a slotted device: *(a)* creating a bight, *(b)* inserting into a carabiner, *(c)* attaching to the harness via the belay loop, and *(d)* locking the carabiner.

Some harnesses don't have belay loops, and they require the belay device to be oriented so that the bight of rope is in a horizontal position instead of vertical. In this case, the brake end of the rope will exit the device on the brake-hand side, which should be the same side as the anchor.

Belaying the Climber

A belayer can maximize friction by maintaining all of the bends in the rope while belaying. More bends means more friction, which ultimately makes it less difficult for a belayer to hold a climber weighting the rope. Consequently, a very small belayer can hold a very large climber when an effective belay system is used. However, this relies entirely on the assumption that the belayer's brake hand is always on the rope. If the brake hand releases the rope for any reason, even momentarily, friction is compromised and the belay becomes inadequate. A functional belay ensures that the climber is able to move up the rock with the trust that a fall will be caught by the belayer—but without concern that the rope will hinder the climbing experience.

To belay a top-roped climber on a slingshot system, start by setting up the belay and getting into a good belay position. Remove all of the slack from the system; tighten the rope between the climber and the belayer, and remove slack between the belayer and the anchor (if being used). Place your left (guide) hand around the side of the rope going up to the top anchors, and place your right (brake) hand around the brake end of the rope (one hand's width from the belay device). If you are not right-handed, you may switch the actions of your left and right hand. Lock off the belay device by pulling the brake line sharply down toward the ground creating a sharp bend against the device. Attention is crucial in belaying because the belayer is the one who will catch the climber during a fall. To catch a fall, the belayer simply bends the rope down and locks off the belay device. Friction is created when the belayer pulls the brake line of the rope down sharply across the belay device. Your brake hand can rest by your thigh or behind your buttocks while maintaining a firm grip on the climbing rope.

To begin belaying, follow these steps:

1. To brake, pull your brake hand down below the device and near your thighs (see figure 7.4a).
2. Pull rope through the belay device with your brake hand, and pull down on the rope with your guide hand (see figure 7.4b).
3. While still locked off in brake, bring your guide hand below your brake hand (see figure 7.4c), and slide your brake hand back toward the belay device (see figure 7.4d).
4. As your climber ascends, return your guide hand to the line going to the climber and repeat the process (see figure 7.4e).
5. If your climber is stationary, remain in the position described in step 3 (see figure 7.4f). Note: If your climber is not moving, staying at step 3 will increase your line of vision, conserve energy, and provide a "fall-ready position" known as the brake position.

Figure 7.4 Top-rope belaying. The brake hand is always in control of the rope, and the guide hand moves to aid in that quest.

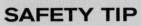

SAFETY TIP

Belaying can be done in many ways. The methods described in this book are recommended because they provide easy rope management techniques that maximize friction during climbing. As you become more confident in your climbing skills and you learn other belay techniques, you should always ask these two questions: Does this technique maximize friction in the system? Does it minimize mistakes during rope handling?

Lowering a Climber

When a climber is ready to come down—either after finishing a climb or because she can't progress any farther—you can easily lower the climber to the ground. To do this, follow these steps:

1. Pull all of the slack out of the belay system.
2. Lock off the belay device by going into the brake position (see figure 7.5a).
3. Hold the brake line with both hands and let the rope slowly slide through your two hands (see figure 7.5b). The climber needs to have her full weight on the rope in order to be adequately lowered.
4. Once the climber is securely on the ground, pay out slack in the rope so she can untie her knot.

Figure 7.5 Appropriate braking position for lowering a climber. Note that both hands are functioning as brake hands. This provides additional friction and control.

SAFETY TIP

The belayer needs to be located very close to the rock. Although this is a little less comfortable for the belayer, it is far safer because the rope ascends the rock directly, instead of at an angle. The angle created when a belayer steps away from the rock can cause protection pieces to pull or can increase the length of a climber's fall because the belayer is pulled toward the rock introducing more slack into the system. It can also result in the belayer being dragged across the ground.

If a climber is lowered too fast, an injury can occur, or the rope can be damaged. Occasionally, the brake end of a climbing rope will become twisted and will need to be untangled before you can continue to lower your climber. When this happens, keep your brake hand on the rope, and shake or spin out the twists in the rope.

Lead Belaying

During lead climbing, the climber moves up the rock and places protection as he goes. As the climber moves above the last piece of protection, the potential for a fall increases. Generally, the climber will climb up the rock until he finds an effective location for an anchor. The belayer is responsible for providing rope to the climber as he moves up the route.

Belayers should not attempt lead belaying until after having a complete and proficient understanding of the slingshot belay. Though the initial setup is similar to a slingshot belay and the brake hand is always in the braking position as the lead climber ascends the route, lead belaying requires a higher level of skill. Lead belaying carries a much more serious burden—when the lead climber falls, he gains speed, and when speed and weight are combined, forces multiply. Catching a lead fall could cause a belayer to be jerked off the ground or into the anchor. Any time the belayer is moving, the chances of the brake hand releasing from the rope go up. Therefore, a lead belayer needs to be extremely attentive and prepared to catch a fall. This may include being attached to an anchor that accounts for upward pull.

As the climber advances up the route or prepares to clip into a piece of protection, the belayer's job is to provide enough rope. If the climber downclimbs or pulls out more rope than needed for a clip, the belayer's job is to take in the surplus slack maintaining a vigilant belay. The belayer always maintains the brake position with the brake hand, but pulls slack through the device using the guide hand as the climber moves or pulls up rope to clip protection. The rope should not hinder the climber from moving up. Also, the belayer must minimize fall distances for the climber by making sure there is no excess slack in the system. A good lead belay will end with the climber never having to excessively verbalize his needs—because the belayer has anticipated those needs. The lead belayer also acts as a second set of eyes for the climber. The belayer may identify when gear is not clipped correctly, when the rope gets behind the climber's leg, or may spot a piece of protection that is likely to cause problems for the leader as he moves up.

Top Belaying

As mentioned earlier, top belaying implies that the belayer is on top of the cliff and the climber is climbing toward the belay station. In all top belays, the belayer must be attached to the anchor in order to avoid falling. Top belaying closely resembles the slingshot belay because the rope is tight between the climber and belayer and a fall would generate minimal force.

Yet, on fifth-class terrain, a fall would result in the climber placing all of her weight on the belay station. Therefore, belaying right off the harness straight down to the climber could be difficult to hold and could also be very painful (see figure 7.6). On fifth-class terrain, a top belay directly off the body is not recommended. In fourth-class terrain or extremely low-angle situations, the top belay off the body is a functional tool that can be used by experienced belayers to hold a small fall or slip.

Figure 7.6 Belaying directly off the body is not recommended in most fifth-class vertical situations as other, more secure techniques are available.

Slingshot Revisited

Several methods can be used to effectively belay a climber from the top of a cliff. The first is to attach the rope to the anchor and then belay using a slingshot (see figure 7.7). The belayer is attached to the anchor with a clove hitch or figure eight on a bight; the belayer is weighting the anchor. The rope from the climber goes through the anchor and into the belay device, which is attached exactly like the slingshot belay. This system is secure, allows the belayer to escape the system quickly if a rescue is needed, and places the force on the anchor instead of on the body of the belayer.

Figure 7.7 Top belaying using a slingshot or "redirect" through the anchor.

TECHNIQUE TIP

The belayer should extend his attachment point at least an arm's length away from the anchor so that the redirect system works better. If the belayer is too close, the redirect will be challenging to manage. One way to accomplish this is to attach yourself to the anchor using the rope from the belayer's harness and a clove hitch (see figure 7.7).

Belaying Off the Anchor

Belaying directly off the anchor is an excellent technique. This can only be done with auto-locking devices such as a Petzl Reverso, the Black Diamond ATC Guide, or the Munter hitch (which is not auto-locking). To set up a belay off the anchor, connect the auto-locking device to the master point with a locking carabiner. Feed a bight of rope through the device, and use a second carabiner loaded against the spine at the retainer to make a brake. If the belayer cannot pull in any slack, the system is rigged incorrectly. The rope going to the climber should be on top of the device (see figure 7.8). As the climber moves up the rock, the belayer pulls in the slack. If the climber falls, the device locks off.

One difficulty with using an auto-locking device (such as the ones mentioned) is paying out slack once the device has been weighted. The easiest way to deal with this issue is to ask the climber to unweight the rope. If the climber cannot unweight the rope, a block and tackle must be set up to release the brake bar. Thread the Prusik back through a higher point on the anchor and the brake bar as many times as possible. Slowly apply pressure until the brake bar releases. This can be dangerous, and a Prusik line should also be attached to the harness and the brake line. Because of this challenge, this system may not be the best choice if you anticipate lowering the climber back to the ground. This is a skill that must be practiced in a controlled environment and should be well rehearsed. However, if the climber ascends all the way to the anchor, a new system can be used to descend.

Additional Belaying Alternatives

Although the three major types of belaying (slingshot, lead, and top) remain constant in this section, the tools used to maintain safety do not. In this section, we'll look at alternative techniques for belaying, including mechanical devices and the Munter hitch.

Figure 7.8 *(a)* Belaying directly off the anchor using an auto-locking device. Note that the live strand going to the climber is on top. The belay line is on the bottom. *(b)* A close-up of this belay system. The clove hitch is the belayer's attachment point.

TECHNIQUE TIP

Learning to lead belay with a mechanical device is challenging because the device wants to keep slack from being provided—and the lead belayer's responsibility is to provide slack. Thus, you should practice this skill with a competent partner on easy climbs to get a feel for how best to provide slack. It is best to read the manufacturer's recommended belay techniques and learn them! If peers belay differently, consider asking why.

Mechanical Devices

Belaying with mechanical devices is an excellent option. When used correctly, mechanical devices are reliable and can make both the climber and belayer feel more secure. A belayer can use mechanical devices for slingshot, top belays, and lead belays. The challenge is making sure that device is used correctly. Feeding rope out to the leader is a particular concern, and is shown (see figure 7.9a). Additionally, mechanical devices cannot thread two ropes at one time; therefore, require the climber to use a different technique when rappelling. Mechanical belay devices are not fallible. Most accidents with mechanical devices occur when the climber is lowered. Figure 7.9b shows the correct brake position for the rope. Figure 7.9c shows how to properly lower a climber.

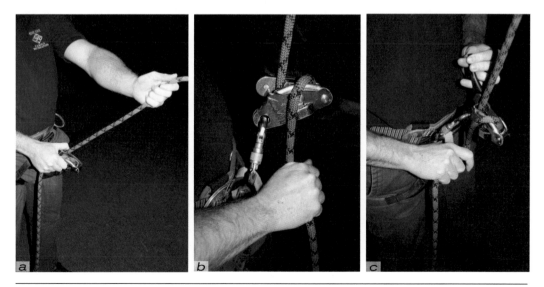

Figure 7.9 Belaying with a mechanical device: (a) feeding slack out with the device, (b) correct brake position, and (c) appropriate lowering position.

CLIMBER TIP

Learn the Munter hitch well. Being able to use this knot in a variety of conditions will increase your ability to adapt quickly as situations change while climbing. It will also provide a backup belay device if another option is not available.

Munter Hitch

Knowing the Munter hitch is absolutely essential for the new climber (see chapter 6). Eventually, all of us drop our belay device or leave it at home by accident. The Munter hitch can be used to rappel and belay, and it can replace any of the devices previously discussed. Additionally, when weight is a concern, the Munter hitch is a very effective belay technique. The drawback of the Munter is that it tends to twist the rope. This twisting causes ropes to wear out a bit quicker, and it can make a belay station a little tougher to manage.

Be aware of one significant difference between the Munter and the other belay devices discussed in this chapter. The brake position on the Munter is not down. It is actually straight out and slightly up from the body (see figure 7.10). Otherwise, the belay process is the same for slingshot, lead, and top belays. The belayer must always maintain control of the brake line on a Munter because it has no auto-locking capabilities; this is especially important to note when using a top belay (see figure 7.11).

Figure 7.10 Brake position when utilizing the munter hitch.

Figure 7.11 Belaying directly off the anchor using a Munter hitch during a top belay.

SAFETY TIP

From a few feet away, partners can do a squeeze check to confirm that carabiners are locked and to check harness buckles, knots, and belay attachments. This should occur every time a new belay is initiated.

Communication Techniques: Minimizing Friction Between Partners

Minimizing friction between climbing partners is accomplished both by maintaining a good relationship and by using effective communication between the pair. Once you have established a partnership, it does not matter what terms are used when climbing together. However, standardizing communication techniques among climbers makes it easy to communicate when you find a new partner.

Climbers should remember two important concepts regarding communication. The first is that a redundancy check should always be done before climbing; this should be built into the process. In other words, before leaving the ground, the climber and belayer should double-check each other by asking and answering several questions (covered later in this section). This should include checking each other's harnesses, the belay system, and each other's attention.

The other concept is that a belayer cannot read minds (at least most can't). Therefore, the belayer cannot know what the climber wants unless it is vocalized. It is one thing to have the basic communication skills down, but it is another to express your needs to the belayer when you are feeling a little scared. At the same time, an inattentive belayer is the worst kind. Inattentive belayers do not keep partners for very long because the partners cannot trust the belay or because the climber eventually gets hurt.

With that in mind, specific language is helpful when double-checking your partner and expressing your needs. Table 7.1 provides a list of standardized terms used to maintain good communication between partners and to ensure that they double-check each other.

Belay commands can be separated into three categories: before the climb, during the climb, and after the climb. Without good communication, friction between partners is increased—and in a worst-case scenario, a major accident could occur. The commands are fairly standardized and are essential for safe climbing. The commands are also short and distinct so they can be easily understood when your climber is far above or below you.

After the climber and belayer have double-checked themselves and their partner, they are ready for commands. The climber initiates the climb by asking, "On belay?" This question asks for confirmation from the belayer that she is ready to start belaying. The belayer responds with "Belay on" after the belay rope is taut and attention is focused on the climber. When the climber says "Climbing," this informs the belayer that the climber is about to start. The belayer responds with "Climb on," giving the climber permission to proceed.

Table 7.1 Communication Terms Used in Climbing

Terms	Explanation
Before the climb	
"Let's do a double check"	Used by the belayer or climber to indicate the need to confirm that harnesses are doubled back, the climber is tied in correctly, carabiners are locked, and the belayer is set up correctly
"On belay?"	Asked by the climber to confirm that the belayer is ready to start belaying
"Belay on"	Used by the belayer to respond to the "On belay?" command and to indicate that the belayer is ready
"Climbing"	Used by the climber to indicate that he is about to start
"Climb on"	Used by the belayer to respond to the "Climbing" command and to give the climber permission to proceed
During the climb	
"Slack"	Used by the climber to indicate a need for more rope
"Take"	Used by the climber to indicate a need for the rope to be tight
"Up rope"	Used by the climber to indicate that too much rope is in the system
"Falling"	Used by the climber to indicate that he is falling and that the belayer should be ready
"Ready to lower"	Used by the climber to indicate a desire to come down
"Lowering"	Used by the belayer to indicate a controlled descent for the climber
"Rock!"	Yelled any time anything is falling (belay devices, carabiners, rocks, and so on)
"Rope!"	Yelled before throwing a rope down the cliff
"Clipping"	Used by the climber to signal the belayer to pay out a little rope to allow the climber to make the clip more easily
"Clipped"	Used by the climber to indicate that the clip has been made and to take in extra rope
After the climb	
"Off belay"	Used by the climber to indicate he is safe and finished
"Belay is off"	Used by the belayer to confirm that the climber is no longer on belay

During the climb, if the climber's rope is too tight, the climber can say "Slack" so that the belayer knows to pay out some rope. Conversely, if the belay rope is too loose, the climber can say "Up rope" so the belayer knows to tighten up the belay. Any time the climber needs to rest and weight the rope, she can call out "Take" or "Tension." The belayer then knows to pull all the slack out of the rope, move the rope into the brake position, and prepare for the rope to be weighted.

When a climber is ready to come down, she simply says "Take" to have the slack in the rope removed and then says "Ready to lower" to signal the belayer to start the descent. The belayer will respond by saying "Lowering" before taking any action. At the end of a climb, the climber will say "Off belay," and the belayer's response is "Belay off." This ends the responsibility of the belayer to catch the climber. When leading a route, the lead climber will shout "Clipping" to signal the belayer to pay out a little rope to allow the climber to make the clip more easily. "Clipped" tells the belayer that the clip has been made and to take in extra rope.

Other commands that are useful in climbing include "Falling" (used to prepare the belayer for a fall), "Rock" (used to alert others in the area that rocks or other items are falling), and "Rope" (used when a climber is dropping or pulling a rope to the ground).

Summary

Belaying is often neglected as climbers become more comfortable with climbing. Many times, a climbing area is a social outlet and a fun community. Remember that belaying is a part of a very serious partnership. You should enjoy the local climbing community, but when belaying, you must only focus on the climb and the climber. This chapter covered some of the various belay techniques that climbers use. After becoming comfortable with the skills presented here, you can consider other belay techniques or styles. A variety of techniques have been developed over the years that climbing has been a sport. Some are better than others, and proficiency at belaying is essential. Always remember that safety is paramount. Minimize stress and friction within the human partnership, and maximize the friction in the technical belay system. This will help you have a long and safe climbing career.

Now that you have read about the importance of managing friction through proper belay techniques, the next chapter will enable you to explore the importance of establishing systems that provide protection when you or your partner climb.

CHAPTER 8

Building Climbing Anchor Systems

Good, solid anchors are the foundation of technical climbing.

John Long

In this chapter, we'll look at how climbers build safe anchor systems. Anchor systems can be composed of either natural or artificial anchor points. By understanding and applying a few basic principles, you can quickly develop the skills necessary to build safe anchor systems for climbing.

This chapter also provides tips of the trade that will help new climbers move rapidly through the construction of anchor systems. Needless to say, to develop skills at building anchor systems, you will need additional learning experiences that go beyond this text. Understanding the strategies and principles presented in this chapter is essential; however, you must also put them into practice by partnering up with an experienced and talented climbing instructor or colleague. Therefore, you should read this chapter, practice your basic skills, and then make sure you go out and build as many anchors in as many environments as possible. If you do this, you will soon master the art and the science of building safe climbing anchor systems.

What Are Climbing Anchor Systems?

When people begin enjoying the sport of climbing, especially in the great outdoors, they eventually come across the everlasting question—What is holding the rope up there? The short answer is an anchor system.

An anchor system is composed of three main components: (1) anchor points, (2) a rig, and (3) a master point (see figure 8.1). The anchor points are the individual components that anchor the system to something solid. The rig interconnects all the anchor points to the master point, which is a connection point where the force of a fall can be applied so it is evenly distributed to all anchor points via the rig. In other words, when a climber falls, the master point takes the load and distributes the force to all anchor points via the rig. This is a simple system that is very effective when well built.

Anchor Points

The anchor points can be natural or artificial in nature. Examples of natural anchor points include trees, boulders, rock formations—in brief, anything that is considered solid and that can be rigged to build an anchor system. Artificial anchor points are made of specially designed pieces of climbing protection known as stoppers, hexes, wired nuts, tri-cams, slider nuts, big bros, and cams (see chapter 5). These pieces are placed temporarily in cracks

Figure 8.1 The anchor system is composed of anchor points, a rig, and a master point.

found in rocks; they are often referred to as "clean protection" because they are removable and do not damage the rock fissures they are placed in. Fixed protections are also a type of artificial anchor point, but they are permanently placed in cracks or in the rock itself. Pitons (which are now rarely used) are placed in rock fissures with the aid of a hammer, while bolts with clipping hangers are drilled directly into solid rock.

The Rig

A rigging system is used to interconnect all pieces of an anchor system. Climbers can use different equipment to create a rig. The cordelette is often tied into a loop using a double fisherman's knot and is then used to rig anchor systems. A triple fisherman's knot is tied when using cord such as Spectra because of the slicker properties of the sheath and the narrower diameter. Webbings with a length of 2 to 8 feet (61 to 244 cm) can also be used to build anchor rigs. Webbings, often called sling, are flat woven synthetic fibers made of nylon, Spectra, Dyneema, or Dynex. Like the cordelette, webbings are commonly sewn together to create a loop, and the looped webbing is used to build anchor rigs. If the webbing is a classic 1-inch-wide (2.5 cm) tubular nylon sling, the webbing will have to be tied in a loop using a water knot.

The Master Point

The master point is formed at the apex of the rig in the direction a falling climber would pull on the anchor system. The master point is created when two locking carabiners are clipped to the rig's apex (see figure 8.2). Preferably, these carabiners will be pear shaped since this design offers more strength and more space at the master point for clipping equipment or rope. However, if a climber is short on gear, a locking carabiner can be combined with a nonlocking carabiner to form the master point. In the worst-case scenario, two nonlocking carabiners can be used as long as their gates are placed opposite and opposed.

Figure 8.2 Two pear-shaped locking carabiners.

Purpose of an Anchor System

Anchor systems have an obvious overall purpose—keeping climbers safe by holding them during and after a fall. As John Long said, "Good, solid anchors are the foundation of technical climbing." In other words, without a good anchor system, a person cannot climb safely when using a climbing rope. However, not all anchor systems have the same specific purpose. Some anchor systems are designed to have the climbing rope pass through the carabiners at the master point—for example, a slingshot top-rope anchor system, which is used in a single-pitch setting where the anchor is above the climber (see figure 7.7 on page 169). Other anchor systems are designed to hold on to the belayer, a belay device, or the climbing rope with their master point, such as in a multipitch climb. (Appropriate anchors and multipitch climbs will be examined in chapter 11.) Climbers often refer to the latter as a belay anchor system.

Whether the system is for top-rope climbing or multipitch climbing, all climbing anchor systems are built according to a few basic principles. You must understand these principles when building anchor systems. The acronym ADDRESS can be used to remember the seven principles, which include the following: angle, distance, direction, redundancy, equalization, shock load, and strong. This series of principles not only allows you to build safe anchor systems, it also helps you assess the overall quality of your anchors.

Principles of Safe Climbing Anchor Systems

In this section, we'll look at the seven basic principles that are essential to understand when building an anchor system. These principles are based on good risk management practices as well as factors related to physics that influence the performance of any anchor system. The following includes a description of each component of the acronym ADDRESS:

- **Angle.** The anchor system should not have a V-angle exceeding 60 degrees at the master point. Ideally, this angle should be 30 degrees or less. Notice that when the V-angle of an anchor system increases in degree, the force on individual anchor points increases exponentially; therefore, instead of distributing less force on individual anchor points, the force actually increases (see figure 8.3).

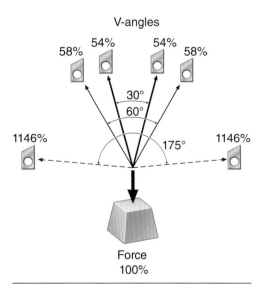

V-angles

58% 54% 54% 58%

30°
60°

1146% 1146%
175°

Force
100%

Figure 8.3 Effect of V-angle on the force applied to anchor points.

Adapted, by permission, from C. Luebben, 2004, *Rock climbing: Mastering the basic skills* (Seattle, WA: Mountaineers Books).

- **Distance.** On a top-rope setup such as a slingshot, the master point should be placed over the edge of the cliff to let the climbing rope run free of friction. On a multipitch climb, the length of a belay anchor should be appropriate in order to place the master point above the belayer's harness—ideally, the master point should be at about the chest level of the belayer.

- **Direction.** The master point should be placed just above the climbing route to avoid pendulum swings from a falling climber.

- **Redundancy.** The anchor system should be redundant. This means that it should have more than one independent anchor point and more than one piece of equipment at its critical points (i.e., two carabiners at the master point).

- **Equalized.** The tension on each anchor point should be equal to all other anchor points. This means that when you pull on the master point, you can see that the pulling force is evenly distributed on each of the anchor points. This principle is often the most difficult to apply to an anchor system, but there are ways to quickly do this, such as using a self-equalizing webbing or using a knot to create a pre-equalized anchor.

- **Shock load.** As a safety rule, climbers need to avoid potential shock load on their anchor system, especially systems that are built with clean protections. However, in certain situations—such as when the system is built on sound bolts or solid natural anchors—you can allow for a minimum elongation (i.e., 1 to 5 inches [2.5 to 12.7 cm]) of the system should an anchor point blow. Shock loading can be dealt with in two ways: (1) avoid it or (2) reduce it. To avoid shock loading, you must create a pre-equalized anchor system. That means tying all the strands of the rig above the master point with a large knot (see figure 8.4). To reduce shock loading, you can also create a self-equalized anchor system using an "improved sliding X." By tying overhand knots in each arm of the sliding X, you can minimize the shock load and the effect of a potential elongation if one arm of the anchor system fails (see figure 8.5).

Figure 8.4 Creating a pre-equalized anchor system.

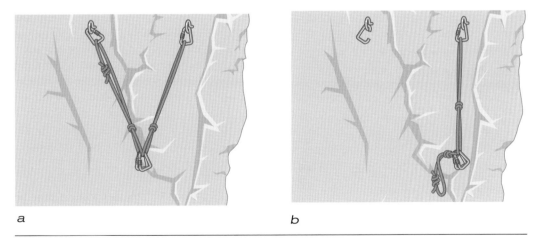

a   b

Figure 8.5 Comparing an improved sliding X *(a)* before and *(b)* after extension.

- **Strong.** Obviously, a good anchor system must be strong—strong enough to hold not only the weight of a climber and his belayer, but also any forces that a climber fall could generate in both top-rope and top-belay applications. You need to know that each individual anchor point would be able to hold the climber's weight and much more. If you do not feel that way about any of your anchor points, then you should not use the anchor system, or you should have more anchor points to increase the strength of your anchor system.

SAFETY TIP

Redundancy is regularly perceived as the most important characteristic of a good and safe anchor system; yet, most climbers often use single rope (9.8 to 11.0 millimeter) to climb. Therefore, although climbers embrace redundancy in anchor systems, they do not see any problem with climbing on a single rope. In reality, if properly used and maintained, a modern climbing rope has little to no possibility of sudden failure. So you should not view the single-rope dilemma as an inconsistency. It is simply a safe and appropriate exception to the rule, much like the larger tree or boulder that is so big and strong that a climber simply anchors it twice instead of using another anchor point.

The Art of Building Anchor Systems

Many experienced climbers will say that building anchor systems is an art. It is considered an art because no two climbing routes are the same and most anchor systems are built under unique conditions requiring quick adaptations based on the environment and the available gear.

To effectively build climbing anchors, you will need to develop automated skills. You must have an instinctive way of conceptualizing the components of the anchor system (i.e., anchor points, rig, and master point) based on (1) the environment at the top of the climb or pitch, (2) your equipment, and (3) the purpose of the system (i.e., slingshot top-rope or belay anchor). In addition, to develop your art, you will need to master the following skills:

Know Your Knots:

- You must be able to select the appropriate knot for the job.
- You should be able to tie all your knots (well dressed and well set) efficiently and rapidly.
- You should be able to assess the integrity of each knot by simply looking at it from a distance (refer to chapter 6 for information on all knots).

Sequence Your Actions:

- You should see in your head all the appropriate steps you will perform to build the anchor system.
- When building pre-equalized anchors, you should remember to always load your master point to help you adjust the tension on the rig. For instance, when building a slingshot top-rope anchor, you simply need to clip the climbing rope to the master point so it pulls on it before you adjust the tension on the rig. (More details will be given on this sequence later.)

Know How to Adjust Tension on a Knot:

- You should be able to take or give slack in a webbing or cordelette connecting the anchor points by simply adjusting a knot, such as the double bowline, the clove hitch, and the water knot (also called the ring bend).

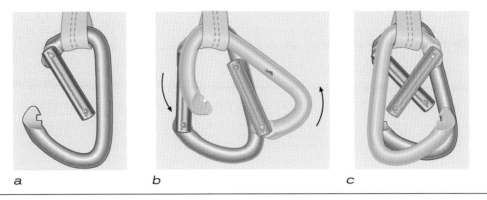

a   b   c

Figure 8.6   Placing carabiners in opposite and opposed directions.

Know How to Use Carabiners:

- You should be able to open, place, or remove a carabiner from a piece of equipment rapidly and smoothly (without confusion or difficulty).
- You should be able to quickly (and without confusion) place carabiners in opposite and opposed directions (see figure 8.6).

Sequencing Your Actions When Building an Anchor System

As previously explained, sequencing your actions properly will greatly improve your efficiency at building anchor systems. So, when building your anchor system—either for a top-rope climb, a single-pitch climb, or a multipitch climb—you should remember the sequence of actions described in the following sections.

Top-Rope Climb

For a top-rope climb, follow these steps when building an anchor system:

1. Identify the climbing route, and distinguish landmarks at the bottom to help you recognize the climb when at the top. Marking the bottom of the climb with a bright piece of clothing can be helpful when setting up a top rope.

2. Approach the top of the climb carefully. ALWAYS secure yourself when working near the edge. If you need to stand 6 feet (1.8 m) away from the edge or closer, you should be secured to a solid anchor point such as a large tree or a boulder. An easy way to do this would be to set a rope with a stopper knot at the end that extends to the edge of the cliff; then connect yourself to the safety line via a Prusik knot clipped to your harness. This method will give you security and mobility.

3. Scan the top of the climb and choose your anchor points once you have identified the top of the climb. Select the anchor points based on the following:

   a. Position—The anchor points should be near each other or far away from the edge to allow a small V-angle at the master point.

b. Distance—The anchor points should not be so far from the edge that your gear will not reach the edge of the cliff unless you combine many pieces together.

c. Access—The anchor points should be easy to access. Their position should not jeopardize your safety.

d. Impact—The anchor points and their surroundings should not be environmentally affected (e.g., soil compaction, vegetation trampling or damage).

4. Secure your first anchor, then proceed toward the edge to build your master point.

5. If you are building a pre-equalized anchor, ALWAYS load your master point with the climbing rope. This will help you when it comes time to equalize the tension of the last anchor point.

6. Build your second and third anchor point. Equalize the tension on the system at the anchor point, not at the master point.

7. Double-check all your knots and carabiner gates and your overall system. Basically, ADDRESS your anchor system before allowing people to climb.

Single-Pitch Climb

For a single-pitch climb, follow these steps when building an anchor system:

1. Once you reach the top of the climb, secure yourself before building your anchor system. Depending on the climb, you can place a good pro, sling a natural anchor, or clip a bolt. You can use short webbing or a daisy chain to connect your harness to the anchor point.

2. Scan the top of the climb and choose your anchor points. Select the anchor points based on the following:

a. Position—The anchor points should be near each other and above your waist so that it will be easy to transfer your weight to the anchor points when you are ready to be lowered down with the rope.

b. Strength—Especially when building an anchor system with protections, you should make sure that you use cracks in the rocks that are part of the main wall (and not just an unstable flake or chock stone in a larger crack).

3. If you are building a pre-equalized anchor, connect all your anchor points before pulling and tying the webbing or cordelette in the direction where you want to place the master point. This will help you equalize the tension on your anchor system.

4. Double-check all your knots and carabiner gates and your overall system. Basically, ADDRESS your anchor system before allowing people to climb.

5. Pass the climbing rope through the carabiners at the master point, and reconnect it to your harness before being lowered down.

Multipitch Climb

For a multipitch climb, follow these steps when building an anchor system:

1. Once you reach a good belay station on the climbing route, secure yourself before building your anchor system. Depending on the climb, you can place a good pro,

sling a natural anchor, or clip a bolt. You can use short webbing or a daisy chain to connect your harness to the anchor point.

2. Scan the section of the climb above and below you and choose your anchor points. Select the anchor points based on the following:

   a. Position—The anchor points should be near each other and above your waist so that it will be easy to belay your climbing partner. Place the main anchor system (i.e., two or more anchor points with a downward pull) above you. Then look below for an upward-pull placement since this anchor system will also be used to protect the lead climber during the following pitch.

   b. Strength—Especially when building an anchor system with protections, you should make sure that you use cracks in the rocks that are part of the main wall (and not just an unstable flake or chock stone in a larger crack).

3. If you are building a pre-equalized anchor, connect all your anchor points before pulling and tying the webbing or cordelette in the direction where you want to place the master point. This will help you equalize the tension on your anchor system.

4. Double-check all your knots and carabiner gates and your overall system. Basically, ADDRESS your anchor system before allowing people to climb.

The Science Behind Anchor Systems

People often say that rock climbing is playing with gravity. And since gravity will never give us a break, we have to accept that some laws of physics will always be involved in rock climbing, especially when using equipment to protect us from a fall. Therefore, the science of building anchor systems for climbing requires that you know a few general concepts in basic mechanics.

Perhaps you remember from your high school science classes that a newton is a unit of force that is defined as the force required to accelerate a mass of 1 kilogram at a rate of 1 meter per second. A kilonewton (kN) equals 1,000 newtons. A practical way to explain this is to simply say that 1 kilonewton equals about 225 pounds. Another way to think about it is to imagine that 1 kilonewton is about the equivalent of a professional football linebacker hanging on a rope. The static force placed on the rope by the weight of the linebacker is the equivalent of 1 kilonewton. Climbing equipment such as carabiners, pieces of protection, webbing, and cordelette are approved by the UIAA, which indicates the minimum tensile strength of the equipment in kilonewtons. Table 8.1 presents a few commonly used types of climbing equipment and their corresponding minimum tensile strength.

You also need to understand a few concepts about the most basic pulley system. When you look at climbing from a physics point of view, you soon realize that top-rope and lead climbing always involve a pulley system. In top-rope climbing, the pulley is found at the master point. In lead climbing, the pulley is found at the carabiner holding the rope after a lead fall. Of course, we are not talking here about a real pulley that spins but simply about the physical effect on the rope and, most important, the anchor system. When a rope is running through a fixed carabiner, with a mass weighting the rope on either side of the carabiner, this essentially creates a simple pulley system that provides a 1:1 ratio. This ratio obviously means that no mechanical advantage is provided through the system—that is why trying to lift a climber by simply pulling on the

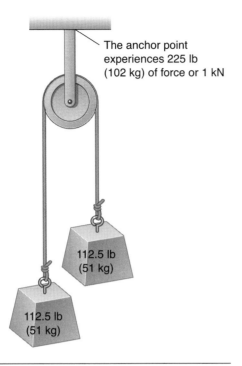

The anchor point experiences 225 lb (102 kg) of force or 1 kN

112.5 lb (51 kg)

112.5 lb (51 kg)

Figure 8.7 Pulley system with a 1:1 ratio.

rope is nearly impossible. However, a 1:1 ratio also means that the mass supported by the master point (in the case of a top-rope setup) is more than just the mass of the climber. The mass of the belayer must also be supported. For instance, without taking every physical factor into consideration, if you have a weight of 112.5 pounds pulling down on one side of the pulley (i.e., master point) and another 112.5 pounds weighting the other side, there will be a total of 225 pounds or 1 kilonewton of downward force on the pulley and whatever the pulley is anchored to (see figure 8.7). This analysis is true if the weights are static, meaning that they are carefully loaded on the pulley without being dropped.

You can see why anchor systems need to be built with strength in mind. Fortunately, modern climbing gear is designed not only to be light but also to offer large amounts of tensile strength (see table 8.1). For instance, staying with the football player metaphor, properly using a carabiner that is tested at 25 kilonewtons would allow 25 linebackers—each weighing about 225 pounds—to hang from the rope, and the carabiner would not break. This should reassure you that if you use your gear properly and apply the ADDRESS principles, you will climb on very safe anchor systems.

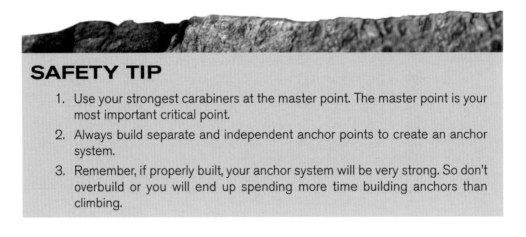

SAFETY TIP

1. Use your strongest carabiners at the master point. The master point is your most important critical point.
2. Always build separate and independent anchor points to create an anchor system.
3. Remember, if properly built, your anchor system will be very strong. So don't overbuild or you will end up spending more time building anchors than climbing.

Table 8.1   Minimum Tensile Strength for Climbing Equipment (UIAA Requirements)

Equipment	Purpose	Minimum tensile strength
8 mm accessory cord	Building anchors	12.8 kN (2,880 lb)
9 mm static rope	Anchor point extension	15 kN (3,375 lb)
8 mm Dyneema sling	Building anchors	22 kN (4,950 lb)
9/16 Spectra sling	Building anchors	27 kN (6,075 lb)
1 in. tubular webbing	Building anchors	18 kN (4,050 lb)
D-shape nonlocking carabiner	Connecting gear	20 kN (4,500 lb)
D-shape locking carabiner	Connecting gear	25 kN (5,625 lb)
Piton	Building anchor point	25 kN (5,625 lb)
Bolt	Building anchor point	25 kN (5,625 lb)
Stoppers, size 6-13 (Black Diamond)	Building anchor point	10 kN (2,250 lb)
Walnuts, size 4-10 (DMM)	Building anchor point	12 kN (2,700 lb)
Rocks, size 2-10 (Wild Country)	Building anchor point	12 kN (2,700 lb)
Tri-cams, size 1.5-7.0 (Lowe)	Building anchor point	11-20 kN (2,500-4,500 lb)
Camalots, size 1-4 (Black Diamond)	Building anchor point	16 kN (3,600 lb)
Friends, all sizes (Wild Country)	Building anchor point	14 kN (3,150 lb)

Scoring Scheme for Designing and Assessing Anchor Systems

In this section, we'll discuss a scoring scheme that you can use when building climbing anchors. This scoring scheme provides you with a simple and logical way to design and assess your anchor system. The scheme is a discretionary scoring system that requires you to have a good understanding of the basic principles and the science behind climbing anchors.

The scoring scheme presented here requires that all climbing anchor systems reach an overall score of 10 or above. So, what creates the overall score? In this scheme, a natural anchor point can receive a score ranging from 0 to 5. For instance, a large, well-rooted, healthy tree will likely get a score of 5. At the same time, a fixed artificial anchor point, such as a bolt, can also get a score ranging from 0 to 5. A well-placed bolt in a solid rock will likely get a score of 5. However, in this scheme, a removable artificial anchor point (i.e., active or passive protections) can only get a score ranging from 0 to 4. For example, a well-placed "walnut," "friend," or piton can get a high score of 4.

From this scoring scheme, you can conclude that when using only solid natural anchors, the minimum number of anchor points needed to create a safe anchor system is two—for an overall score of 10. But, there is an exception to this rule.

Imagine that the top-rope site you are using has a large healthy pine tree (i.e., 3 feet [91 cm] in diameter). Any experienced climber—or anyone with common sense—would feel safe using only that anchor point for climbing since it is by far the strongest component of the system. However, you need to understand that a single large tree or boulder (scoring an indisputable 5) should be used *twice* to create two solid independent anchor points (and thus reach the overall score of 10). By anchoring your system twice to the same large tree or large boulder, you respect the redundancy principle even if you use the same anchor point twice.

Conversely, if you are being presented with a handful of small trees that cannot receive an individual score of 5, you will be required to use more than two trees to reach an overall score of 10 or above. As you can see, the scoring scheme involves simple arithmetic and common sense. Typically a diameter of 6 inches is the minimum for a live and healthy tree to be considered a climbing anchor.

For artificial anchors, if you use only solid fixed artificial anchor points (i.e., anchor bolts), the minimum number of anchor points needed to create a safe anchor system is two—for an overall score of 10. Again, this score is correct only if each bolt is properly placed in solid rock and judged to warrant a maximum individual score of 5.

Finally, if you use only solid but removable artificial anchors (i.e., passive or active pieces of protection), the minimum number of anchor points needed to create a safe anchor system is three—for an overall score of 12. This is true and safe only if each piece of protection is properly placed.

Assessing natural, fixed, and removable anchor points will be more carefully explained later in this chapter. In the meantime, table 8.2 summarizes the scoring scheme proposed for building and assessing climbing anchor systems. Study it, understand it, and memorize it. This scoring scheme will make your life easier when it is time for you to build your first anchor systems.

Table 8.2 Anchor Point Scoring Scheme

Type	Maximum score	Minimum required	Possible overall score
Natural	5	2	10
Artificial (fixed)	5	2	10
Artificial (removable)	4	3	12

Mixed Anchor Systems

If you use a mixed anchor system—meaning that you combine natural and artificial anchor points—you can still use the scoring system presented in this chapter. All you have to do is combine the individual score for each anchor point and aim to reach a total score of 10 or above.

For example, you can anchor a tree that scores 5 with two artificial pieces of protection, each scoring 4, to get a grand total of 13. The possibilities are limitless, and since no two climbs will be the same, you should be ready to adapt your anchor system to whatever situation you are facing. Just apply the principles of the scoring scheme to build safe climbing anchor systems.

Selecting and Scoring Natural and Artificial Anchor Points

What makes a solid natural or artificial anchor point? This is where a lot of experience building anchor systems becomes useful. Until you gain this experience, you can use a series of guidelines that will help you develop sound judgment when evaluating various anchor points. These guidelines are presented in accordance with the scoring scheme that was just discussed.

Natural Anchor Points

A tree will receive the maximum score of 5 if it meets the following criteria:

- The tree is 6 inches (15.2 cm) or larger in diameter (see figure 8.8).
- The tree is alive.
- The tree's root system does not move when you push on its trunk.
- The tree shows no signs of rotting, insect infestation, or fire burn.

Figure 8.8 *(a)* Healthy tree with a good diameter, and *(b)* an unhealthy tree that shows signs of rotting and a poor root system.

A tree lacking any one of these characteristics will receive a score from 0 to 4 based on how precarious it appears. Here you will have to use your judgment. But needless to say, when using these trees, you will need more anchor points to build your anchor system.

Note: Trees scoring less than a 3 should be avoided.

A boulder will receive the maximum score of 5 if it meets the following criteria:

- The boulder is larger than 4 feet (122 cm) in diameter (i.e., too big to put your arms around it). See figure 8.9.
- The boulder is placed directly on a flat surface, not perched on small stones.
- The boulder is placed on a surface that slopes away from the climbing edge.
- The boulder is solid and cannot be moved or tilted by pushing on it. Use your legs to perform this test. Lie down on your back and push the boulder with both of your legs, as if you are in the gym doing a leg press.

A boulder lacking any one of these characteristics will receive a score from 0 to 4 based on how precarious it appears. Here again, you will have to use your judgment. But if a boulder can be moved with your leg press, don't even think about using it.

Note: An unstable boulder should never be used because the potential failure of a boulder could be catastrophic.

Figure 8.9 *(a)* Boulder with a good diameter and in a stable position, and *(b)* boulders too small and with an unstable position.

A rock formation (i.e., chicken heads, flakes, horns, chockstones, needle eyes, and so on) will receive the maximum score of 5 if it meets the following criteria:

- The rock formation is an integral part of the rock or bedrock (see figure 8.10).
- The rock formation is solid—no hollow sound or vibrations when you tap on it.
- The rock formation has no cracks.
- The rock formation is shaped in a way that will allow it to hold a sling in place.

A rock formation lacking any one of these characteristics will receive a score from 0 to 4 based on how precarious it appears.

Note: An unstable rock formation should never be used because the potential failure of a rock formation could be catastrophic.

Fixed Artificial Anchor Points

An anchor bolt will receive the maximum score of 5 if it meets the following criteria:

Figure 8.10 An example of a good and reliable rock formation.

- The bolt shaft is placed perpendicular to the rock surface.
- The hanger lies flat on the rock.
- The entire surface of the hanger makes contact with the rock.
- The nut holding the hanger is not loose.
- The bolt does not show any rust.
- The bolt is placed in a reliable rock.
- The bolt hanger is oriented in the appropriate direction of pull.
- The bolt is not placed under any overhangs.
- The bolt is not an old one-quarter-inch compression bolt. See figure 8.11 for a good and reliable bolt.

An anchor bolt lacking any one of these characteristics will receive a score from 0 to 4 based on how precariously it is placed. See figure 8.12.

Note: Anchor bolts scoring less than a 3 should be avoided.

Figure 8.11 An example of a good and reliable bolt.

Figure 8.12 An example of an unreliable bolt.

Removable Artificial Anchor Points

A passive piece of protection (i.e., nuts, stoppers, walnuts, tri-cams, hexagons, and so on) will receive the maximum score of 4 if it meets the following criteria:

- It is placed in a reliable rock fracture or formation.
- It is as large as, or larger than, a thumb.
- It is placed appropriately for its direction of pull.
- It has a large surface of contact.

A passive piece of protection lacking any one of these characteristics will receive a score from 0 to 3 based on how precariously it is placed.

Note: Pieces of protection scoring less than a 2 should simply not be used. Doing so would require you to build an anchor system with four or five anchor points. Keep it simple!

A piton or knife blade will receive the maximum score of 4 if it meets the following criteria:

- The piton is placed in a reliable rock fracture or fissure.
- The piton is not cracked.
- The piton is driven to (or almost to) its eye and is very solid and secure.
- The piton is placed appropriately for its direction of pull.

Figure 8.13 An example of an unreliable piton.

Note: Although pitons and knife blades are often left in cracks for long periods of time, they are technically considered "removable" artificial anchor points. Plus, the very nature of these pieces of protection does not always allow climbers to ascertain the reliability of the part of the piton that is hidden in the rock.

A piton or knife blade lacking any one of these characteristics will receive a score from 0 to 3 based on how precariously it is placed (see figure 8.13).

Note: Pieces of protection scoring less than a 2 should simply not be used.

An active piece of protection (i.e., friends, cams, link cams, camalots, and so on) will receive the maximum score of 4 if it meets the following criteria:

- It is not overcammed (i.e., less than 90 degrees). See figure 8.14.
- It is not undercammed (i.e., more than 120 degrees). See figure 8.15.
- It is offering good contact on all lobes.
- It is placed appropriately for its direction of pull.

An active piece of protection lacking any one of these characteristics will receive a score from 0 to 3 based on how precariously it is placed.

Note: Active pieces of protection scoring less than a 2 should be avoided.

Figure 8.14 This piece of active protection is overcammed.

Figure 8.15 This piece of active protection is undercammed.

Shock Loading Anchor Points

As explained earlier, shock loading an anchor point means putting excessive stress on that anchor and the equipment connected to it. Even though this is exactly what happens every time a lead climber falls on a piece of protection, shock loading a climbing anchor system is totally unnecessary and should be avoided. However, because the use of presewn webbing is so popular, building anchor systems with the infamous "sliding X" is still a prevalent practice. Remember that a "sliding X" anchor system will always include a potential for a shock load if one anchor point fails.

To prevent shock loading problems when building anchor systems, let's add a few more guidelines to our set of principles:

1. Anchor points that received an individual score of 5 *can* be shock loaded.
2. Anchor points that received a score of 4 or less *cannot* be shock loaded.

This means that building an anchor system using a sliding X on two solid bolts is acceptable. However, building an anchor system using a sliding X on three solid pieces of protection, such as three well-placed walnuts, will not be acceptable because of the potential shock load.

Furthermore, you need to learn the proper way of building a "sliding X" anchor system. For years, the sliding X was taught or presented in climbing publications as the simple double-strand "V" webbing with a twist in one of the strands (see figure 8.16). This simplistic version presents two serious problems: (1) It includes a shock load that

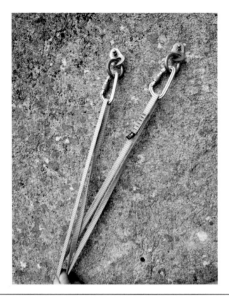

Figure 8.16   Standard sliding X.

Figure 8.17   Improved sliding X.

is proportional to the length of the webbing—the longer the webbing, the longer the shock load. (2) It provides no redundancy if the webbing fails.

A solution to these problems is the improved version of the sliding X (see figure 8.17). Notice that by placing two overhand knots near the apex of the "V," you not only minimize the length of the shock load, you also create redundancy within the system. Consequently, the improved version should be the only one used when building a sliding X anchor system on two solid bolts (each scoring a 5 in the scoring scheme).

Multipitch Climb Anchor System

When you are leading a route on a multipitch climb, building an anchor system is quite similar to building any other anchor system. The difference is that all anchor systems built on a multipitch climb will require a piece of protection with an upward pull. If you build with pieces of protection, the main anchor system must be built with at least three pieces interconnected to create a single anchor's master point. However, you will also need a piece of protection placed below the anchor system and connected to the master point. This piece of protection will create a redirectional anchor point that will allow your anchor system to be used not only with a downward force but also an upward force.

Because you are on a multipitch route, having an upward-pull anchor system will be essential—you and your belayer will need it when you start leading upward from that anchor system.

Building an Anchor System With Opposing Anchor Points

This technique is used only in dire situations—that is, when horizontal or vertical cracks do not allow a piece of protection to be used with the proper direction of pull toward the master point's resting position. Imagine a horizontal crack with no constriction outward but only two V-shaped pinches in the crack, one going to the left and one going to the right, 1 to 2 feet (30 to 60 cm) apart from each other. The only way a passive piece of protection (such as a nut or a stopper) will hold in the sideways pinches is if the direction of pull is horizontal. In this case, you can use two opposing pieces of protection to build an anchor point (see figure 8.18). Notice that we are not talking about an anchor system here, since this technique creates a very large V-angle where the direction of pull is applied. Remember, the larger the V-angle, the more force is applied to

Figure 8.18 Example of two opposing pieces of protection in a horizontal crack.

both the anchor points and the webbing holding them. So, again, this technique can be used as one component in a larger anchor system.

To connect the pieces of protection, follow these steps (see figure 8.19):

1. Set the nuts or stoppers properly in each constriction.
2. Clip a sling to one of the protections via a carabiner and then pass it through the carabiner of the opposite protection.
3. Pass the end loop of the sling between its own strands and then through the same carabiner one more time.
4. Clip the end loop in the sling.

Figure 8.19 *(a)* Connect sling to one of the protection's carabiner, then feed it through the second protection's carabiner. *(b)* Pass the end loop of the sling between its own strands. *(c)* Clip sling through the same carabiner one more time.

CONSUMER TIP

If you plan to do a lot of multipitch climbs, you might want to look into getting a pair of Alpine Equalizers (made by Trango). The Alpine Equalizer is designed to quickly equalize up to three anchor points. Based on the research done by Jim Cormier at Cormier Mountaineering, the Alpine Equalizer is a light presewn rig made of super-strength webbing. It is ideally suited as a self-equalizing anchor system, but it can also be turned into a pre-equalized anchor by tying an overhand knot in the center loop or by tying clove hitch knots at each anchor point. The rig is available in 6-foot (183 cm) and 3-foot (91 cm) versions. Visit www.trango.com to find more information about the Alpine Equalizer and to see an instructional video.

Examples of Classic Anchor Systems

This section presents illustrations of the classic anchor systems (thus pleasing the visual learners). This includes anchor systems designed for specific situations, such as a top-rope climb with a belay from below or above, a single-pitch climb, and a multipitch climb. Note that many of the systems for single-pitch climbs can also be used during a multipitch climb. Remember that the main difference between a belay anchor for a single-pitch climb and one for a multipitch climb is that the latter will always need additional anchor points designed to pull upward to protect the next pitch.

For each included anchor system, a brief explanation is provided on why the system or the rigging technique is used. Finally, an analysis of each system is provided based on the use of the ADDRESS principles.

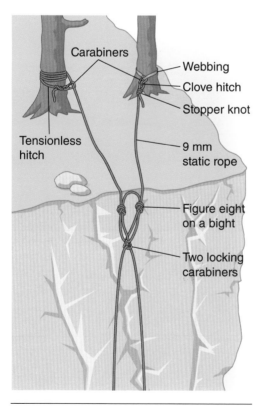

Figure 8.20 Two-points natural anchor system pre-equalized with extension.

Top-Rope Climb

Two-points natural anchor system pre-equalized with extension

This is a classic and effective way to build a good anchor system (see figure 8.20). This system is often used by experienced climbers when these two conditions are met: (1) The climber can approach the top of the climb safely via a trail or an easy scramble on an adjacent route, and (2) the top of the climbing site is flat and safe to work around.

Notice that a single nine-millimeter static rope is used to build the rigging while keeping redundancy in the system. The two figure eight knots (tied on a bight) at the master point literally create two distinct ropes, one for each anchor point.

Finally, notice that the construction of the anchor system started with the tensionless hitch on the left tree. Once the master point was created and loaded with the climbing rope to create tension on the system, the second anchor point (i.e., right tree) was connected via a clove hitch tied to the carabiner clipped to a webbing. The clove hitch was used here because it allows for a quick and easy adjustment of the tension on the entire system. Don't forget that the load strand in the clove hitch must be on the spine side of the carabiner. Add a stopper knot to secure the loose end of the rope after the clove hitch or tie a figure eight in the end of the rope and clip to the carabiner to "close."

Angle.   The angle at the master point is below 60 degrees, which will greatly reduce the stress on each anchor point and the respective rigs. The length of the webbing around the tree is long enough to keep the angle of its apex at less than 60 degrees.

Distance.   The master point is placed over the edge of the cliff, allowing the climbing rope to run freely.

Direction.   Even if both anchor points are not forming a perfect triangle with the master point, the master point hangs just above the climbing route; therefore, no pendulum swings will be experienced by the climber after a fall.

Redundancy.   The system is redundant because it uses two separate anchor points (i.e., trees), two independent rigging systems, and two locking carabiners at the master point. Notice that the clove hitch is tied to a single carabiner because a failure of the carabiner would not be catastrophic—the other line would still hold the weight of a fallen climber.

Equalized.   The tension in the system has been equalized by adjusting the distance on the right line in the rig.

Shock loading.   A potential shock load has been eliminated by using two separate knots at the master point, which also creates a pre-equalized system.

Strong.   The system is strong because each tree can easily be given an individual score of 5. Therefore, the system's overall score reaches 10, which means it is safe to use for climbing.

Redundant single-point natural anchor system pre-equalized with extension

This system is not commonly used, but it is appropriate in certain situations where a number of strong anchor points do not exist (see figure 8.21). In this situation, you may

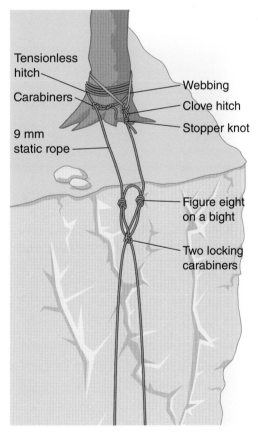

Figure 8.21   Redundant single-point natural anchor system pre-equalized with extension.

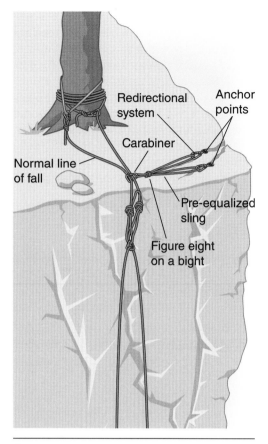

Redirectional system

Anchor points

Carabiner

Normal line of fall

Pre-equalized sling

Figure eight on a bight

Figure 8.22 Redirected redundant single-point natural anchor system pre-equalized with extension.

use a single "bombproof" anchor such as a large and well-rooted tree or a large and stable boulder. Although the system uses a single anchor point, redundancy is still present in the system because the anchor has been rigged twice. The setup for this anchor system is the same as the previous one.

Angle. With this system, the angle at the master point is virtually zero, which is technically ideal.

Distance. The master point is placed over the edge of the cliff, allowing the climbing rope to run freely.

Direction. One drawback of this system is that the "bombproof" anchor has to be directly above the climbing route. However, it is also possible to use a single large anchor that is slightly to the right or left of the climbing route; in this case, the rigging must be redirected so the master point hangs above the climb. The redirect can be accomplished using a smaller anchor such as a tree or using a piece of protection (see figure 8.22). Don't forget that the redirect anchor is not designed to hold weight but only to reposition the direction of the rig.

Redundancy. The system is redundant because it uses two separate anchor lines and two locking carabiners at the master point. Notice that the clove hitch is tied to a single carabiner because a failure of the carabiner would not be catastrophic—the other line would still hold the weight of a fallen climber.

Equalized. The tension in the system has been equalized by adjusting the distance on the line attached to the webbing.

Shock loading. A potential shock load has been eliminated by using two separate knots at the master point, which also creates a pre-equalized system.

Strong. The system is strong because the "bombproof" anchor can easily be given a score of 5. The overall score reaches 10 because the anchor has been rigged twice.

Two-points natural anchor system pre-equalized with a belay from the top

When a climbing route is only accessible from the top, an anchor system may be set up that includes a belay from the top. This system is different from an anchor used on a multipitch climb because the belayer's position will often force the climbing rope to run over the edge of the cliff. This problem will be corrected by placing an edge protection pad, empty backpack, or jacket under the rope to avoid rope abrasion.

The belayer will be anchored to the system via a butterfly knot placed on one of the anchor lines. The belay device will be placed directly at the master point. Depending on the type of belay technique used, the belayer could be positioned either beside the master point (see figure 8.23) or in front of the master point near the edge of the cliff (see figure 8.24), which would allow the belayer to keep an eye on the climber.

For this system, two tensionless hitches are used. The equalization of the system can be accomplished at the master point by simply pulling the anchor line in the direction of the climb and tying two separate figure eight knots. To avoid equalization problems with this setup—and to secure yourself at the top of the cliff—make sure that you, the belayer, tie and clip yourself to the butterfly knot before tying the master point.

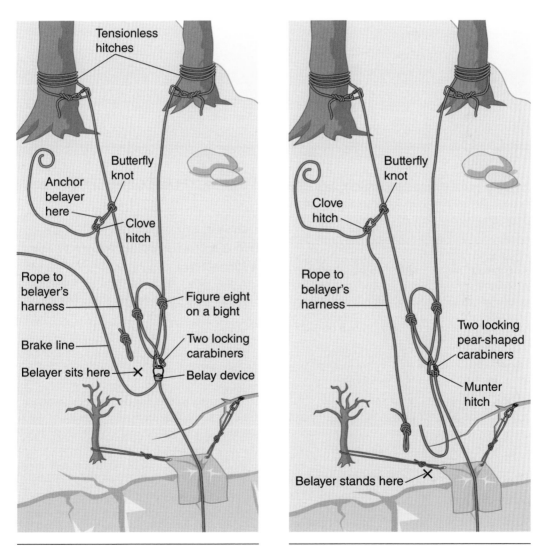

Figure 8.23 Two-points natural anchor system pre-equalized with a belay from the top (with the belayer beside the master point).

Figure 8.24 Two-points natural anchor system pre-equalized with a belay from the top (with the belayer in front of the master point).

This setup will allow you to lower climbers as well as belay them back up. This is often essential when climbing over a seashore, over a lake, or over the edge of a deep canyon.

Angle. The angle at the master point is below 60 degrees, which will greatly reduce the stress on each anchor point and the respective rigs.

Direction. In this system, like in many others, you must be sure that the belayer's position does not interfere with the direction of pull on the master point. The belayer needs to be positioned in line between the master point and the climber; otherwise, the situation is dangerous for the belayer and the climber. If the belayer is not positioned properly, a fall from the climber would create a pendulum on the belayer, which could lead him to lose his grip on the brake rope.

Redundancy. The system is redundant because it uses two separate anchor lines on two separate anchor points. Two locking carabiners at the master point complete the need for redundancy at all critical points.

Equalized. The tension in the system has been equalized by simply tying two separate knots to create the master point.

Shock loading. A potential shock load has been eliminated by using two separate knots at the master point, which also creates a pre-equalized system.

Strong. The system is strong because a score of 5 can easily be given to each anchor point. The overall score reaches 10.

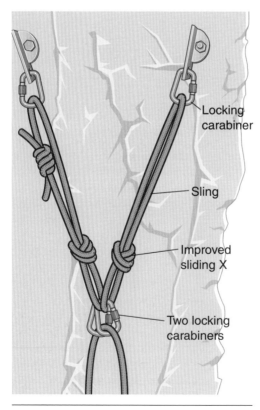
Locking carabiner

Sling

Improved sliding X

Two locking carabiners

Figure 8.25 Two-points artificial (bolts) anchor system self-equalized with limited extension.

Single-Pitch Climb

Two-points artificial (bolts) anchor system self-equalized with limited extension

This setup is also a classic in the world of climbing, especially around sport climbing crags (see figure 8.25). A seven-millimeter cordelette or a sewn webbing (Spectra) works best for this quick setup. Once you have secured yourself to one of the bolts, you should build your anchor system by placing a carabiner at each climbing anchor. Then clip the cordelette or webbing to each carabiner. If you are using a cordelette, both ends will need to be tied together with a double fisherman's knot. This should form a large triangular loop. Now pull the line between each anchor, twist it half a turn to create a sliding X, and bring it down to meet the other line. Place two locking carabiners at the master point.

Next, to reduce the potential shock load, tie an overhand knot on each strand of the rig so that the strands sit about 3 inches

(7.6 cm) above the master point. You have now quickly built—with a minimum amount of equipment—a self-equalizing anchor system with a limited extension.

From here, feed the climbing rope through the master point, and after removing your safety clip, let your belayer lower you down.

Angle. The angle at the master point is below 60 degrees, which will greatly reduce the stress on each anchor point and the respective rigs. If the angle is larger than 60 degrees, you should use a longer cordelette or webbing—this will reduce the angle at the master point.

Direction. In this system, the sliding X setup allows the master point to be multidirectional, so the master point pulling direction can vary.

Redundancy. The system is redundant because placing a knot on each strand of the rig creates two separate anchor lines on two separate anchor points. Two locking carabiners at the master point complete the need for redundancy at all critical points.

Equalized. The tension in the system is self-equalized by the sliding X.

Shock loading. A potential shock load has been reduced by placing knots on each strand of the rig.

Strong. The system is strong because a score of 5 can be given to each anchor point. The overall score reaches 10.

Two-points artificial (bolts) anchor system pre-equalized

This setup is quite similar to the previous one; however, this time a pre-equalized anchor system is created (see figure 8.26). To build this system, you can again use cordelette or webbing and follow similar steps at the beginning.

Place carabiners on each bolt hanger, and clip the cordelette or webbing to each carabiner. Pull the line between each anchor and bring it down to meet the other line. Now pull all lines to the exact position where the master point will rest, and tie a large figure eight on a bight. Place two locking carabiners at the master point.

From here, feed the climbing rope through the master point, and after removing your safety clip, let your belayer lower you down.

Angle. The angle at the master point is below 60 degrees, which will greatly reduce the stress on each anchor point and the respective rigs. If the angle is larger than 60 degrees, you should use a longer cordelette or webbing—this will reduce the angle at the master point.

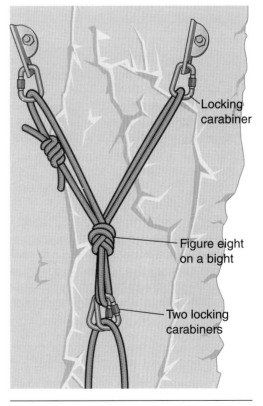

Figure 8.26 Two-points artificial (bolts) anchor system pre-equalized.

Direction. As with all pre-equalized anchor systems, the direction of pull on the master point must be determined. If the master point is created even slightly off the direction of pull, the anchor point will not share the load when a climber falls on the system.

Redundancy. The system is redundant because placing a knot at the master point creates two separate anchor lines on two separate anchor points. Two locking carabiners at the master point complete the need for redundancy at all critical points.

Equalized. The tension in the system is self-equalized by the figure eight being tied correctly on the bight to form the master point.

Shock loading. A potential shock load has been eliminated by the figure eight tied on the bight.

Strong. The system is strong because a score of 5 can be given to each anchor point. The overall score reaches 10.

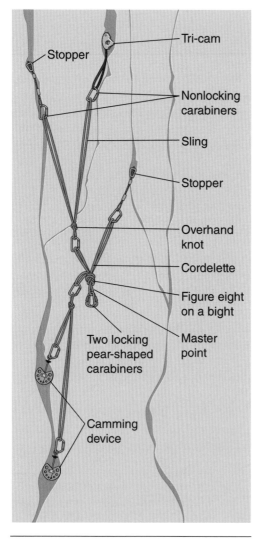

Figure 8.27 Five-points artificial anchor (protection) system pre-equalized.

Multipitch Climb

Five-points artificial anchor (protection) system pre-equalized

Examples of belay anchor systems for multipitch climbs are numerous, but they all share the same basic construction. The anchor system should protect from forces pulling downward in order to protect the second. The system should also protect from forces pulling upward in order to protect the lead climber during the following pitch. This means that all the protections should support each other when forces are applied.

A classic way to accomplish this is to place three pieces of protection with a downward pull and one or two pieces of protection with an upward pull. Both sets of protections are then rigged together to hold the master point between them (see figure 8.27).

Pre-equalizing all anchor points is essential, especially since the system is built with artificial pieces of protection that might be compromised by a sudden dynamic force created by a shock load.

To build this anchor, you will first need to build the top anchor points. This means that the three downward-pull pieces of protection are placed first. The two closest pieces of protection are then rigged together with a pre-equalized webbing;

the third piece is left alone, waiting to be connected to the entire anchor system via a cordelette. Next, two other pieces of protection are placed below with an upward pull. These pieces are also rigged together with a pre-equalized webbing. (Note that a single piece of protection with an upward pull will often be enough to secure the belayer and the leader during the next pitch.) Finally, all the elements of the system are rigged together with a long, pre-equalized cordelette to form the master point. With this setup, the master point can be pulled upward or downward without compromising any of the downward or upward pieces of protection. This technically renders the master point multidirectional.

With this system, the climber will use a clove hitch to anchor herself to the master point using the strand of climbing rope attached to her harness. Although she will belay from her own harness, she will use the master point to perform a redirected belay. This technique not only keeps the belayer in a secure position, it also makes good use of the anchor system, which will take the brunt of the force in case of a fall from the second. Once the second has reached the belay station, he will secure himself to the anchor system by adding his own carabiner to the master point and connecting his strand of the rope to it using a clove hitch. This system looks complicated when both climbers are together at the belay station, but with some hands-on practice, you will see that the setup is not very confusing. Nevertheless, multipitch climbing does require an excellent understanding of belay anchor construction.

Angle.   The angles created between the downward-pull pieces and the master point are below 60 degrees. The same can be said about the angles between the upward-pull pieces and the master point. The only angle that is larger than 60 degrees is the one formed at the master point between the upward and downward pieces. However, this angle does not compromise the integrity of the anchor points because the downward- and upward-pull anchor points work separately. This means that the downward protections are affected only by downward forces and that the upward protections are affected only by upward forces.

Direction.   As with all pre-equalized anchor systems, the direction of pull on the master point must be determined. The load must be equally distributed to the downward-pull pieces as well as the upward-pull pieces when the master point is pulled either downward or upward. Remember, to be truly multidirectional, a master point must be able to move in various directions while keeping equal tension on all anchor points.

Redundancy.   The system is redundant because the rig interconnects many pieces of protection—three with a downward pull and two with an upward pull. Two locking carabiners at the master point complete the need for redundancy at all critical points.

Equalized.   The tension in the system is self-equalized by the figure eight being tied correctly on the bight to form the master point.

Shock loading.   A potential shock load has been eliminated by the figure eight tied on the bight on the webbings and on the cordelette forming the master point.

Strong.   The system is strong because a score of 4 can be given to each anchor point. The overall score reaches 12 for downward forces. For the upward forces, don't forget that the belayer will take a large amount of the forces generated by a falling lead climber; therefore, the upward-pull pieces don't need to score above 10 in our discretionary scoring scheme. The forces on these pieces will be much less than the forces on the downward-pull pieces.

Summary

An anchor system is composed of three parts: (1) at least two anchor points, (2) a rig, and (3) a master point. The construction of effective and safe anchor systems is based on a few essential principles. These principles include adequate *angle*, proper *distance* for the master point, appropriate *direction* of pull on the anchor points and the master point, *redundancy* at all critical points, *equalization* of the tension on all anchor points, reduction or elimination of a potential *shock load*, and finally, an overall anchor system that is *strong*. The acronym ADDRESS can help you remember these principles.

Anchor points can be created by using either natural features (such as trees, boulders, and rock formations) or man-made objects called climbing protections. These climbing protections can be fixed, or permanently placed in the rock (i.e., bolts, pitons). They may also be temporarily placed in rock fissures (i.e., chocks, cams, and so on).

From a physics point of view, properly built anchor systems are very strong. Although climbers need to understand how strong these systems can be, they should also know that building anchor systems effectively is an art. To achieve a high level of comfort building climbing anchors, you need to understand the seven principles of ADDRESS. You also need to master four essential sets of skills: (1) knowing how to tie climbing knots, (2) sequencing your actions when building anchor systems, (3) knowing how to adjust tension on a knot, and (4) knowing how to use carabiners.

Understanding the strategies and principles presented in this chapter is important; however, you must also put them into practice by partnering up with an experienced and talented climbing instructor or colleague.

CHAPTER 9

Strength and Grace: Techniques for Movement on Rock

Technique is our protection.

Chuck Pratt

Prolific American climber Chuck Pratt states it best: "Technique is our protection." Fluid and confident movement and good technique are at the foundation of rock climbing. Although rope work, hardware, and anchor systems all prove critical in our ability to climb and explore, the deciding factor ultimately boils down to whether or not we have the skill and strength to execute the moves. Strength may sometimes substitute for lack of skill and vice versa; however, climbers should strive for a healthy combination of strength and skill in order to work toward ever-improving performance. This chapter provides basic information on proper technique for climbing on varying terrain, as well as tips and ideas that will help you in your overall progression.

General Tips and Techniques

Though specific types of climbing often call for certain techniques, several basic principles should be applied to any terrain you climb. How do you climb a ladder? This question might seem silly, but the answer provides the first step toward gaining proper technique for rock climbing. Obviously, to get up the ladder, you hold the rungs with your hands, move your feet up a rung, and stand up. Your upward progress is primarily gained through your legs.

This bit of information is extremely important. The more you use your legs, the more energy you conserve in your arms. When first getting out on the rock, most people tend to concentrate on the wrong appendages. It is very easy to depend too much on your upper body, especially your hands. Although your hands are important for maintaining balance, you will find that proper footwork will increase your confidence and performance quickly, making climbing more enjoyable.

Even before touching the rock, you should have a plan put into place. This plan, however rough, might entail visualizing your intended route, evaluating potential troublesome sections, and committing to memory good rest stances and possible hazards that exist (see figure 9.1). Once en route, you need to be constantly aware of your

Figure 9.1 Climb like a hawk—situational awareness. You must use your sense of sight. Beginning on the ground, you should study the route and identify certain features. Good climbers continuously observe and make adjustments.

surroundings. People often get tunnel vision when climbing. By constantly reminding yourself to look around, you will undoubtedly find better solutions that will save you both time and strength. Look ahead for potential sequences, and look below to find good footholds.

Balance is the key to efficient and safe climbing (see figure 9.2). Observing a talented climber move gracefully and effortlessly over difficult terrain is often both a humbling and inspiring experience. It is particularly humbling if you just spent an hour working yourself up the same route, and it is inspiring because it shows you what is possible. Though obviously strong from many days of climbing, talented climbers appear as if they exert little energy. Why is that? The easy answer is that they are good. The more involved answer is that they have the confidence within themselves and the knowledge of how to use and position their body in ways that allow for smooth, efficient movement. The first step in gaining confidence in your movements is learning how to maintain control and balance. Balance is directly influenced by the weight distribution of the climber's body.

Keeping your weight centered over your feet is the first step in maintaining balance. The second step requires you to keep control while in motion. Big dynamic moves are always exciting, but in reality, the majority of the movements are made statically. This is done by looking ahead and deciding what particular movements might do to your body positioning and how they will affect your balance. If you determine that the move will throw you off balance, you then need to determine what can be done to compensate and keep you under control.

Figure 9.2 Balancing.

While climbing, if you never feel stable and balanced, you are burning the valuable resources needed to get you to the top. The moment your balance becomes off center, you must compensate by using additional strength in order to keep yourself on the rock and off the rope. This extra effort may tire you out and cause you to fall.

Flagging

Flagging is a technique used by climbers to maintain balance (see figure 9.3). By extending a foot for counterbalance, a climber may be able to maintain positive pressure on a sideways hold that is off to the side.

Figure 9.3 Climber adjusts her center of gravity by "flagging" out a leg. The suspended foot serves as a counterbalance.

Flagging can help avert a fall. When you release one point of contact, if your body opens up (i.e., "barn doors"), your weight will not be properly lined up and distributed. Work on repositioning yourself in order to prevent this imbalance.

The Match

In climbing, the term *match* essentially means to swap or change. Whenever you change your hands or feet on a particular hold, you are matching. Matching hands, feet, or hands and feet are all very common while climbing. The most obvious time a climber matches is during a traverse, which involves moving horizontally (see figure 9.4). While moving horizontally, you are using the same holds for both your right and left sides (both hands and feet). However, the match is a common practice when moving up as well. While making upward progress, the hand-to-foot match occurs when using a low hold with your hand and then high-stepping and making the switch with your foot (see figure 9.5).

When matching, you need to think ahead and then check to see exactly how much room there is to work with.

Figure 9.4 Hand-to-hand match.

Figure 9.5 Flexibility is key for the high-step hand-to-foot match.

When matching feet, the climber will often have to hop off one foot while planting the other in its place. Other times, a climber may need to place one foot on top of the other. Once one foot is on top of the other, the lower foot slides out, allowing the upper foot to replace it seamlessly (see figure 9.6).

Static Versus Dynamic

The majority of moves performed while climbing lie within reach of one another. Though possibly requiring a stretch, holds can typically be reached statically from a fixed stance or position. Occasionally, however, a climber is faced with the challenge of obtaining a feature that lies out of reach but is needed to make progress. The one option

Figure 9.6 Foot-to-foot match.

in this situation is to perform a dynamic move—a move that requires a jump or lunge. Typically more committing than static moves, dynamic moves range from short lunges to gain as little as an extra inch to all-out throws for multiple feet. The term *dyno* is used to describe dynamic moves that require all points of contact with the stone to be lost because of the distance between holds (see figure 9.7).

Figure 9.7 Dyno. Set up, launch, and stick it! Failure to reach the desired hold usually results in a fall.

TECHNIQUE TIP

To gain a little extra distance on a big dyno, try adjusting your aim to a point just beyond your desired hold. This often helps you get just enough extra distance to successfully complete the move.

The combination of balance, situational awareness of the rock around you, and an awareness of your body's position on the rock will help you execute the specific moves outlined in more detail in the following sections.

Rock Features

In a nutshell, rock climbers climb two types of features: rock faces and cracks (see figure 9.8). These two categories can be further broken down into more distinct and refined classes. The term *face climbing* can refer to cliffs with extremely overhanging features as well as to low-angled, featureless slabs. Similarly, the cracks you climb can be as narrow as your fingertips or as wide as your wingspan. Between each of these extreme examples lies a wide variety of terrain. The following sections cover basic techniques that will give you an understanding of how to climb both face and crack climbs. You should realize that no amount of literature can make up for actual time spent on rock.

Figure 9.8 Comparing (a) a crack climb to (b) a face climb.

Face Climbing

As the name implies, face climbing refers to climbing rock faces as opposed to cracks. When face climbing, the climber uses features or irregularities on the rock face. These irregularities can be used to gain positive forces in many different ways by both hands and feet. A certain feature might begin as a crimp for your hand, become a side pull, and then end up an edge for your foot after performing a hand-to-foot match. Combining different movements and techniques efficiently takes on the character of an intricate dance performed in the vertical world. The movements, techniques, and features that make up this dance vary considerably; they are tools in the climber's tool belt for success.

Handholds

Holds used for face climbing are simply irregularities in what would otherwise be a blank face. The task for a climber is to use these features for efficient movement. For both hands

Figure 9.9 Jugs are defined as large, positive holds that are easy to hold on to.

and feet, the holds used come in a variety of shapes and sizes. This section provides an overview of common features encountered and the proper techniques used in taking advantage of them. Remember to use your sense of sight as well as your sense of touch to find good handholds.

The **jug** (see figure 9.9) is a super friendly hold that inspires great confidence whenever encountered. It is characterized as a large hold that is easy to grasp and maintain.

Depending on the size of these features and the amount of purchase needed, **edges** can be gripped in two ways: the open-hand grip (see figure 9.10a) and the closed-hand grip, also called a crimp (see figure 9.10b). Each method has its place. For larger edges, the open-hand grip is used. In this grip, the climber grasps the edge with the palm open and fingers extended. The crimp is used when the edge gets small enough that

Figure 9.10 (a) Open-hand grip and (b) closed-hand grip.

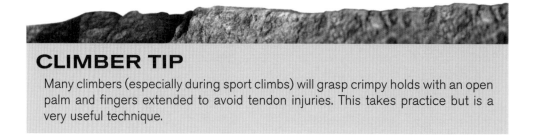

CLIMBER TIP

Many climbers (especially during sport climbs) will grasp crimpy holds with an open palm and fingers extended to avoid tendon injuries. This takes practice but is a very useful technique.

the amount of force needed cannot be generated with the open-hand grip. The crimp is performed by placing the fingertips on the edge and then bending the knuckles to apply more force on the fingers. The thumb can also be placed on top of the fingers and used for greater power. Be aware that while crimping is more secure and provides better purchase, it does put more stress on fingers and tendons, which is a common mechanism for injuries.

Pockets can vary greatly in their size and shape. They can be deep, wide, and positive, accepting up to four fingers and feeling similar to a jug (see figure 9.11). Pockets can also be shallow, sloping, and narrow. When pockets are not wide enough to accept multiple fingers side by side, a climber can sometimes use stacked fingers, applying downward pressure on top of one another.

A **sloper** will often include some type of feature to hold onto other than its texture. When broken down to their basic form, sloping holds require the climber to use downward pressure to generate as much friction as possible between the palm of the hand and the rock (see figure 9.12). Although this feature may simply be a variation in the slope angle or a small seam that enables a crimp, the combination may prove necessary to make the hold adequate.

Figure 9.11   A good example of a three-finger pocket.

Figure 9.12 Chalk is especially useful on sloping holds, allowing the climber to increase the amount of friction and avoid slippage.

Body Tension

Body tension is extremely important and is often used while climbing. It is especially important when using holds that produce forces that push the climber away from the wall. The side pull, gaston, and undercling are all movements that require certain amounts of body tension to keep the climber in balance.

Performed just how it sounds, a **side pull** differs from holds used with a downward pull in that the side pull is held vertically with the power being generated by pulling inward toward the climber (see figure 9.13). Side pulls may often require flagging in order to generate the appropriate counterbalance.

Similar to the side pull, the **gaston** is performed using a vertical hold; however, the gaston involves using a different direction of pull. To perform a gaston, the climber grasps a hold and pulls outward. Climbers will sometimes use a double gaston to climb a wide crack. Both hands pull in opposite

Figure 9.13 Side pull.

Figure 9.14 Double gaston.

Figure 9.15 Undercling.

directions on the sides of the crack, as if the climber is trying to pull the crack apart (see figure 9.14).

With an **undercling,** the climber's palm faces up as he or she utilizes positive features with upward or outward pressure to keep his or her body close to the rock. By pulling the body into the rock, the climber produces more downward pressure, creating more secure footholds (see figure 9.15). In steep terrain, the undercling helps keep the climber's hips close to the rock, and it allows for extra reach because it is easily used from a lower position.

The **mantle** is a series of moves that culminates in having your feet end up where your hands began. The climber begins with the hands hanging from a ledge above (see figure 9.16*a*). As the climber moves upward, the hand position changes from pulling downward to pushing upward and locking the elbow (see figure 9.16*b*). The climber works the feet up and brings them to the ledge, starting the process of a hand-to-foot match (see figure 9.16*c*). The mantle often requires

Figure 9.16 Mantle.

significant arm strength and hip flexibility. The mantle is most often used for gaining a ledge.

Footholds

Although your feet are used to gain purchase on holds, you should remember that your legs will be doing the majority of the work. In modern times, climbing shoes have advanced significantly. Because climbing with your feet is so important for balance and efficiency, you need to develop a keen sense of your climbing shoes' capabilities and develop trust in your footwork. Edging, smearing, and hooking are three techniques used to gain friction on rock with climbing shoes.

When a climber is **edging**, the straight, stiff part of the climbing shoe is used (see figure 9.17). This move can be performed with both the inner and outer edge of the foot. Inside edging is one of the most commonly used footholds. Stiff soles edge better than flexible soles.

Figure 9.17 Edging.

Two types of **hooks** fall under the category of edging: the toe hook and the heel hook (see figure 9.18). Though a climber will occasionally use a hook for upward progress,

Figure 9.18 Heel hook on overhang.

hooks are primarily used as balancing mechanisms to keep the climber situated comfortably on the wall. An example would be hooking your toe around a feature to keep your body from swinging outward. An example of a hook being used for upward progress comes when working to surmount an overhang. The heel can be placed on the lip of the overhang and can be used to generate extra downward pressure, adding assistance to the pull of the upper body.

Figure 9.19 Smearing.

As opposed to edging, when a climber is **smearing,** the climber uses the flat, flexible part of the climbing shoe. When smearing, the climber works to achieve the greatest amount of friction possible between the rubber on her shoe and the rock itself (see figure 9.19). Two main factors come into play here: (1) the amount of surface area between the shoe and the rock, and (2) the angle of force (i.e., climber's body weight). When smearing on nearly sheer surfaces, you should look for inconsistencies or tiny features that will provide additional pur-

Figure 9.20   Slab footwork.   **Figure 9.21**   Stemming.

chase, adding security to the placement. Some climbs only have a move or two requiring friction; other climbs, such as slabs, are primarily made up of friction moves (see figure 9.20). Footwork on this sort of terrain requires good body positioning. By keeping your body away from the rock, you are putting more weight over your feet, which in turn offers a greater amount of friction.

Stemming is important for all types of climbing. Climbers primarily use stemming in corners where they can smear their feet and push on either side, effectively generating opposing forces to keep the climber in place. Corners or dihedrals are often home to cracks (see figure 9.21). With proper body positioning and balance, stemming often affords the climber a great no-hands rest.

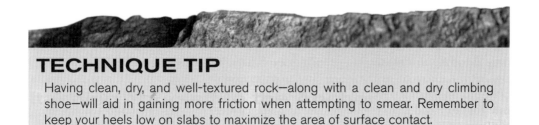

TECHNIQUE TIP

Having clean, dry, and well-textured rock—along with a clean and dry climbing shoe—will aid in gaining more friction when attempting to smear. Remember to keep your heels low on slabs to maximize the area of surface contact.

Crack Climbing

Techniques for crack climbing differ from those used for face climbing. While on a face, the climber is grasping holds and irregularities. In crack climbing, climbers lodge their hands into the crack to gain body-supporting purchase and then upward movement. The goal is to jam some part of the climber (whether it's the hand, foot, knee, arm, or body) into the crack, get it locked off, and use that jam for upward progress. Crack climbing can test inventiveness and creativity. At times, crack climbing can also be painful. There are no rules for crack climbing; by experimenting with different hand- and footholds, each climber gains a better understanding of what is possible.

Depending on the type of rock and the nature of the crack, climbers often tape their hands and fingers with athletic tape to keep their digits and skin intact (see figure 9.22). Cracks range in size from being just big enough for fingertips (i.e., 1 or 2 centimeters) to being a full-body chimney (i.e., 3 to 5 feet [91 to 152 cm]). Because of this broad range, many different techniques are used for different crack sizes. The relationship of body size to crack size is the critical element and will vary depending on climber size. A jam that feels secure to one climber can be shaky and insecure to another (see figure 9.23).

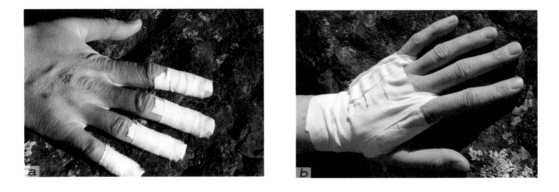

Figure 9.22 *(a)* Finger taping, *(b)* hand taping palm down, and *(c)* hand taping palm up.

Figure 9.23 A fine example of crack-climbing technique. The climber uses a variety of jamming techniques with both hands and feet rather than using features on the nearby rock face.

Figure 9.24 Here is an example of a finger lock with the fingers down. The climber gains additional purchase in the crack by flexing her fingers.

Figure 9.25 By flexing the hand, friction is increased on the walls of the crack, supporting the weight of the climber. This is a good example of a mid-sized hand crack.

Fingers

A good finger lock can be a very secure placement, but at the same time, it can cause pain. After inserting your fingers in a vertical crack, torque your hand to its palm side until it becomes secure (see figure 9.24).

Hands

The hand jam is a commonly used move in crack climbing, and when used correctly, it can become a comforting and stable handhold. The climber uses the fingertips, the back of the hand, and the palm as three points of contact. Once inserted in the crack, the hand can be flexed and made bigger, ensuring a nice snug fit. Also, the thumb can be tucked under the palm for added strength (see figure 9.25).

Fists

As with hand jams, a good fist jam is a very solid hold (see figure 9.26). Depending on crack size, the fist can be inserted either horizontally or vertically.

Figure 9.26 Fist jam *(a)* vertically and *(b)* horizontally.

Off-Width Cracks

Although they have the potential of being tedious, painful, and just plain grunt work, off-width cracks are rewarding objectives. Following are several common techniques that will prove beneficial when climbing off-width cracks:

• **Hand or fist stack.** This technique involves using both hands in conjunction when filling the crack. The hand or fist stack is used when the crack is too wide for a single fist jam (see figure 9.27).

Figure 9.27 Different variations on the hand or fist stack.

• **Arm bar and arm lock.** When the crack is wide and deep enough to fit either the full length of your arm or your arm bent at the elbow, you can use the arm bar or the arm lock. When a climber is performing the arm bar, the entire length of the climber's arm is in the crack. With the palm pushing on one side and the elbow applying pressure on the other, the arm bar is locked into place. The arm lock or "chicken wing" is performed by bending the arm and inserting the elbow first in the crack; the climber then uses opposing pressure to create a secure placement (see figure 9.28).

Figure 9.28 Arm bar and arm lock.

Figure 9.29 An example of a toe jam.

Foot or Toe Jam

The foot jam is an extremely stable—yet sometimes painful—foothold (see figure 9.29). The sequence is composed of two main motions: First, the climber inserts the foot into the crack as parallel to the sides as possible. Second, the climber twists the foot by bringing the knee up and inward. Foot jams are such good footholds that they are sometimes difficult to remove from the crack. A toe jam is useful for smaller cracks that are too small to accommodate the entire foot.

Chimneys

A chimney is a wide crack that accepts your entire body. When climbing a chimney, you should face one side of the crack and push your feet, back, hands, and knees against the sides of the crack; you then work these points of pressure in conjunction to make upward

TECHNIQUE TIP

When first starting out, you must be careful not to overjam. Overjamming is essentially putting too much force on a particular jam, which in turn burns energy quicker. After setting a jam, you can back off, decreasing the amount of force, until just before the jam might slip. Although this may feel less secure, it allows for a more efficient use of energy.

Figure 9.30 Using the arms as stabilizers, the climber gains upward motion by repositioning the feet and applying both horizontal and vertical pressure.

progress (see figure 9.30). When lead climbing a chimney pitch, consider where your gear is racked. Placing all of your protection on a shoulder sling allows you to move it out of the way. If gear is on the harness, it can be very uncomfortable and impede movement.

Lieback

To perform the lieback, you grab the side of a crack with both hands and then walk your feet up to a comfortable height, somewhere between knee and waist height. You use the opposing forces of pulling hands and pushing feet to establish yourself (see figure 9.31).

The lieback is often used to overcome sections of off-width crack. Though seemingly stable and easy, liebacks put loads of stress on your arms and often leave you in

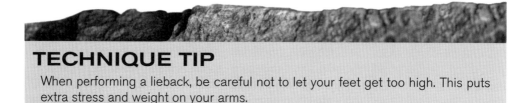

Figure 9.31 Lieback.

precarious positions. Climbers who are not well versed in crack-climbing techniques often resort to the lieback. This might work on short sections, but it is an inadequate substitute for honing your crack-climbing skills. The lieback is physically demanding, making energy conservation difficult. The lieback also positions the climber in ways that make placing protection in the crack much more difficult. However, the lieback does have its place and is an important skill to master.

Overhang Climbing

When the terrain you are climbing becomes overhanging, you are simultaneously decreasing the amount of weight on your feet and compensating with an increased amount of upper body strength. Though decidedly more strenuous, body tension, strength, and endurance can make overhang climbs easier and more enjoyable.

- **Body tension.** By pulling your body closer to the face, you are increasing the amount of weight over your feet (keeping your hips in). This helps out your arms, but it does require a lot of core strength and control, which is centered around your abdominal muscles.

- **Strength and endurance.** At certain points in all climbing, technique gives way to the need for more power. It is inevitable that someone who climbs regularly will get stronger; however, if you are always climbing slabs, you will not build the muscles necessary for steeper climbs.

At Rest

When you have the opportunity to rest, take it. While climbing, many people do not recognize when they have an opportunity to rest. This may be a full-blown no-hands rest or just a partial rest that enables you to shake out one arm at a time. Whichever it is, using it to its fullest might prove instrumental in allowing you to successfully complete the route.

No Hands

The no-hands rest is the saving grace on many climbs. Not only does it allow you to let go with both hands and depump (decrease the amount of lactic acid flowing through your muscles), it also gives you the chance to comfortably look ahead and evaluate the terrain to come. The simplest form of a no-hands rest comes when standing on a ledge. As routes become steeper and their ledges become smaller, climbers are forced to become more inventive.

A no-hands rest occurs when a climber can fully take the weight off his hands and arms, allowing him time to rest without weighting the rope. These often occur when the climber has good spread-out feet and is located on less-than-vertical terrain where she can lean against the face (see figure 9.32).

Knee Bar

Occasionally, a bent knee can become very well secured by pressing the knee up under a small overhang while maintaining

Figure 9.32 No-hands rest.

Figure 9.33 Knee-bar rest.

Figure 9.34 Skeletal hang rest.

that pressure with a secure foot placement (see figure 9.33). This knee bar gives the climber an opportunity to rest.

Partial Rest

Partial rests allow you to rest one append-age at a time. Though not as ideal as the no-hands rest, partial rests still offer quick rests that can be very helpful before executing difficult moves. Partial rests also provide optimal opportunities for placing gear, allowing a free hand to clip a bolt or place protection.

The skeletal hang enables climbers to relax their muscles by hanging on outstretched arms (see figure 9.34). This reduces tension in the muscles and uses the skeletal structure to bear some of the weight. While great for resting, weighting your skeletal system (arms) can also be incorporated into basic climbing move-ments. Whenever the amount of time spent holding weight with bent arms can be limited, the climber is indeed reducing overall fatigue.

Climbing Safely

You should always test the holds before putting any weight on them. From bulletproof granite to crumbling piles of broken and loose rock, many factors go into the rock quality of a given climbing area. Take the time to understand local geology and the characteristics of different types of rock. Many climbing injuries can be linked to falling rock and broken holds. There is not much you can do to prevent rock fall from above—other than protect yourself with a helmet and have your belayer standing in a safe zone. However, you can prevent injuries related to falls from broken holds and dropped rock by simply testing and evaluating holds before committing to them.

Many rock features can be evaluated with a quick visual inspection. Sure, a nice, clean crack in a blank face is straightforward enough, but what if that splitter crack is splintered into other cracks and has visible loose blocks precariously perched? Obviously, you will want to proceed with caution. When approaching a potentially loose or fragile section, a helpful tactic is to gently hit the area with the side of your fist or the butt of your hand—while doing so, listen for a hollow thud and watch for any movement (see figure 9.35). Although the thud indicates detached rock, it does not necessarily mean the hold is useless. It does, however, give you significant information concerning the next sequence of moves. Once you decide to use a feature that holds some suspicion, you must be sure to treat it as such. You must make sure that you pull down and not out on these holds. By pulling out, you are almost asking for the rock to dislodge. The direct downward pull is your best bet for keeping a suspect hold in place while putting pressure on it.

Figure 9.35 Checking for loose rock.

When a fall occurs on top rope, the chance of serious injury is considerably lower. This is because, with a good belay, the distance of the rope stretch will not exceed a few feet. Conversely, a fall while lead climbing may range from a few feet to well over a hundred. In some instances, falls offer no chance of injury and may actually prove to be quite fun and exhilarating. Other times, climbers may find themselves in "no fall" situations, where the outcome of a fall looks grim and potentially life threatening (e.g., landing on a ledge). Of course, this all depends on the type of climbing you are participating in and the amount of risk you are willing to take.

Always be aware of your surroundings. Whether on top rope or lead, a falling climber should assume an alert body position with hands and feet pushed out in front. This enables the climber to deflect herself and absorb impact while swinging back into the rock. For many people, it is natural instinct to grab hold of the rope during a fall. Avoid grabbing the rope so that your hands remain free. This will enable you to protect yourself against hitting the rock wall and protect yourself when swinging uncontrollably. You can grab a quickdraw to *prevent* a fall and stabilize yourself, but you should never stick a finger in a bolt hanger or grab a quickdraw *during* a fall. In fact, while you are falling, grabbing anything—whether it's a rock feature or gear—is not advisable because it can cause injury.

Summary

Venturing into the vertical world of rock climbing requires flexibility, strength, and overall good technique. Good technique minimizes the amount of strength a climber needs, and it improves efficiency of movement on the rock. For proper technique, you need to focus on the key elements discussed in this chapter—balance, situational awareness, climbing with your legs, using proper handholds and footwork, and climbing like a hawk.

Different features or climbs require different techniques. By getting out and practicing some of the maneuvers discussed in this chapter, you can begin to develop the appropriate techniques for rock climbing.

Remember that proper technique and improved performance come through the confidence gained with experience. Get out, practice these maneuvers and techniques, and become a better, more efficient rock climber. Climb safe!

The old saying "Whatever goes up, must come down" applies to rock climbing. Now that you have read about techniques to help you climb with both strength and grace—enabling you to reach new heights—you will want to learn how to safely descend back to the ground. Chapter 10 will provide you with the technical skills you need to know.

CHAPTER 10

Descending

One climbs, one sees.
One descends, one
sees no longer, but
one has seen.

René Daumal

Descending is the other half of climbing. Being able to make the best decision for descent is an essential skill when rock climbing. Four common methods are used for descending from rock climbs: (1) walking off the top on a trail or on easy terrain, (2) downclimbing either the route you ascended or another route, (3) being lowered off by your partner, and (4) rappelling. The focus of this chapter is rappelling. However, we'll briefly cover the other methods of descending first.

Walk-Offs

One of the safest methods of returning to the base of a rock climb is walking off the top on easier terrain, which will probably not require a rope for safety. Topographic maps, photographs, guidebooks, or drawings of the route will often show the preferred walk-off and level of difficulty. The level of difficulty will generally be class 1, 2, or 3 (see page 68 in chapter 4 for more details).

Downclimbing

Some rock climbs may require you to climb down the same route you ascended or a nearby route that is easier. If you are not using a rope for safety, this can be a very dangerous method of descending. Before you downclimb outdoors on steep terrain, it is a good idea to practice on top rope. To be able to see your feet and find the best footholds, you will need to move your body out away from the rock instead of "hugging" the rock. Before you make each move, you should scan the terrain immediately below you, looking for the most positive holds. Then, try to move only one point of contact (hand or foot) at a time. Climb efficiently and with effective technique, keeping your body in balance and expending the least amount of energy possible. If you and your partner are both downclimbing, the most skilled climber can go first and point out the best holds. If you choose to downclimb roped to your partner, extreme care should be taken so that one climber does not get knocked off balance or fall if the other climber slips. To lessen the length of a fall, gear may be placed by the first person downclimbing and removed by the second. This is called downleading. If you have safer options for descending, you should choose one of them.

Lowering

Lowering your partner is fast and efficient, and it gets the rope down without the risks associated with throwing ropes (i.e., stuck ropes, windblown ropes, and so on). Lowering also sets the rope length for rappel by ensuring that the rope end reaches the ground. For your partner to feel comfortable being lowered, you must lower him smoothly, using a safe and consistent speed. Several methods may be used for lowering a climber. Here are two of the most common methods:

• **Method 1:** mechanical device—If you and your partner are at the top of a climbing route, you can use a plate- or tube-style belay or rappel device. The device is attached to the master point of the anchor with a locking carabiner, and you redirect the rope through another locking carabiner on the brake side (see figure 10.1). If you are on the ground and have belayed your partner to the top of a climb, you may simply lower him to the ground by decreasing the bend of the rope over the edge of the belay device (attached to the belay loop of your harness) and letting the rope slide through. Use two hands on the brake side when lowering.

- **Method 2:** Munter hitch—If the distance is short, say less than 70 feet (21.3 m), a Munter hitch on a pear-shaped carabiner (preferably symmetrical) can be used to lower a climber. The setup for this lowering method can be done quickly. When creating the Munter hitch, be sure to lay the rope flat and avoid introducing twists. If you keep twists out of the hitch, the rope is much less likely to kink as you feed it through while lowering. Longer distances can introduce more twists, so you may choose method 1 for lowering someone over 70 feet. When using a Munter hitch, a symmetrical carabiner allows the rope to move smoothly over itself instead of being forced into a narrower portion of the carabiner. In addition, a pear-shaped carabiner is wide and allows plenty of room for the Munter hitch to ride without moving onto the gate or up the spine. For this reason, narrow carabiners are not suitable for use with a Munter hitch. Refer to chapter 6 for instructions on tying the Munter hitch.

Figure 10.1 Mechanical device being used for lowering.

When using either of these methods to lower a climber from above, you should use a backup in case your hand is knocked off the rope by a twist or some other unexpected occurrence. This backup can be a hitch made with a loop of cord (4 to 8 millimeter depending on the diameter of the rope used to lower) attached to your belay loop. The greater the difference in diameter between the hitch cord and the rope, the more gripping power the hitch has. Examples of appropriate hitches include autoblock, klemheist, and Prusik (see figure 10.2). Be sure to test the hitch and verify that it grabs the rope before you trust it as a backup while lowering a climber.

Figure 10.2 Examples of appropriate hitches: *(a)* autoblock, *(b)* klemheist, *(c)* Prusik.

Rappelling or Abseiling

The final method of descending is rappelling (often called abseiling outside the United States). This is one of the most common ways to descend from a rock climb. Rappelling involves using an anchor to attach your ropes at the top of a climb, adding friction to the rope—generally by means of a mechanical device—lowering yourself down the ropes, and retrieving the ropes to use again. A word of caution: Rappelling is often done at the end of a climb when you are tired and you must trust the system alone; it is not a backup. Therefore, great care must be taken to double-check every part of the system before you begin your rappel. In this chapter, each component of the rappel system is discussed. First, you will learn how to build and inspect a rappel anchor and how to attach the rope to it properly. Next, you will learn about methods of rappelling and how to attach the rappel device to the system. Finally, you'll review information about how to descend whether you are one pitch or multiple pitches from the ground.

Rappel Anchors

The anchor is one of the most important elements of the rappel system—it is the element on which everything else depends. Ideally, a rappel anchor consists of at least two strong protection points that are equalized to share the load. A protection point is a component used to secure the climber to a cliff or ledge, thus preventing a fall. See chapter 8 for a complete discussion on how to build an anchor. You will often find fixed anchors on routes that are rappelled on a regular basis. These anchors may not be equalized, but they may still be safe, assuming they are strong enough for the load placed on them.

Inspecting the Rappel Anchor

Rappel anchors may be natural or artificial. On popular routes that require rappels to descend, artificial anchors (usually bolts, but sometimes pitons or fixed chockstones) are often already in place. Before trusting these with your life, you should inspect them to check their security. A bolt anchor may be suspect if (1) you see streaks of rust below it; (2) the hanger either spins when you push it or is bent; (3) the bolt is an old-style one-quarter-inch bolt; (4) the bolt is the wrong choice for the rock, such as a compression bolt in soft sandstone; or (5) the bolt may be pulled in an outward instead of downward direction when you are beginning your rappel. If you suspect that the anchor is weak, you may choose to back it up with another anchor that you build. If there are nearby cracks, you could place artificial gear—but remember, you will not be able to retrieve it. Some people have been injured or killed from rappel anchor failure because they did not want to leave their expensive gear behind. If you choose, you may back up the anchor for all but the final rappeller. Have the heaviest rappeller descend first with the backup gear in place, and if the primary anchor holds, remove the backup before the last person descends. Obviously, this practice increases the risk for one team member. Many climbers carry a small selection of "leaver gear," or gear that they don't mind leaving behind in such a situation.

Natural anchors are those that use rock features or trees as protection points. When anchor building, some people drape the rope directly around a tree (if the area regulations allow tree anchors), and then pull the rope down when they have rappelled. This may seem to leave no trace since you are not leaving a webbing anchor behind; however, it actually damages both the tree and the rope because of the friction against the tree bark while you are pulling the relatively heavy rope down. Whether you are using a tree, a

SAFETY TIP

If you come to a fixed anchor that already has webbing, be sure to inspect the webbing and the knot carefully before trusting the anchor with your life. Check to see if the webbing is faded, has abraded edges or nicks, has fuzzy spots, feels "crunchy," has rust stains on it, or has been used for rappel without a ring or quick link. Webbing with any of these characteristics is suspect and should be replaced with fresh webbing, preferably in a natural color to match the environment. Avoid leaving multiple slings in place if they are in bad condition. This is trash and should be cut away and taken out of the area in your pack.

rock, pitons, or bolts, it is better to leave a sling with a rappel ring, locking carabiner, or quick link threaded on it, especially if someone else may rappel from that spot later.

Rappel Anchor Positioning

When setting up your rappel anchor, you must be aware of any rope-damaging conditions in that area. Any time the anchor material or rope runs over a sharp edge, you should pad it to prevent damage. Under tension, ropes and webbing can be cut much more easily than you may think. You can use commercially available rope protectors, or you may use backpacks, clothing, and so on. You may have to leave the padding behind, unless you attach the protection to the rope using a cord or string. The padding should be attached to the side of the rope you will pull during rope retrieval to avoid jamming the padding against the anchor system.

Because you will most likely be pulling the rope through the anchor from below after your party rappels, the anchor needs to be positioned so the rope will pull easily. For example, if the anchor is not set over the edge of the cliff, the rope may be difficult to pull because of friction along the ground's surface. The rope may pull rocks or debris off the top onto you, or it may get stuck in a crack. You should carefully consider both the lateral and vertical position of your rappel anchor.

Rappel Anchor Strength

Another rappel-specific consideration is anchor strength. Keep in mind that more force will sometimes be put on the anchor—more than the heaviest person's body weight—because unintentional bouncing or stopping your rappel quickly will increase the load. Complete your rappel slowly, smoothly, and with consistent speed to reduce the stress on the anchor. Because you are putting your complete trust in the rappel system, the anchor must not fail.

Attaching Yourself to the Anchor

You have built your anchor and have considered its position relative to your line of descent. Now it's time to secure yourself to that anchor so you can set up the rest of the system. When you are within 6 feet (183 cm) of a "clean" edge (flat ground or rock with a drop-off)—or farther from the edge but in sloping terrain that has sand, gravel, mud, or ice that may compromise your footing—be sure to attach yourself to an anchor with a tether. This tether should have the following characteristics:

- It should be long enough so you can move freely.
- It should be made of a material that is strong enough to hold if you slip or fall. The best material also has dynamic properties to absorb forces. Even a short fall directly onto a static tether can generate forces high enough to injure the climber or compromise the anchor.
- It should be clipped to an anchor at or above your waist level to minimize shock loading on both the anchor and your body if you were to slip and fall.

What material will you use to anchor yourself? You have several options, including a daisy chain, webbing chain-link, sewn runner, and Purcell Prusik.

Daisy Chain

Many climbers use daisy chains as tethers. However, you must be aware of the following note of caution regarding daisy chains: *Do not clip more than one loop with your carabiner.* The stitching between loops can come out with a load of 700 pounds, which may easily be generated if you slip when sitting or standing with your waist above or even with the anchor's master point. If you have clipped more than one loop, and the stitching comes out, your carabiner will be free of the daisy chain—and you are no longer secured to the anchor.

Webbing Chain-Link

The webbing chain-link tether (Personal Anchor System by Metolius or Chain Reactor by Sterling), like the daisy chain, is an adjustable-length choice for securing yourself to the anchor. However, this product was developed specifically for this purpose and is a safer option. It consists of a series of linked webbing loops, each of which is strong enough to hold a substantial fall. Again, be aware of the material used for the links of webbing. Nylon links will absorb shock loads, while Spectra or Dyneema links will not. The disadvantages of the webbing chain-link system are its bulk and the limited choice of functions.

Sewn Runner

Climbers like to use gear that has multiple purposes or functions. This saves weight and is more efficient. For this reason, a large number of climbers choose to attach themselves to the anchor with a double-length sewn runner. To do this, you first need to girth hitch

SAFETY TIP

When choosing any type of tether, it is important to consider the type of fiber. Materials such as Spectra and Dyneema have very little stretch, so your body takes most of the shock load in a static fall. You can be injured or the anchor components may fail from a fall of only a few feet onto Spectra or Dyneema material.

the runner to your belay loop. You can adjust the length of this tether by tying a figure eight knot in the runner and clipping the locking carabiner into the runner on the side of the knot closest to you. If you need a longer tether, clip the carabiner at the end of the runner. For anchor attachment, nylon runners' shock-absorbing properties make them a much better choice than Spectra.

Purcell Prusik

Some climbers use a Purcell Prusik made with nylon cord (of six or seven millimeters in diameter) to attach themselves to an anchor. This is an adjustable tether (see figure 10.3) that can be attached to your harness by girth hitching the short loop to your harness belay loop. Clip the two loops of the Purcell together to the master point of the anchor as your safety tether. The Prusik allows you to adjust the length easily, and the nylon material is more shock absorbing than other materials.

Preparing the Ropes

Rappelling may be done with single or doubled ropes; however, you would rarely be rappelling on a single line in a rock-climbing situation. Most rappels are done on doubled ropes in one of two ways. If the rappel is short, you should use one rope hanging from the anchor at the middle point of the rope (or at a point at which both ends touch the ground). If the rappel is longer than half the rope length, you should use two ropes. The end of one rope is threaded through the anchor, then joined to the end of the other rope by a knot.

Figure 10.3 Purcell Prusik.

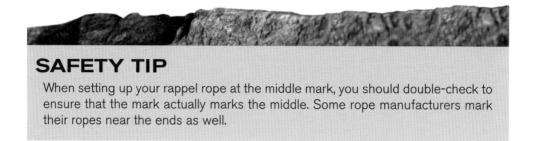

SAFETY TIP

When setting up your rappel rope at the middle mark, you should double-check to ensure that the mark actually marks the middle. Some rope manufacturers mark their ropes near the ends as well.

Short Rappels

When you are rappelling on one rope, you must be able to efficiently find the middle point of the rope. Some ropes come with a factory-made middle mark, usually a section of rope in which the sheath has been marked black. If your rope does not have this mark, you can blacken the middle at home with a rope-marking pen. These are available from rope manufacturers. Do not use a permanent marker such as Sharpie or Marks-A-Lot. Tests have shown that markers not made specifically for climbing ropes may weaken the fibers. Be sure to measure the middle point several times before you mark it because this is difficult to undo. When you are setting up your rappel anchor, you should pull the rope through the rappel ring or quick link until you reach the middle mark. Each side of the rope will be of equal length. Some ropes are bicolor or biweave, and they change color or pattern at the middle point. These are a bit more expensive, but the middle mark cannot wear off. However, if you need to cut one end short because of excessive wear or damage, the pattern change will no longer indicate the middle of the rope.

Long Rappels

If you are using two ropes to rappel, put one end of a rope through the rappel ring, chain anchor, or quick link, and then tie it to the end of the other rope. Climbers use several types of knots to join ropes for rappelling. Knots that join two ropes are called bends. The most common types of bends include a double fisherman's, flat overhand, and figure eight follow-through. Check all of these bends before you rappel to make sure that they are well dressed and pulled tight or set (see figure 10.4).

Figure 10.4 Well-dressed (a) fisherman's, (b) flat overhand, and (c) figure eight follow-through bends.

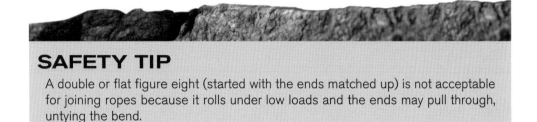

SAFETY TIP

A double or flat figure eight (started with the ends matched up) is not acceptable for joining ropes because it rolls under low loads and the ends may pull through, untying the bend.

Double Fisherman's Bend

If you are using a double fisherman's bend, make sure the tails are at least as long as double the diameter of the knot (at least 4 inches [10.2 cm] for most common climbing ropes). Thicker ropes require longer tails. The double fisherman's is a good choice if your ropes are different diameters. However, this bend tends to catch in cracks more easily than others, possibly causing stuck ropes when you are attempting to recover them.

Flat Overhand Bend

The flat overhand bend is the choice for many rappel situations because it can be tied quickly and because it rides easily over rock surfaces as you are pulling the rappel ropes during retrieval. Some people think this bend looks unsafe; thus, it has the nickname European Death Knot, or EDK. However, the flat overhand is a UIAA-approved method (meaning it has been tested by the International Mountaineering and Climbing Federation) and is used by climbers and guides worldwide. Many people choose to tie another overhand behind the first one as a backup, and they leave long tails (12 inches [30.5 cm]) (see figure 10.5). This bend is strong enough for rappelling, but it is not suitable for joining ropes on a long top-roped climb because of the greater forces involved.

Figure Eight Follow-Through Bend

A third bend that climbers use to join ropes is the figure eight follow-through. A figure eight is tied in one rope, and the other rope retraces it so the ends are pointing in opposite directions. The length of the ends should be double the diameter of the knot (or longer). This bend is easier to untie than the double fisherman's.

As you may know, many accidents in climbing have involved people rappelling off the ends of their rope when the ends do not reach the ground. If you cannot see that both ends are on the ground, you should knot the ends of the rope to prevent them from passing through the rappel device. Any large knot that will stay in the rope will do. One suggestion is a figure eight or figure nine knot on a bight, depending on the size of the opening in your rappel device (a rappel device that is a figure eight style requires a larger knot to block against it). A fisherman's knot, also called a grapevine or stopper knot, is effective for most tube-style rappel devices.

Figure 10.5 Backup to the flat overhand bend.

TECHNIQUE TIP

A figure nine knot on a bight is simply a figure eight knot with an extra wrap around the neck before the end is poked through the hole. This creates a larger knot and shortens the amount of rope you have left. You can also make a figure ten or twelve—just put a few more wraps around the neck.

Getting the Ropes Down

Once you have set up the rappel, how do you get the rope down the cliff? If you lowered your partner, one end is already down. However, if all members in your party are rappelling, you have two choices: throwing the rope or rappelling with the rope.

Throwing the Rope

You can butterfly coil the rope and throw it down in sections. You will coil each half of the rope into two bundles and throw each bundle separately. To do this, hold one end of the rope. Knot the end if you are unsure it will reach the ground. Pull an arm's length of rope and hold the middle of this strand in your hand. Pull another arm's length of rope, moving away from the end, and lay the rope on top of the one in your hand so that a loop about 2 feet (61 cm) long forms on the other side of your hand. Now pull another arm's length of rope and lay the loop across your hand, on top of the single strand. Alternate sides so that the loops form butterfly wings—one on each side of your hand, as opposed to a coil around your hand. To ensure that the coils do not catch on one another, make each coil about 1 inch (2.5 cm) shorter than the last (see figure 10.6). When you have coiled about half of one side of the rope, stop and pinch that bundle between your knees to hold it together as you start another coil with the rope closer to the middle mark. Stop coiling the second section of rope when you see the middle mark a few feet away. You will end up with two bundles, one near the tail of the rope and one near the middle.

Now you can throw this half of the rope down the cliff. You will want to first throw down the bundle nearest the middle of the rope to avoid entangling the rope. Be sure to yell "Rope!" two times before throwing it over the edge in order to warn those who may be below. In addition, make sure you "manage" the other half of the rope—have it secured by clipping it to the anchor so it can't slip through

Figure 10.6 Butterfly coil.

to the ground when you throw the first half of the rope. After the first half is down, coil the second half of the rope in the same manner, yell "Rope!" again, and toss the bundles one after the other.

Rappelling With the Rope

If there are people below you who may be hit by the rope, or if the rope may become entangled (e.g., by wind or rock features), you may consider rappelling with the rope in butterfly coils, hanging from your harness. This allows the coils to feed out through your rappel device as you descend. To do this, butterfly coil one half of the rope, making each coil about 1 inch (2.5 cm) shorter than the last so it will feed out easily without catching underlying coils. Lay the first butterfly coil over a shoulder-length sling that has a carabiner on each end of it. Clip one carabiner to the other, and hang the bundle from your gear sling; the rope should feed out the front. Coil and sling the other half of the rope, and hang it from the gear loop on your other side. Put yourself on rappel with a backup. If you have made neat coils, the rope feeds out smoothly (see figure 10.7). This method may take a bit more time initially, but it may save you the hassle of clearing snags and snarls in the rope on the way down.

Figure 10.7 By preparing ahead of time with neat coils, you will allow the rope to feed out smoothly.

TECHNIQUE TIP

Properly orienting the rappel device based on how much weight you will be putting on the rappel system can help the ropes run smoothly through your rappel device. A tube-style device (e.g., Trango Jaws or Black Diamond ATC-XP) may have one side with notches or fins to provide more friction. If you have a heavy pack, are descending steep or overhanging terrain, or are rappelling with a rope less than 10 millimeters in diameter, you should orient the rappel device so the ropes on the brake side run over these notches. Alternately, on low-angle terrain or with ropes thicker than 10 millimeters, you should use the low-friction side for the brake.

Rappel Devices

On steep terrain, most climbers rappel using mechanical devices. The most common rappel devices are tube style—for example, the Black Diamond ATC, Trango Jaws, and Petzl Reverso. Each of these devices has a head and a tail side, the latter being the side with the keeper that prevents it from sliding out of your reach. For a double-rope rappel, you should push a bight of each rope from the head of the device toward the tail so the bights of rope align with the keeper. Clip both ropes and the keeper through a locking carabiner into your belay loop. Make sure the brake side (or the rope going to the ground) is on the ground side of the rappel device when it's attached to your belay loop. This will make it easier to brake, letting gravity work with you instead of against you (see figure 10.8). Once you have checked that the ropes are oriented properly, you should lock the carabiner gate. The friction generated by the amount of bend in the ropes over the edge of the rappel device controls your speed of descent.

Figure 10.8 Make sure the brake side (or the rope going to the ground) is on the ground side of the rappel device when it's attached to your belay loop.

Figure 10.9 The Pirana is one style of a modified figure eight device that is often used in canyoneering.

Descending devices with a figure eight style have gone out of fashion, mainly because they twist the rope and have less versatile options for friction, both in rappelling and belaying. Petzl makes a modified figure eight device called the Pirana, which has several advantages over the old-style figure eights. The Pirana has multiple modes that can be used to increase friction during a rappel, and it can be easily tied off in the middle of a rappel so you can go hands free. The device has a separate spot to attach it to your harness, so you can go on and off rappel without removing it from your belay loop. You can also rappel more quickly with a Pirana, which may be an advantage in some situations. This style is more effective as a rappel device than a belay device. The Pirana has been used more in canyoneering and rescue work than in climbing situations (see figure 10.9).

What Happens if I Drop My Rappel Device?

If you don't have a rappel device and you need to descend a steep drop, you have several choices of improvised rappel methods.

Carabiner Brake

A carabiner brake rappel is a system that works like a rappel rack commonly used for caving. You need at least one locking carabiner and three nonlocking carabiners to set up this system. Attach the locking carabiner to your harness. This will extend the system off your belay loop to prevent wear from the rope rubbing on it as you descend. Next, clip two nonlocking carabiners—gates opposite and opposed—to this locking carabiner (make sure the gate is locked). Pull a bight of rope through these two nonlocking carabiners. Clip one or more additional nonlocking carabiners around the bight, and then clip them around the ropes to the anchor and slip them over the two carabiners that are opposite and opposed. Now they will act like brake bars. The more carabiners you have clipped around the bight, the more friction you will have on your rappel. Make sure the rope is running across the spine of these brake bar carabiners, not the gate. The oval style of nonlocking carabiner works best for this setup (see figure 10.10).

Figure 10.10 The oval carabiner style works best when setting up a carabiner brake rappel system.

Munter Hitch

If you don't have enough nonlocking carabiners to build a carabiner brake system, you can instead use a Munter hitch on a locking carabiner (a symmetric and pear-shaped carabiner). Even if you are rappelling on double ropes, you can tie a Munter hitch in both ropes together. A big difference in rappelling with a Munter hitch is that you brake by moving the brake strand up toward the anchor instead of down toward the ground. Disadvantages to this method are that it is more difficult to back up and that it tends to twist the ropes (see figure 10.11).

Figure 10.11 A Munter hitch can be used to rappel when you don't have a mechanical device.

TECHNIQUE TIP

While rappelling, to brake using a Munter hitch off your harness, hold the rope strands parallel; the brake strand is held up toward the anchor.

Carabiner Wrap

A carabiner wrap is another method for rappelling using just one locking carabiner. In this method, you simply wrap the rope or cord around the spine of the carabiner approximately five times (the number of wraps will depend on the diameter of the rope, your weight, and the steepness of the descent). Adjust the number of wraps according to the amount of friction you need to safely control your descent. Be sure the wraps are along the spine and that each wrap sits next to the others without overlapping or twisting.

Rappel Backups

Taking your hands off the rope to clear snags can be dangerous if you don't have a backup for your rappel. A backup also provides security in case a falling rock knocks your hand off the brake side of the ropes or in case other unexpected situations arise, such as a bee sting, slippery footing, and so on. When you are using a backup, you should double-check that it is secure and functional before you unclip your tether and begin to rappel. Several methods can be used for backing up a rappel.

Figure 10.12 Tying the rappel line to a pear-shaped carabiner clipped onto the master point (using a Munter-mule combination with an overhand backup knot).

Top-Rope Belay

When you need to back up a person who is a beginning rappeller, you may want to do this from above because the system streamlines a rescue. In this case, you can use a top-rope backup from either the rappel anchor or a separate anchor. The simplest method is to use the same anchor. Attach the rappel rope to the anchor using a locking carabiner. Then, chain two locking carabiners off the master point next to the rappel setup for the belay. Chaining one carabiner to the other for the belay prevents the rappel anchor carabiner and the belay carabiner from pinching together and trapping the rope. The lowest locking carabiner should be a pear-shaped style, because you will be setting up a Munter hitch as the belay mechanism. If the length of the rappel is less than half the rope length, you can use the same rope for both the rappel line and the belay line. In this case, the rappeller descends a single rope. At the middle mark, tie the rappel line to a pear-shaped carabiner clipped onto the master point; do this using a Munter-mule combination with an overhand backup knot (see figure 10.12). Toss the rappel line down the cliff. The rappeller ties in to the other end of the rope (the belay line) with a figure eight follow-through and then puts himself on rappel (see figure 10.13). To belay, tie a Munter hitch on the lower end of the clipped locking carabiners, close to the belayer's tie-in point. Then, feed out rope through the Munter hitch so there is about a foot of slack as the rappeller is descending. If the rappeller needs to take his hands off the rope or loses control of the rappel, you have him on the top-rope backup. If the rappeller gets something caught in the device, such as a shirt or hair, you can tie off the belay line with a mule knot and untie the mule from the rappel line to give slack. After the problem is fixed, the rappeller can continue rappelling, or you can lower him.

Figure 10.13   Using the top-rope belay.

Fireman's Belay

The fireman's belay is another method of backing up a rappel. For the first person down, another method must be used to back up the rappel. When it is the second person's turn, the fireman's belay can be used. The climber on the ground will hold both ropes in his hand or use another method to grab the ropes (e.g., a rope-grabbing hitch). If you are backing up with a fireman's belay, you should leave enough slack in the system to allow the rappeller to continue to move down. If the rappeller loses control, take out the slack by pulling down on the ropes to act as the brake hand, stopping the rappel (see figure 10.14). This method is quick to set up, but a rescue is not as easily performed as with a top-rope belay.

Autoblock Backup

A third popular method used to back up a rappel is an autoblock, or rope-grabbing hitch (using four-millimeter cord), attached to either your belay loop or your leg loop. You should attach the hitch on the brake side of the rope, below your hand. Your pinky finger pushes the hitch down the rope as you rappel. Do

Figure 10.14   Using the fireman's belay.

TECHNIQUE TIP

To extend your rappel device, a basket hitch is stronger than a girth hitch. See chapter 6 (page 144) for a description of the basket hitch. To make this hitch, fold the sling in half and thread it through your harness. Clip the two halves together with the carabiner of your rappel device.

not hold the hitch in your hand because if you lose control of the rappel, you will likely squeeze the rope, and the hitch will not grab with your hand on it. If you have a harness with a belay loop and full-strength leg loops, attach the cord to the leg loop with a girth hitch; your rappel device should be attached directly to the belay loop. However, if you have a diaper-style harness (e.g., a Black Diamond Alpine Bod), the harness may have plastic buckles joining the leg loop straps. These plastic buckles may break or come undone if you use an autoblock on the leg loop. In this case, you may attach the autoblock cord to the harness with a girth hitch, joining the waist belt and the floppy length of nylon webbing between the leg loops. You should extend the rappel device with a sling so that you have enough space between the autoblock and the device. Make sure your backup hitch is short enough that it does not get sucked into the rappel device (see figure 10.15a). With an extended rappel device, watch that your hair doesn't get caught in it as you rappel.

In the past, climbers put the hitch above the rappel device, on the ropes going to the anchor. This is usually not done anymore for several reasons. First, once weighted, your hitch may be very difficult to release in order to continue your rappel, especially if the rappel is free hanging. Second, if you do lose control of the rappel, your full body weight is solely on the hitch. When you put the hitch on the brake side of the rappel device, it only takes a fraction of your body weight to keep the bend in the rope over the rappel device, making your mid-rappel stop more secure (see figure 10.15b).

Figure 10.15 Using an autoblock backup for rappel.

Mechanical Device Backup

A fourth backup method is a mechanical device that grabs the rope, similar to a friction hitch. An example is the Petzl Shunt. The Shunt works with single and double ropes; however, your rappel device must be extended on a sling or draw so that the Shunt can be attached to the rope that goes into the rappel device (see figure 10.16). This device is not as popular because of price and weight considerations.

Rappel Technique

Rappel technique is the skill set needed to descend the ropes. Special considerations are taken before you begin the rappel, while you are rappelling, and when you finish the rappel.

Figure 10.16 Backing up with a mechanical device.

Before You Start

Before you rappel, make sure any long hair is tied back and any loose clothing is tucked in. Leave jewelry such as long earrings, rings, and bracelets at home. These items can get trapped in the rappelling device, causing a more involved self-rescue or assisted rescue. Most climbers don't wear gloves to rappel, because their skin is toughened from climbing and working with ropes. However, if you are a beginner, consider wearing gloves to protect your hands. Gloves made of leather or synthetic leather provide the best grip. Gloves should fit snugly; if they are too large, they tend to get caught in knots and carabiners.

Thread the bights of rope through your rappel device, as discussed earlier. Make sure you have a backup, whether it is a fireman's belay from below, a top-rope belay, a hitch, or a shunt. Double-check your system. Some climbers like to use memory tools for this, such as "your ABCs." *A* is for anchor; check that it is solid and equalized in the direction you are rappelling, and that you are not leaving behind anything clipped to the anchor. *B* is for buckles; check that your harness buckles are doubled back. *C* is for carabiners; see that all lockers are locked and that none of the carabiners are cross-loaded (i.e., loaded against the gate). When you test the rappel, stay attached to the anchor, but weight the rappel device, not your tether. If everything is OK, you may undo your tether and stow it out of the way. Many climbers clip the end of the tether to a gear loop.

During the Rappel

Shout "On rappel!" before you start to alert others to the fact that you are descending over the edge. If the rappel route is steep or overhanging, the start of the rappel can be very intimidating. However, you have checked your system and can now trust it. If the rappel is overhanging, you may be able to sit down and scooch your behind over the edge to begin your rappel. First, you must turn so you are facing the rock. Gently lower yourself into an L position, as if you are sitting on the ground with your legs straight in front of you. Keep your knees slightly bent, not locked, to act as shock absorbers. Your

Figure 10.17   Controlling the speed of your rappel.

feet should be shoulder-width apart to provide stability. If you want to slow your rappel, position your brake hand low and near your hip, putting a sharp bend in the rope over the edge of the rappel device (see figure 10.17). If you would like to rappel more quickly, push your hand away from your body, lessening the angle of the rope's bend over the device. If you kick a rock loose, and there could be other people below you, yell "Rock! Rock!" until the rock has stopped.

For rappels down slab or low angle terrain, you can simply walk backward down the slope, staying in balance and control and rappelling smoothly. Jerky rappels, bouncing, and sudden stops put extra stress on the anchor. Turn to look where you are going.

Finishing the Rappel

When you get to the ground—or to your next rappel station—secure yourself before undoing your rappel device. A rappel station is a convenient spot from which to rappel. If you are still on the cliffside, the rappel station may not have a fixed anchor. If not, you must build an anchor before securing yourself and removing the rope from the belay device. If you are on the ground, make sure you are in balance, especially if the ground is not level. Once you are secure, remove the rope from your rappel device, yell "Off rappel," and move away from the cliff if possible, preferably to a location where your partner can see you. Doing so facilitates communication and gets you out of the rock fall zone. Once everyone in your party has finished the rappel, you will retrieve your rope by pulling one end. Make sure any end knots have been untied before you pull. See Rope Management on page 251 for more information on rope retrieval.

Challenging Conditions

Certain rappels will require special techniques and skills to perform safely. These may include descending over a roof, rappelling far away from the rock face with a backpack, having to get onto rappel when the anchor is hanging over the edge of the cliff, or discovering that you need the use of both hands during your rappel.

Roof or Overhang

If you come to a roof, make sure you lower your behind below the level of your feet. Keep your feet on the edge of the roof until your head is below the roof (see figure 10.18). If your feet slip off the edge before your head is clear, you could smack your face into the rock. Keep your body parallel with the rock face, and release both feet at the same time, absorbing the shock with your legs if you swing in.

Wearing a Backpack

Another challenging situation is when you are wearing a heavy backpack while performing a free-hanging rappel in which your feet are too far away from the rock to touch it. In this situation, you'll find that it is uncomfortable to stay upright without stressing your abdominal muscles. A good solution is to hang your backpack from a sling.

Figure 10.18 If you come to a roof when lowering, be sure to keep your feet on the edge of the roof until your head is below the roof.

The sling is girth-hitched to the haul loop on your backpack and is clipped into the belay loop of your harness (or into the carabiner of the rappel device). While you are rappelling, the backpack hangs between your legs.

Awkward Start

You may encounter a situation in which the anchor for a rappel hangs down over the cliff edge. This presents a problem when you are standing on top. You have put yourself on rappel, but now how do you start? Downclimbing and then falling onto the anchor may cause a shock load to the system, causing personal injury or anchor failure. Possible solutions include using another rope to lower everyone except the last person onto the rappel, or using a secondary rappel to get onto the primary rappel.

A secondary rappel is simply a rappel begun from a safe location that allows you to lower yourself onto your primary rappel. First, make sure you are secured to the rappel anchor. Then, reach over the edge and grab the two ropes of the primary rappel. Put yourself on rappel on the primary system, and make sure you have a backup. Next, you'll set up your secondary rappel. Attach a length of six- or seven-millimeter cord to the anchor, ensuring that the cord will reach over the edge and below where you will hang to begin your primary rappel. Using this cord, create a Munter hitch on a separate locking carabiner (pear shaped) attached to your harness belay loop. This is your secondary rappel system. From a safe location, rappel on the cord over the edge until you are weighting the primary rappel. Your primary rappel's backup will hold you in this location. Now you may pull the end of the cord through the Munter hitch, dismantling the secondary system, and continue rappelling on the primary system. You will not be able to retrieve your cord or the anchor (see figure 10.19).

Figure 10.19 Creating a secondary rappel.

TECHNIQUE TIP

I was rappelling on a windy day once, and the ropes blew around the corner out of sight. Still above them, I stopped to yank them back under me. Much to my dismay, I found that the ropes had snagged on something I couldn't see. Luckily, I knew how to tie off my rappel device so I could clear the snag using both hands. Once you rappel too far and your ropes become taut, you will be unable to continue rappelling and will have to ascend in order to free the tension caused by the snagged rope.

Tying Off Mid-Rappel

What if you need to stop in mid-rappel and go hands free? Suppose there is a perfect photo opportunity, or maybe you have to clear some snagged ropes. If you have a rope-grabbing hitch or device, you may simply let go with your brake hand. If you are being belayed from above, you can communicate to your belayer that you want to stop and be hands free. Wait for a positive reply. If you are being belayed with a fireman's belay, two-way communication is also very important. If you have no backup, several methods may be used to tie off a rappel.

Thigh Wrap

One method for tying off a rappel is to wrap the brake end of the rope around your thigh several times. Before you remove your brake hand, you must be sure you can trust

TECHNIQUE TIP

A load-releasable knot, such as the mule knot, is useful when you want to untie the knot while you or your partner is hanging on the rope.

that the wrap won't slip (see figure 10.20). If there is a chance the wraps can unwind, clip the free rope (going to the ground) through a locking carabiner attached to your leg loop or gear loop.

Blocking Knot

If you are on a low-angle slope and you are able to unweight the rappel, you can tie a blocking knot behind the rappel device. This can be any knot that will stay tied and that can't pass through the rappel device. Figure eight or figure nine knots on a bight are good choices.

Mule Knot

A third method used for tying off mid-rappel is the mule knot. Whether you are using a tube-style device or a Munter hitch to rappel, the mule knot is useful because it is a load-releasable knot. This means it can be untied while you are hanging on it (unlike a figure

Figure 10.20 The thigh wrap is one method used to tie off the rappel.

eight on a bight). If you are rappelling on a Munter hitch tied around a pear-shaped carabiner, you should tie the mule knot above the Munter around the rope going to the anchor. First, create a loop several inches in diameter, using the brake strand. Lay the loop across the rope going to the anchor. Now form a bight of rope using the brake strand, wrap it around the rope going to the anchor, and poke it through the loop you created previously. Pull it snug so the mule knot backs up against the Munter hitch. The mule needs a backup knot, so tie an overhand, finishing it so the end points up toward the anchor. The backup knot should also be snug against the mule knot. This is a very secure method of tying off. For more information about the Munter mule knot, see chapter 6.

If you are rappelling with a tube-style device, the tie-off with a mule knot is similar to when using a Munter hitch. However, you will use friction to your advantage to increase security. The first step is to take the brake strand and poke it through the locking carabiner that attaches the rappel device to your belay loop. Pull a bight of this strand up and create a loop. Lay the loop across the rope going to the anchor. The rest of the mule knot is tied the same as previously described. The only difference is that your tube

Figure 10.21 The mule knot with a tube-style device.

device is locked off in a position with the most friction between the rope and the device (see figure 10.21).

When you decide to start rappelling again, make sure your brake hand is on the rope as you undo your tie-off. Continue your descent.

Multipitch Rappels

Many climbing routes require more than one rappel to reach the ground. Having an efficient team can increase your safety in the mountains.

Efficient Teamwork

Efficiency means, in part, that every team member is completing a necessary task at any given time. Thus, if the next rappeller can be setting up to go on rappel as you are undoing your system at the bottom of your rappel, your team can move faster. This can help the team avoid getting stuck in the dark or in a storm. The following is an example of moving efficiently.

If you have rappelled with a rope-grabbing hitch or mechanical backup, once you reach the ground, you can pull extra rope through the rappel device and backup before removing them. At this point, you may call "Off rappel!" which indicates that the next rappeller can begin to set up her system. She can pick up the rope off the surface at the top, and she will have enough slack that she is not pulling on your rappel device as you are removing it from the rope. If she needs a backup for her rappel, you can just leave your rope-grabbing hitch attached to the rope and use it like a fireman's belay. If she is using a different backup system, you can take off the rope-grabbing hitch, and if possible, move back to a point where she can see you. If you are at a mid-rappel station, you should locate the next anchor in a spot that is out of the rock fall zone from rappellers above.

Lowering Versus Rappelling

Another way to increase efficiency is to lower all the climbers except the last one. Lowering tends to be faster than rappelling.

Line of Descent

When you set up your rappel, take note of the location of the next rappel station. Traversing (descending at an angle instead of directly below the anchor) while on rappel can be difficult, and if you slip, it may cause a pendulum fall. What will happen if you have a pendulum fall? Will you hit a rock or a tree? Will the rope slip over any sharp edges between you and the anchor? A rope under tension could be cut if it scrapes along a sharp edge. You should also note whether there are any loose rocks that could be knocked off a ledge as the rope slips. It is often better to rappel straight down instead of traversing. However, if the route has many loose rocks, you can rappel to an anchor or secure spot slightly to the side. This way, when you pull your rope, you will not be pulling loose rocks onto yourself or your rope.

Rope Management

If the descent is steep or overhanging, you may want to bring two ropes so you can tie them together and do longer rappels. If the descent is on slab terrain, you may be able to downclimb more efficiently than rappelling—if the terrain is safely within your downclimbing ability. Consider using time-saving measures such as butterfly coiling the rope and rappelling with it on your harness (see the discussion earlier in this chapter for details). Rope management is a key to being efficient. The last person to rappel before your team pulls the rope should make sure the ropes are separated as he rappels. This person can separate the ropes by running a gloved finger between them as he rappels. He could also separate them by clipping the carabiner on a quickdraw from his harness to one of the ropes and letting the rope slide through. Regardless of the method, the ropes will pull much more easily if there are no twists, especially if friction is high because the rappel anchor is set back from the cliff edge.

When the last team member finishes each rappel, you will need to pull the rope. Stuck ropes can dramatically increase your time to descend. Therefore, when you pull the rope, make sure you have it aligned away from cracks and features if possible. Untie any end knots, and make sure the two ropes are not crossed over one another or twisted together. If you have used two ropes joined with a knot and threaded through a rappel ring, quick link, or fixed anchor, then the only rope that will move is the proper one to pull; pulling on the wrong end will only jam the rope-joining knot against the metal anchor piece. However, if you choose to use webbing alone, you will need to remember which rope to pull once you finish the rappel. If you pull the rope that is opposite the side with the knot in it, you risk jamming the knot between the webbing and the rock—and your rope may get stuck. In this case, choosing two ropes of different colors allows you to remember which one to pull (e.g., "pull blue"). As you are pulling the rope down, your partner can stack it neatly on a ledge; if the terrain is steep or overhanging, your partner can make a lap coil by butterfly coiling the rope across her tether. When you get to the knot that joins the two ropes, you can stop pulling and begin to untie the knot, while your partner continues pulling on the second rope. Make sure you have managed the end by tying it off to the anchor so the rope can't fall off the cliff. When you have the rope-joining knot untied, you can thread one end through the rappel anchor and tie it to the end of the other rope to join them together for the next rappel. When your partner finishes pulling the second rope, you are ready to rappel again.

Stuck Ropes

What if your rope gets stuck? Not only can a stuck rope decrease your efficiency in descending, but it can also cause your party to become stranded partway down a mountain. If your rope becomes stuck, avoid yanking blindly with brute force. First, change the angle from which you are pulling. Perhaps the rope is not stuck, but looped over an obstacle, and changing your angle of pull may free it. If this doesn't work, try whipping the rope in waves or side to side. Finally, pull hard using several team members' body weights or using mechanical advantage. Be careful that you don't get hurt if the rope pops free unexpectedly. If none of these methods are successful, you may have to ascend to free the rope.

Assuming that you have enough rope, the safest way to ascend is to lead the pitch as a backup. As you ascend, place protection along the way while sliding a rope-grabbing hitch (attached to your belay loop) on the stuck side until you reach the troublesome spot. If you do not have enough rope to back up an ascent of the stuck side, you may consider waiting for a rescue instead of risking an unprotected fall if the rope were to become freed.

Self-Rescue

You need to know what to do if your partner gets stuck partway down a rappel. This can happen if your partner is rappelling and gets a shirt or hair stuck in the rappel device. It can also happen if the rappeller realizes she is going down the wrong way, if she rappels into a knot that was left in the rope, or if she doesn't have enough rope to reach the next station. In these situations, your party may have to self-rescue. The first choice would be for the rappeller to rescue herself. Do not attempt to cut a stuck object out of the rappel device while you or anyone else is hanging on the taut rope. It is very easy to accidentally nick or slice the rope and create a much worse situation.

Top-Belayed Rappel

If the problem is that something has caught in the rappel device, the solution is simple if you have set up a top-belayed rappel as the rappel backup. The rappel rope is secured to the anchor using a Munter mule knot, and the belay is provided by a Munter hitch. In this situation, you can dismantle the belay, untie the mule knot from the rappel line, and lower your partner to the bottom using the Munter hitch that remains. Alternatively, you can allow your partner to clear the caught item. First, tie off the belay line with a mule knot. Second, untie the mule knot from the rappel line. Third, feed slack through the rappel line until your partner can clear whatever is caught in the rappel device. Fourth, take up the slack on the rappel line, and retie the mule knot. Fifth, untie the mule knot from the belay line, and tell your rappeller that she is free to rappel again.

Unweighting the Rappel

If the backup to the rappel is not a top belay, the simplest solution for a snagged rappel device calls for the rappeller to have an extra sling or cord, preferably at least 48 inches (122 cm) long. The rappeller uses the material to create a hitch above the rappel device; this hitch includes a foot loop hanging down. The rappeller steps into the foot loop, creating slack in the ropes of the rappel device, and clears the snag. Then she pulls slack up through the rappel device, reweights it, and removes the hitch and foot loop to continue the rappel.

Ascending the Rope

If a rappeller realizes that he is going the wrong way and needs to ascend the rope, he may use two slings: One is a foot loop, and the other is attached to the rappeller's belay loop. The rappeller slides each hitch up the rope, alternating between the two hitches and unweighting the one he wants to slide. Since the rappeller is only attached to the rope by one of the hitches, a backup is necessary for safety in case the hitch attached to the belay loop slides. When ascending, climbers commonly use a figure eight knot on a bight in the climbing rope below the foot hitch; the knot is clipped into the belay loop with a locking carabiner. Every so often (8 to 15 feet [2.4 to 4.5 m]), the climber ties another figure eight knot in the rope and clips it into the locking carabiner (after dropping out the last one he tied).

If your party needs to self-rescue and the rappeller does not have any extra slings and carabiners with him, you will have to develop a different plan. If you have another rope up at the anchor, you can assist using a hauling system.

Hauling

Two basic hauling systems used in climbing are the C haul, which provides a 2:1 mechanical advantage, and the Z haul, which provides a 3:1 advantage. When the C haul is set up, it resembles the letter *C* in shape. The Z haul looks like a *Z*. Mechanical advantage is needed at the anchor only if there are not enough people in your party to haul the weight of the rappeller. Don't waste time setting up a mechanical advantage system if you have enough human power to directly haul your team member straight up. If you decide to haul directly (without setting up a hauling system), use a backup hitch on the rope, attached to a secure anchor, so you can let go in case you need a rest break.

C Haul

The setup for a C haul is simpler than that for a Z haul. You can use a C haul in the following situations: when you only need to haul a short distance, when the climber can assist the haul by pulling as she walks up a slope, or when you have multiple haulers to assist. When setting up hauling systems, if you are dropping a rope to the rappeller, you should first make sure that you manage the end of the rope. This means that you must tie it off to the anchor so it can't be dropped off the edge. To set up a C haul (creating a 2:1 mechanical advantage through a pulley system), follow these steps:

1. Create a bight in the rope that is tied off to the anchor. This loop will be lowered down to the rappeller.
2. Clip a carabiner into this loop and lower it to the rappeller.
3. When the loop reaches the rappeller, she will clip it into her belay loop. Ask her if she can assist the haul by pulling the rope that is moving toward her as you haul. This is the line opposite the one you are pulling, or the line attached to the anchor.
4. You or your group pulls the rope until the rappeller unweights the rappel line, freeing her stuck hair or shirt from the rappel device or allowing her to untie the knot in the rappel rope. If the rappeller needs to be hauled to the anchor again, have the climber self-belay on the rappel line as a backup (see figure 10.22).

Figure 10.22 The C haul: self-belaying on the rappel line as a backup.

Z Haul

Suppose you are the only one at the anchor, and the rappeller is much heavier than you. Or perhaps the rappeller is so far down the rope that a loop won't reach him. In these situations, you can set up a

Z haul. With a Z haul, the rappeller won't be able to assist, and the hauling is hard work. For every 3 feet (91 cm) of slack you pull in, the rappeller only moves up 1 foot (30 cm).

For the Z haul, the rappeller needs to be attached to a separate rope, which you will lower to him. To do this, follow these steps:

1. Manage the end of the rope by tying it to the anchor so it can't fall off the cliff.
2. Tie a figure eight on a bight in the other end of your hauling rope.
3. Attach a carabiner to the bight in the figure eight. If the rappel is overhanging, slide the carabiner down the rappel line to your partner. On the other hand, if the rappel is low angle, the carabiner may become trapped, so you must lower the figure eight to the rappeller, if possible.
4. Have the rappeller clip the carabiner into his belay loop.

While the rappeller is attaching himself to the extra rope, you can begin setting up the haul system. You will need two loops of cord or webbing—about 24 inches (61 cm) in length—and several carabiners. To set up the system, follow these steps:

1. Attach a locking carabiner to the master point of the rappel anchor, and clip the haul rope through it.
2. Tie a rope-grabbing hitch (such as a Prusik, klemheist, autoblock, or Bachmann) to the haul rope going to the rappeller. Clip a carabiner into the loop of cord that is left, and attach this hitch to the master point of the anchor. This is called the ratchet, and it stops the rope from sliding down when you let go.
3. Tie another rope-grabbing hitch (below the first) on the haul rope going to the rappeller. Clip another carabiner into the loop that is left over. This hitch is called the tractor, and it pulls up on the rope going to the rappeller.
4. Clip the rope through the carabiner attached in the previous step, and pull the rope up toward the anchor (see figure 10.23). Your rope should form a Z shape coming from the rappeller up to the ratchet hitch at the master point, down to the moving tractor hitch, and back to your hand. Be sure to communicate with your partner so he will be ready when you begin to haul.

Figure 10.23 The Z haul: clipping the rope through the carabiner.

To haul, you must first be sure that you are secure and tethered to the anchor if necessary. Move both hitches as far as possible downslope from the anchor. Then haul in the rope until the hitches are close together, and gently let out rope until the rappeller's weight comes on to the upper ratchet hitch. Now you can move downslope and reset the lower tractor hitch as far downslope as possible. Repeat until the rappeller can fix the problem or until he is up at the anchor with you again.

Summary

Descending is a necessary part of climbing. It can be dangerous because you must often trust your body weight entirely to the anchor system and ropes. Whether you are a world-class climber standing at the top of El Cap or an enthusiastic beginner practicing new skills, you must employ proper techniques to descend. In this chapter, we have covered various methods of descending, including walk-offs, downclimbing, lowering, and rappelling. You have learned about rappel anchors, preparing the ropes, and various rappelling methods. In addition, you've reviewed specific techniques that can be used in challenging situations that you may encounter while rappelling. Practice these techniques with a focus on efficiency and safety, and your confidence and judgment in the mountains will thrive.

CHAPTER 11

Lead Rock Climbing

Climb the mountains and get their good tidings. Nature's peace will flow into you as the sunshine flows into trees. The winds will blow their own freshness into you, and the storms their energy, while cares will drop off like autumn leaves.

John Muir

After spending countless weekends top-roping at the local crag or following partners up multiple pitches, many beginning climbers find that they want to experience the thrill and satisfaction of leading a climb on their own—to climb on the "sharp end" of the rope. Lead climbing involves climbing a route while intermittently placing or clipping protection (either permanent bolts or gear you place in a crack). While lead climbing, you will also be belayed by a partner from below. The belayer pays out rope as you move upward, offering protection in the event of a fall.

Lead climbing allows you to test your rock-climbing skills in a less controlled environment, resulting in a more challenging and eminently more satisfying experience. This type of climbing requires a greater level of commitment and increased awareness of variables such as weather conditions, loose rock, rope handling, run-outs (spans between available protection), and so forth. At the same time, the exhilaration and sense of personal accomplishment that accompany ascending a route while on lead are unmatched by other forms of roped climbing. Moreover, although climbing in this style involves a greater amount of risk than top-roping, it opens up a wide range of possibilities and experiences; you can climb steeper and longer routes, something simply not possible while being protected from the top. Furthermore, to ascend a route—to climb from bottom to top without falling or resting—requires that you actually lead it.

So far in this book, you have been introduced to the mechanics of rock climbing—how to belay, rappel, tie a variety of knots—and have been exposed to some basic climbing skills, such as how to grip holds and how to edge. You are now ready to take the next step and learn how to lead. This chapter helps you in this process, introducing you to the fundamentals of lead climbing. Topics discussed include belaying, reading guidebooks and topos, racking gear, lowering off climbs, clipping bolts (or other types of protection), placing protection, managing the rope, and knowing how to fall, to name a few. We focus on two forms of lead climbing—traditional and sport.

Traditional climbing is a style of lead climbing that involves placing your own gear (typically in cracks) as you proceed upward. Sport climbing, a more recent style of climbing, involves routes that are entirely protected by fixed protection, typically bolts. Because of the accessibility and lower risk levels associated with sport climbing, most climbers nowadays begin leading on short, well-bolted routes. In this chapter, to provide some historical continuity, we discuss traditional climbing first, then sport climbing.

You should only begin leading routes after you have spent sufficient time mastering fundamentals in more controlled environments. A book on rock climbing is no substitute for expert, one-on-one instruction and experience. Repeated and progressive learning opportunities with a mentor or guide are indispensable in learning how to climb. The written word cannot convey all the information, wisdom, and skill necessary to safely lead a wide range of climbs. Therefore, you should never presume to have mastered all the necessary skills from reading a text—or even from seeing a video or attending a one-day session at a climbing school.

All that said, "On belay!" Let's start climbing.

Traditional Lead Climbing

The first people up the mountain didn't find bolt hangers or preset rappel anchors waiting for them. They brought some tools, took the rock on its terms as they found it, and fashioned ways to keep themselves safe as they ascended. Today, traditional

It's a round trip. Getting to the summit is optional, getting down is mandatory.

Ed Viesturs

lead climbers continue in that spirit. They also add an ethic of preserving the natural environment and protecting it from undue damage or unsightly artificial intrusion. Jeff Achey, editor-at-large of *Climbing Magazine,* reflects, "Key to the feeling is invoking the spirit of mountain and crag, the inherent hazards and joys. As a trad climber, you can't be squeamish. You'll be up on the cliffs when it rains. You'll use loose handholds. On a great day maybe you'll get lost, cold, scared, and hungry. And when you get back, a can of beans never tasted so good, and the campfire feels like the warm embrace of Mother Earth herself" (Achey, 1999, p. 108).

Before the Climb

Failing to plan is planning to fail, so before you hurry to the crag, you need to give some quality attention to where you intend to climb and which tools you will need. See chapter 4 for more information.

Route Selection

Traditional routes are those that caught the eye of early climbing pioneers—natural and classic lines that follow grand crack systems, commanding features, chimneys, inside corners, or outside arêtes. But how do you know if a route is right and ready for you? Your appetite for a particular route or area may be whetted by reading an article in a climbing magazine or by hearing stories from other climbers. More definitive information can be garnered from climbing guidebooks. If you are a beginner at traditional lead climbing, you should pick routes that have a difficulty level below your actual ability. This will enable you to get acquainted with the area and its peculiar character and demands. The guidebook will give guidance on any of the numerous variables that will determine success or failure at a particular area:

- Physical difficulty and grade of the route
- Availability of protection, or lack thereof, and the most appropriate gear for the particular rock
- Clarity of route finding, landmarks, and descent routes
- Character (steep, overhanging, slab, run-outs)
- Hazards (loose rock, wildlife such as pigeons and snakes, lightning and other weather patterns)
- Remoteness and accessibility to medical care or rescue assistance (e.g., local emergency numbers)
- Regulations such as permits, private land, seasonal closures, and camping restrictions

Your willingness to lay out the cash for a local guidebook may offset hours of frustration that can result from route finding in a new area. It can also help you avoid getting into a climbing situation that is over your head or getting lost on the descent because of faulty advice from someone you just met. Remember, though, that some information may have changed since the book was printed (such as permit requirements, regulations, and so on).

Inexperienced lead climbers sometimes have an ego-driven tendency to select initial routes that are graded right at the limit of their ability. However, a better strategy is to start out with routes several grades lower than your ability, especially if you are coming into traditional leading straight from the world of gym climbing or sport climbing. You must remember that, especially if you are new at placing protection, you are probably going to spend double the amount of time on this route as you would spend simply toprope climbing or sport leading and clipping quickdraws. Therefore, you don't want to be at your limit of endurance and skill. Even if you are capable of something more difficult, there is no shame in climbing a moderate or intermediate route. The important thing is that you can do it with safety and confidence while amply protecting your partner or party. Keep this in mind: The wider the base of the pyramid, the higher its point can rise. The more moderates you complete, the stronger your confidence grows, and the greater your capacity becomes for pushing to higher challenges.

Equipment Preparation

With guidance from guidebooks or local climbers, you should be able to identify the type of protection equipment needed for a particular area. For example, tri-cams are a must for the horizontal cracks in the Gunks of New York, while Seneca Rocks in West

ROCK CLIMBER TIP

"Trick tripling" your 12- or 24-inch (30.5 or 61.0 cm) runners allows them to be carried compactly on the gear sling or harness. They can then be easily elongated if extending the placement is desirable to avoid generating excess rope drag in the protection system.

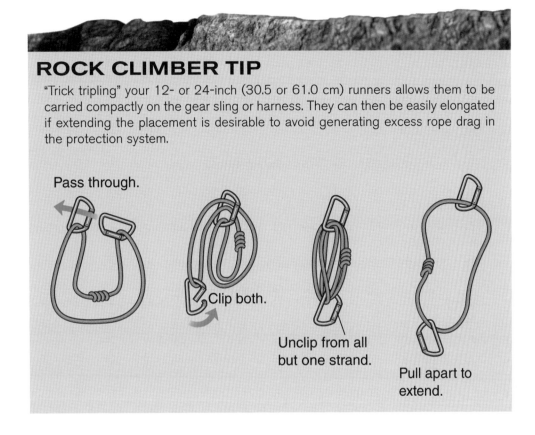

Pass through.

Clip both.

Unclip from all but one strand.

Pull apart to extend.

Virginia eats up stoppers and passive protection. Types of protection and anchoring options were covered extensively in chapter 8, so we will not repeat that information here. Another important part of preparation is organizing your "rack" for efficiency and safety.

Leaders organize their gear in different ways. Some prefer to distribute their equipment entirely on the gear loops of their harnesses so that nothing is hanging around the shoulders. Another style is to have the protection on an over-the-shoulder gear sling. With this style, the protection can be handily passed between leaders when "swinging leads." Regardless of which approach you choose, similar pieces are usually clustered together, and less frequently used pieces are put around the back. Carrying five to seven nuts per carabiner will give you a range of ready options when selecting a piece for a crack. Some leaders have a gear sling on each side: one for protection pieces and the other with preclipped and "trick-tripled" slings and quickdraws (two carabiners on each). Each climber will discover and develop his preferred style of gear arrangement. I like to have all the gates on my carabiners opening up and out. Being consistent with your preferred methods makes you efficient, and practicing with those methods makes your situations more predictable and your performance more fluid. In addition to the protection chosen—stoppers, hexes, camming units, slings, and quickdraws (see chapter 5 for a discussion on gear)—the following additional items may be helpful for the traditional lead climber:

- Rope of the appropriate length. Consulting the guidebook, you should ascertain that your rope is long enough for the route you are selecting. Using a 50-meter rope on a 180-foot (55 m) pitch is going to cause a problem! Also consider your method of descent—if you plan to lower off or rappel, make sure the length of your line is at least double the route height. See chapter 10 for more specifics on descending.

- Two nut tools for dislodging stuck gear (one for you and one for your second, who "cleans" the route).

- Pocket knife or multitool for cutting old slings from belay stations, tinkering with cams, or opening jammed locker carabiners.

- Small rescue pulley for rescue situations or simply assisting your second through a difficult crux.

- Two rescue or Prusik loops for rescue situations, fixed-rope ascending, or rappel backups when descending.

- At least one wide-mouth carabiner or pearbiner for Munter belays, plus several extra locking carabiners for anchor building.

- One or two cordelettes (18-20 feet or 5-6 meters) for building belay anchors.

- A guidebook attached to a cord loop, or quick cards with route information and descent routes.

- A water bottle clipped to the back of your harness (using a cord loop and duct tape); some routes can take longer than a top-rope or sport line, and you won't be returning to your pack for a while.

- Hiking footwear clipped to the back of your harness; this will depend on the descent options available. Sometimes you can lower off permanent anchors or rappel down, but other times, your descent may require hiking or an extensive walk-off.

- A small headlamp and a few first aid supplies (for abrasions and open wounds); this can be particularly useful for multipitch situations. Many traditional lead climbers have a story to tell about when a simple effort turned into a "rope-stuck-in-a-crack, late-night-in-the-dark-rappel" epic.

- A small fanny pack or streamlined climber pack for leader or second; this can contain a good number of the miscellaneous items.

Finally, before you cast off, you should be aware of some additional equipment issues for your partner. These will be addressed later in this chapter (see Seconding and Cleaning the Route on page 270).

Climbing the Route

So you have chosen a route within your capabilities, geared up, tied in, and checked over your partner's knots and belay arrangement. As you begin to climb, you are already looking for gear placements. You have many things to consider as you begin your traditional ascent.

SAFETY TIP

Personal Training for Leading

Every climbing outing, even a top-roping day, can be an opportunity to develop and refine the skills needed for successful lead climbing. While waiting for your turn on the top rope, you can walk around the base and place numerous nuts and cams, then clip in a sling and stand in each one to test its soundness and direction of pull. Place clusters of gear close to the ground and then connect and equalize them as you will need to do when building anchors in between pitches on a long traditional route. Chris Tate, a wilderness first aid instructor, wisely admonishes, "Test the system," meaning that in many areas of outdoor skills and pursuits, you should try out the skills frequently and in varied but controlled sessions before your life depends on them.

Having the Right Strategy

As a beginning trad leader, your rule should be to protect early and often. *Early* means shortly after leaving your belayer's stance—this way, if you do fall, your belayer's anchors will not take the entire load. *Often* means that you recognize that in a fall, every protection piece (and its connecting slings, and so forth) will absorb some of the shock of the fall. So the more pieces taking the shock, the more the load is distributed, and the lower the impact on any one part of the system.

Remember that you are essentially unprotected from a ground fall until you get your first protection piece in; therefore, you must take this first assignment seriously. Then, as you reach a total height nearly double the height of your first placement, you again risk "cratering"—"taking a grounder," hitting the bottom, and getting hurt badly—until your second piece is in and solid. Experienced trad leaders know that the early stages of the pitch can be the most dangerous, because of the potential for a ground fall and because of the limited rope available to absorb the shock. Though more dramatic, a fall from 60 feet (18.3 m) above your belayer can be much safer than one from 15 feet (4.5 m) up, all other factors being equal.

While leading, you can add a few verbal signals to help ensure continual and clear communication with your partner. Many leaders will say "Little slack" for the rope draw-up, "Clipped" when they have snapped their rope into each piece, and then "Moving" to signal that they are ready to continue their ascent. These signals are very helpful when the route takes you out of the sight line of your belayer, which occurs with many trad lines. When climbing in a location where several other parties are within earshot, many climbers make standard practice of attaching a name to every signal (e.g., "On belay, Fred" or "Climb on, Joe").

Choosing and Placing Protection

The protection system you devise will be a combination of natural features (trees and rock features such as horns and flakes); passive devices (stoppers and hexes); active, camming, or expanding devices; and existing permanent anchors (bolt hangers, fixed pitons, and nuts embedded in cracks from previous parties). There are countless ways to construct safe anchors—as well as some unorthodox approaches (a friend of mine once jammed his nut tool into a hairline crack, tied it off short, and clipped it; this is not recommended, but it gave him some peace of mind!).

Be aware of the tendency of some placements to lift out with rope drag (i.e., the friction that the trailing rope exerts on the placement carabiners, especially if the carabiners introduce angles into the rope line). This can often happen on your first placement if your belayer is positioned away from the wall. A multidirectional placement or an opposition setup can correct this problem (see chapter 8, page 194).

You should be ready to add a second protection piece before any section of the route that looks particularly challenging or beside any placement that looks questionable. In the event of a big fall, you will never regret the additional time that you took to back up your protection. In addition, you should clip into existing fixed pitons or bolt hangers if they still appear to have integrity. Clipping in and then tugging hard on the sling will help you decide if these fixed anchors are still reliable or if they have loosened or corroded over time. If one of these anchors fails in a fall, it has still taken some of the total shock load. But be ready to back it up with one of your own pieces if you have any reason for doubt about its dependability.

Be sure to extend your protection pieces with ample use of quickdraws and short slings. Your goal is to trail a relatively straight line. A zigzag pattern will generate increasing drag—as a result, by the time you are 50 feet (15.2 m) from your belayer, you will feel as if you are pulling a truck up the cliff (see figure 11.1). Just below overhangs, you should be very attentive to extending, so the rope is not pulled in underneath a roof to reach a placement. Some people may think that extending here lengthens the potential distance of a fall, but if the additional force of a nonextended placement causes the protection piece to rip out, you will be falling a whole lot farther until your next piece catches you! The same applies to any time you transition from horizontal to vertical (as in moving along a ledge and then ascending a headwall at the end). This corner turning will severely drag on your rope, so you should soften the bend by extending copiously with long slings.

When choosing the appropriate piece, I usually unclip the host carabiner from my gear sling and hold up the five to seven nuts on it to see which one I think will work. When I have my candidate, I slot it into the crack and play with it until either I am satisfied or decide I need to choose another for a better fit. When I have a fit, I unclip it from the host carabiner and return the unused set to my gear sling. Then I turn to my quickdraw rack and select a sling with carabiners to extend the piece and clip in my rope. If necessary, I may join two slings to get the desired extension. I finish by giving some energetic yanks to make sure the nut is there to stay in the event of a big tug (me falling!).

A traditional route following a chimney or crack system can have a healthy share of loose rock—much more than a clean and steep face studded with bolt hangers. You should thump on the rock on each side of your placement to ensure that you have not used an expanding crack or loose flake. Warn your belayer if you are going to move over something broken, and be very aware of what you haul on or how you drag your feet as you come onto ledges; a small pebble hurtling from 50 feet (15.2 m) above can ruin someone's day.

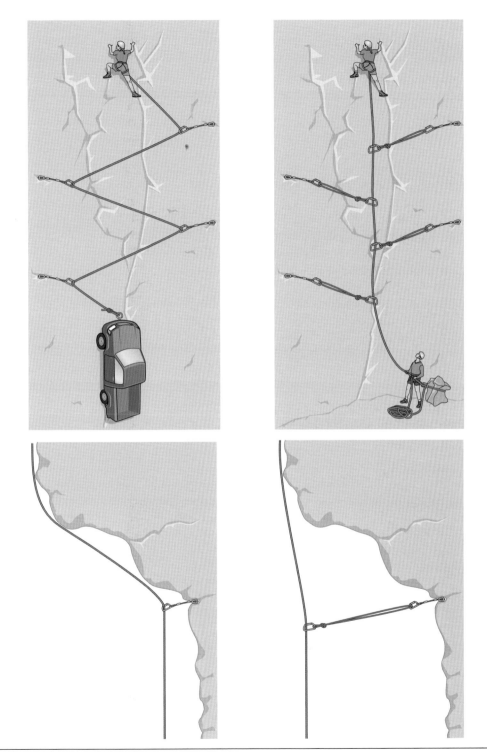

Figure 11.1 Appropriately extending placements dramatically reduces rope drag.

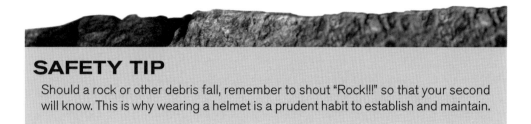

SAFETY TIP

Should a rock or other debris fall, remember to shout "Rock!!!" so that your second will know. This is why wearing a helmet is a prudent habit to establish and maintain.

Avoiding Dangerous Tendencies

Beginning traditional leaders have a few dangerous tendencies, and these call for brutal honesty with self and partner. One is to place "psychological pro." While climbing, if you haven't placed any protection for a while and you start to get a little nervous, you may be tempted to simply throw in a nut or cam and clip in without ensuring that it is truly a sound placement. The ensuing assurance is actually false security, but leaders fall for it because they have a need to see something between themselves and their last dependable—and far-off—piece of protection. Another dangerous tendency can be to keep "running it out" because either you cannot find a good placement or you can't find a decent stance to stop. Needless to say, consequences here can be dire. When this happens, it is usually because the aspiring leader chose a route over his head. The solution—if the person survives this trauma and still wants to return—is to approach the next climb with more humility and less self-consciousness about the route grade.

Falling and Bailing

Sport climbers fall a lot—in fact, some believe that not falling at some point during the day means they are not climbing at their limit. But in the trad world, not all the routes are as steep and clean as the 5.11s and 12s of the sport world. Traditional routes include chimneys to jam in, ledges to collide with, slab faces to abrade your skin on, and trees to swing into. In addition, although traditional leaders work to place good gear, they know intuitively that there is something less permanent and solid about a nut that they have placed compared to a bolt drilled or epoxied into a rock. In short, in the trad world, climbers don't look for excuses to fall, and in fact, they would be happy to return home day after day having not fallen at all. For traditional climbers, the adventure is not in the airborne thrill—it is in the exploring of the vertical environment and in being able to use their tools and skills to pass across it and not leave a trace. For the trad climber, falls are interruptions in the joy of climbing—and sometimes, catastrophic ones.

That said, falls will happen. Here are some strategies to help you avoid the most desperate consequences of a fall:

• Try to make placements from the most economical and energy-conserving stance, rather than make them as early as possible. Many falls happen as a leader is frantically trying to set a piece before his stance is well established, or after he has wasted too much energy standing on something marginal.

• Be watchful of places where falls carry added complications (above ledges or slabby low-angle faces). Double up your protection any time you are uncertain of a placement or if you are climbing near your grade limit.

- Don't allow the rope to get passed around behind your heels. Numerous leaders have been flipped upside down because they were not attentive to rope position when they came off.

- After a fall, stop the action, analyze the situation, and allow your rope to recover from the shock. Ask yourself these questions: "Is my protection still good, or was some part of my system compromised?" "Am I injured in any way?" "Did I lose or damage any critical gear?" "Is my belayer still on board?" "Am I climbing over my head on this route?" "Did I dislodge anything loose that has become a new hazard?"

At times, a climber will need to bail, or retreat, from a route. For example, one fine morning I was leading Pleasant Overhangs—a delightful three-pitch classic on the west face of Seneca Rock in West Virginia. I pulled up onto the large ledge of the first belay, only to come face to fang with a four-foot black snake that had made it up there before me. Following the time-honored practice in American mountaineering of yielding to the first party to ascend on a given day, I notified my belayer that I would be lowering off (and rather pronto, I might add). Sometimes climbers may get off route and into steeper

Identifying and overcoming natural fear is one of the pleasing struggles intrinsic to climbing.

Alex Lowe

terrain than they can handle. They may drop a critical piece of gear, or they may find that the equipment they have is not adequate to protect the route they are on. Weather may interrupt climbers' plans, or encroaching darkness may suggest that they pick it up another day. The flexibility (and humility) to change plans is the first (and some would say, the most important) survival trait that climbers have. King Solomon was not a mountaineer, but he seems to have understood something about the human tendency to fall in love with a plan, even at the expense of rationality and flexibility: "The prudent see danger and take refuge, but the simple keep going, and suffer for it" (Proverbs 27:12). Chinese philosophers also teach the value of adaptability: "The rigid person is a disciple of death; the soft, supple, and delicate are lovers of life" (Tao Te Ching).

A plan is simply a climber's best attempt to forecast conditions and design appropriate strategies. But when the conditions are different than anticipated, the strategies that are dependent on them must be reconsidered. Therefore, the best climbers are always reevaluating and tinkering with the plan, continuing to fit it to present realities. Rigid unexamined adherence to plans or rules is always dangerous. "Rules are for fools," quipped Paul Petzoldt, founder of the National Outdoor Leadership School and cofounder of the Wilderness Education Association. Preserve an open and flexible mind, adapt and change as necessary, don't attach your ego to completing the trip as planned, and you will successfully avoid becoming a disciple of death—the deceased adherent of an inflexible plan.

If you need to bail, COMMUNICATE with your belayer so he knows exactly what this change of plans is going to mean and what his role will be. Back up any protection you are going to be lowering or rappelling from—remember, the $7 you may need to sacrifice for that irretrievable carabiner, nut, or sling is a pretty good price to pay for the life (or lives) you are preserving. And when you get down, if you experience mild disappointment at not having finished what you started, remind yourself of what Ben, my longtime climbing partner, would say in such situations: "The rock will be there . . ."

Finishing the Route

At the end of your pitch, you may face several scenarios. You might top out onto a ledge or top area, or you might stop at a belay stance between pitches in a multi-pitch situation. Your stance may be a spacious ledge or mountaintop, or you might be clipped to an anchor and hanging in your harness. You might be planning to lower off or rappel to clean your own route, or you might be planning to set up a top-anchor situation so your partner can climb up and join you. Furthermore, you might arrive at three nicely drilled bolts with hangers that you can easily clip into, or you might find that you need to construct an anchor from scratch with your own tools.

Lowering Off

If you are planning to lower down off permanent anchors, you must communicate clearly with your partner. Several accidents in recent years have involved leaders and belayers who did not communicate and had different ideas about what was going to happen at the top. If the leader expects to be lowered down, and the belayer thinks that he must clear the rope so the leader can set up a rappel, these climbers will have—in the words of long-time park ranger and author Jim Burnett—"a very melancholy situation." This occurred to an experienced climber in March of 2002 at Lumpy Ridge in Rocky Mountain National Park. After a 110-foot (33.5 m) fall and multiple broken bones and internals, this individual has learned the lesson that we reinforce here: COMMUNICATE, be clear, and ask again if you are unsure (Williamson, 2003, p. 65).

If you must construct an anchor from your own tools to lower off, you need to accept the fact that you will be sacrificing some gear at the top for safety's sake. Create a solid anchor—don't be a minimalist just to save money. One climber made this mistake when he was lowering off a route at the Heart Creek Slabs in Alberta. This climber was lowering with rope running through a sling when the rope burned through the webbing. The climber fell to the base of the climb and sustained a fractured pelvis. Experienced climbers will know right away what happened here—they know that nylon running on nylon has the potential to generate a high amount of heat, and they are aware of nylon's low melting point. THIS CLIMBER WAS TOO CHEAP TO LEAVE A CARABINER AT THE TOP! (Williamson, 1995, p. 4). Similar accidents have happened when leaders have decided to back off a route but refused or neglected to place a second piece backing up their primary anchor because it would be irretrievable. There are stories of long falls after the leader back-cleaned lower pieces and then fell on a single top anchor that failed (Williamson, 2000, p. 49). What a price to pay for being stingy!

Bringing Up a Partner

If you are staying at the top and bringing your partner up to you, you should keep yourself on your partner's active belay until your anchor is rigged and you are safely clipped in. Overlap your security systems; don't take yourself off your partner's belay until you're protected. In a relay race, the baton is often dropped during the handoffs. Similarly, in lead climbing, critical errors are often made during these transitions.

Where possible, belay off your anchors instead of your own harness. The Munter hitch with a pear-shaped carabiner is ideal here, but other belay devices can be used as well; the line should be redirected at the anchor or master point (see figure 11.2). This disengages you from the loading of the system and avoids the trauma of you being tugged toward the edge if your partner falls. If your partner needs to hang in order to

Figure 11.2 Belaying off the anchor frees the belayer from carrying the load if the climber falls or hangs.

use both hands to remove a protection piece, you can lock off the rope and support her without taking the load on your person. This also sets you up much more appropriately to give assistance (in several forms) if your partner struggles through a difficult section. See chapter 10 for more details.

The higher and the farther back from the edge you can set your master point, the more useful this anchor will be if you find yourself in the situation of needing to construct a 2:1 or 3:1 pulley hoist (i.e., a C haul or Z haul system). Remember to place padding, such as a pack or jacket, to protect the rope from rock abrasion (see page 253 in chapter 10).

If you have another pitch (or more) to go, you should be sure to set up your anchor with at least one up-slotted piece—usually positioned below the belayer's waist and positioned to resist an upward pull. You are anticipating that your belayer will be using this same anchor to belay you on the next pitch, and you know that she will need something to resist being lifted.

Pull up remaining slack until you are tugging on your partner's harness. When she says, "That's me," you can call out "Stand by" as you clip in your belay device. When prepared, call "Ready here," and your partner will initiate the belay sequence ("On belay"). As you bring up rope, you can flake it loosely on the ledge, or you can stack it butterfly style over your knee or over an anchor line. This is especially important in a hanging belay situation. I witnessed a hanging belayer on Crack of Dawn on The Face of a Thousand Pitons at Seneca Rocks, West Virginia, with his rope loop dangling way down the cliff as his partner ascended. The wind carried it and whipped it around, interfering with the efforts of a neighboring climbing party. Because of the high potential for snagging and tangling, you should manage your rope compactly whenever possible.

When your partner reaches your stance, apply the overlap principle again by having her anchor in before you take her off your live belay. Discuss which system you will use for your belay stance anchors. Some options include (1) tying a clove hitch on your partner's rope—2 to 3 feet (61 to 91 cm) from her harness—and then clipping this into your master point, (2) having your partner preset with a daisy chain on her harness and clipping this into your anchor, or (3) using a Munter mule to connect your partner to the anchor (if belaying your partner using the Munter hitch). This last method means that you will not have your pearbiner to take with you on the next pitch. If your climb ends at the top, have your partner walk back to a clear safe zone away from the edge before unroping.

Seconding and Cleaning the Route

Following a traditional leader carries some special responsibilities. As the second, you will be providing the leader with the belay he is depending on to keep himself (and you) safe. You will also be the one who collects the gear from the route.

Preparing for the Climb

The climbing ability of the two partners should be roughly similar. This will help avoid the situation where a leader has to haul his less adept partner through all the difficult parts of the climb. The second should also have a fairly good understanding of knots, belay technique, and even self-rescue. Situations can arise in which the belayer is the one left conscious to figure out how to bring down an injured leader, how to lower or rappel both climbers to safety, or how to escape the belay and go for help. Even in normal situations, the second will be left to break down anchors and manage equipment unsupervised, so fundamental skills such as knot tying and belaying should be automatic. In addition, being responsible for removing gear means that the second will be spending longer periods standing on the route (longer than when top-roping or sport climbing, which have a more continuous flow). Traditional leading should never involve an overzealous leader dragging a novice out to the crag to climb—there are too many variables and risk factors.

The second and the leader should discuss their plans extensively. They should both understand what will happen at the top (lower off, top belay, or rappel) and how the leader wants the climb conducted. Both should be reasonably familiar with the route description so that either one can raise questions if things are not going as planned.

Before the climb begins, you (the second) should tie into your end of the rope so you get a check before your leader leaves (or tie a knot in the end if planning to lower the leader off). Tying in or tying off the far end of the rope to yourself or the anchor also effectively "closes the system" so that there is no chance of a drop if you must lower the leader off the route. Unfortunately, each year we hear stories of leaders falling because the tail end of the rope ran out through the belay device during a long lower. As the second, you should gather your equipment near at hand in case you need to manage a situation while anchored at the base. This equipment should include a water bottle if the belay is going to be long, cordelette and extra carabiners for belay escape, and weather gear if there is any threat. You should be helmeted (correctly fitted and fastened) since you will be in the fall line of any dislodged rocks or dropped gear. Each partner should have a nut tool to pry or poke protection pieces out of cracks. If you do not have gear loops on your harness, you will need an over-the-shoulder sling to rack gear on as you clean it. Some climbers who are seconding a route also place a billiard-ball-size rock in their chalk bag to use as a hammer on the nut tool for removing particularly stubborn stoppers or hexes.

Making the Climb

As the leader climbs, the pair will gradually create an understanding about how much tension is needed in the line. The second can develop an intuitive feel about when to release slack for clip-ins. As the leader signals his intentions, the second should provide a reply to every signal (e.g., "Thank you") so the leader knows that communication is alive and active. For long pitches, the second can also help the leader by providing feedback about the length of cord remaining ("20 feet . . . 15 feet . . ."). Though the guidebook may suggest certain belay stances, sometimes leaders choose to string two pitches together into one; in these cases, available rope length remaining can be vital information.

When seconding a route for a beginning trad leader, you should provide as much moral support as possible. This type of communication can be very important. You can affirm the leader's placements, upward progress, and construction of the protection system. Reassurances about the belay ("Try what you need to; I've got you") are music to the ears of a leader. Leaders also often appreciate gentle feedback about their actions ("Probably time to get something in" or "You might want to extend that a little bit more").

As the leader finishes the pitch, the belayer must be clear on each stage of the transition and must keep an active belay until told "Off belay" from above. Don't assume, and don't get sloppy about details—COMMUNICATE.

As the second climber, you will be removing the protection equipment and transporting it up to your leader. If you are able to modestly organize the gear as you collect it, you will save time and create efficiencies when you reach the belay stance with your leader. As you approach a nut or cam, you should dislodge it first, before unclipping it from the rope. This way, if you lose your grip on the nut or cam when dislodging it, it will simply slide down your rope to your harness, rather than falling into the abyss. After the gear is dislodged, you should sort it on your gear sling or harness loop, doubling or tripling up any slings so they are not dangling at your knees or feet. Even partial organization goes a long way—you don't want to arrive at the belay stance looking like a yard sale. You may use the nut tool (and your hammering rock) to remove any stubborn pieces, and if you need both hands, you can ask for a lockup from above.

Finally, as you arrive at the belay, you should hand your leader a locking carabiner so he can anchor you in. Then sort the gear by handing the leader one piece at a time so he can rebuild his rack. Get acquainted with the anchor system and master point, because you might be the one dismantling the system later. Offer any feedback on the route or placements, and get signals straight for what comes next—another pitch, a walk-off, or a roped descent.

Third Member of the Party

Occasionally, the traditional leading party will have a third or fourth member. This does not change the fundamentals, but it does introduce a few additional issues. One of these issues is route selection. Ideally, the route selected would have belay stances or ledges large enough to comfortably accommodate the group. If hanging belays are called for,

Arriving at one point is the starting point to another.

John Dewey

the leader will need to have a well-practiced system for receiving and anchoring one partner, and then belaying a second.

For route pitches with a length that is less than half the rope length, the second partner can simply be clipped (two carabiners) at the midpoint of the rope with a butterfly knot; the third member can then be tied in at the far end. For any pitch longer than this, a second rope should be used. The leader ties in standard style to rope 1, and the second ties in (also standard style) to the opposite end of rope 1. The second then ties in one end of rope 2 as a trailing line (off the back of the harness), and the third party member ties in to the other end standard style. Rope 1 is used to belay the leader from below, and then the second from above. As the second is climbing, he is also presetting rope 2 to be used to belay the third party member from above.

The second climber still cleans the route, so the third climber has little responsibility other than to top-rope ascend the pitch. However, if one of the two followers is weaker or less experienced than the other, the weaker member should be the second climber but should be instructed to simply unclip his rope from each protection piece as he comes to it. The third climber can then take out the pieces as he ascends.

In some situations, the second may need to back-clip his trailing line to a piece as he passes it. For example, this may be necessary when the second is traversing a horizontal ledge and wants to protect the third from a big pendulum fall. It can also be done if clipping the line will keep the rope from drifting into a crack (or behind a flake) and jamming.

Reprise

Modern climbing has evolved to the point of having numerous sub-disciplines—artificial or indoor climbing, top-roping, traditional leading, sport leading, ice climbing, and mountaineering. While the early pioneers tended to be generalists, many climbers today discover a niche and roost there—usually for reasons of access and expense. When considering traditional leading against the backdrop of the others, probably only mountaineering calls for a broader range of skill and knowledge. Traditional leading requires competence and precision in numerous areas (movement and technique, rope work, creating anchors and protection systems, route finding, risk and incident management, backcountry rescue, and first aid). It also requires the judgment and versatility to use those skills in different environments and situations. Those who ascend a mountain or rock face using traditional means of protection—and then walk away leaving no trace of their passing—enjoy a sense of intimacy with the mountain and its features that few other experiences can parallel.

Sport Climbing

As mentioned earlier, sport climbing involves routes that are entirely protected by fixed protection (typically bolts). During the 1980s, sport climbing took the world by storm. In Europe and the United States, vast expanses of stone—considered by many traditional climbers as being too short to be interesting, impossibly steep, or lacking features adequate for placing protection—caught the attention of a new generation of climbers. Intent on pushing the limits of what most considered impossible, this new group of climbers sought to establish routes that would allow them to develop and test their abilities. Armed with cordless power drills and commercial-quality bolts, route developers quickly started to establish difficult climbs, challenging the existing ground-up ethic of traditional climbers by bolting routes from above, on rappel. Despite generating controversy, sport climbing grew in popularity as glossy magazines started featuring photos of Lycra-clad athletes scaling futuristic bolted routes, inspiring a generation of climbers and helping to legitimize this new style of climbing.

Since then, sport climbing has evolved into its own athletic enterprise, independent of traditional climbing. In sport climbing, the goal is testing one's physical limits and gymnastic capabilities, rather than placing gear, navigating long approaches, or route finding. Sport climbers—many of whom have never placed their own gear—have developed their own rules, nomenclature, crags, and, yes, even clothing lines. Because of the athletic requirements of modern sport climbing, climbers who wish to excel spend countless hours in the gym, performing weight training and aerobic conditioning as well as training specifically for their projects (the routes they want to complete). See chapter 2 for an extensive discussion of physical training for climbing.

Most sport routes are less than a single pitch (less than one rope length), making them accessible. Most routes also feature bolts placed at regular intervals. This removes much of the danger associated with falling, making these sorts of routes relatively safe. Moreover, because sport routes typically feature fixed anchors, descending is easy.

Not all bolted routes are without risk. For instance, at Joshua Tree National Park in California—an area that maintains a strict ground-up ethic—it is not uncommon to encounter long run-out sections (the distance between bolts), rusted one-quarter-inch bolts, hangers of dubious quality or origin (on older climbs, some bolts are adorned with homemade hangers), and poor bolt placements. As a result, even a relatively easy bolted route on moderate terrain can quickly become a source of terror for a lead climber.

With shiny bolts leading the way up a route, it is easy to forget that climbing is inherently dangerous; the moment you step off the ground, you face the possibility of falling. Unfortunately, injury and death do occur in sport climbing. Accidents are rarely caused by equipment failure; rather, they occur because of lapses in human judgment or attention. Regardless of the style of climbing or the length of the route, venturing into the vertical realm is inherently risky—simple errors can be fatal. As a climber or a belayer, you must approach your task with diligence—your life and your partner's life depend on it. Do not assume that a route is safe or well protected just because it is bolted. As discussed in the upcoming section, before setting out, you should consult a guidebook and determine if the route is suitable given your level of skill and experience.

Sport Climbing Gear

To start sport climbing, you only need to purchase a limited amount of gear. Because sport climbing involves a great deal of falling, the equipment you purchase should be of the highest quality. You should also check your equipment frequently for wear or damage. See chapter 5 for a more complete discussion of equipment.

Rope

First, you need a UIAA-rated dynamic rope that is at least 10 millimeters in diameter, 60 meters (197 feet) long, and preferably dry treated. Thinner ropes, while popular, are less durable and can support fewer falls, making them less suitable for a beginning climber. At the same time, you should make sure your rope is long enough for the types of routes you will be climbing—climbers sometimes hit the ground (this is called "decking") because their rope is a few meters too short. Be sure to tie a knot in the end of the rope; this will prevent you from decking if you misjudged the length of the route.

Finally, ropes that are dry treated—that is, impregnated with a waterproofing agent—pass through protection more easily than untreated ropes. Dry-treated ropes also resist dirt, grime, and moisture better (although they are not waterproof), making them ideal for leading. Ropes degrade quickly when exposed to dirt and ultraviolet rays; therefore, you should not step on your rope, drag it through the dirt, or leave it exposed to sunlight for extended periods. A number of companies make rope bags that you can rest your rope on while belaying. These bags can also be used to store your rope when not in use.

Quickdraws

To clip into bolts, you need to purchase a set of quickdraws—a set of 10 to 20 will do when you are first starting out. A quickdraw consists of two carabiners connected together by a sewn runner. Quickdraws are used to connect your rope to a bolt hanger—the "top" carabiner is clipped to the bolt, while the "bottom" carabiner is clipped to the rope. Quickdraws (or simply, "draws") are manufactured in a variety of lengths and come with different-size carabiners. For a general-purpose rack, select draws that are between 8 and 12 inches (20.3 and 30.5 cm) in length and that include carabiners that fit your hand and are easy to clip. Before starting a climb, clip the top carabiners of your draws to the gear loops on your harness, making sure there is an equal number on each side of your body.

The benefit of using quickdraws, rather than single carabiners, is that they "straighten out" the route you are leading—like extending slings while traditional climbing, using quickdraws allows the rope to proceed more directly up a route, resulting in less "zigzagging" of the rope between bolts (see figure 11.2). This helps to reduce rope drag and limits the likelihood that the rope will unclip from the carabiner during a fall. A quickdraw clipped to a bolt also gives you something to grab onto when you need to get back to a high point after a fall (back to where you were before you came off).

Helmet

Rock fall is an ever-present danger in rock climbing. To protect yourself against falling "missiles," you should always wear a helmet while at the crag, whether climbing or belaying. Even a small rock builds up a great deal of momentum as it falls, packing quite a punch when it hits the human body. Each year, falling debris strikes numerous climbers in the head. In some instances, the climber is critically injured or killed. Modern helmets are lightweight and less restrictive than earlier models, making them relatively comfortable to wear for extended periods.

Belay Device

For belaying sport climbs, you need to purchase an auto-locking belay device, such as a Petzl Grigri. Auto-locking belay devices are safer than friction belay devices (assuming you have been trained in their use and you never take your brake hand off the rope). They also allow you to deliver a more dynamic belay to your climber, providing a softer, less jarring "catch."

Guidebooks

As with trad climbing, you should consult a guidebook for the crag where you are climbing. This will limit the likelihood that you will get in over your head on a route. A guidebook will point you in the direction of suitable and fun climbs. Guidebooks come in a wide variety of styles and quality, but most include information about the rock, guidelines for camping, and the names and ratings of routes. Many guidebooks also include detailed descriptions of routes (topos), including the length of the route, the first climbers to ascend the route, the number of bolts, the type of anchors, and whether the route is safely bolted or not.

Do not assume, however, that the topo is correct; many are not—rock breaks and bolts are often miscounted, changing the characteristics of a route. Use your own judgment. Take extra draws and do not be afraid to back off a route if it gets too exposed, too difficult, or too run out; there is always tomorrow to try again. When first starting to lead, you should choose a route that is two or three grades below what you climb on a top rope. So, if you climb 5.10c on top rope, your first lead might be on a 5.8. It is easier to learn the mechanics of leading by climbing on a route that is not physically taxing or challenging for your level of skill.

Climbing Partner

When lead climbing, having an experienced partner is as important as having the proper rope or quickdraws. Your climbing partner must know how to belay, how to operate an auto-locking belay device, how to lower off climbs, and so forth. An inexperienced belayer will compromise your safety (be more likely to drop you) and may also make the process of leading more difficult. Less experienced belayers often have a difficult time feeding the rope smoothly, understanding commands, and providing enough slack for easy clipping. Especially when you are new to leading, you should climb with someone more experienced than you are. Regardless of your level of experience, it goes without saying that you must make sure your belayer is attentive and capable of holding you in the event of a fall. A belayer who weighs little may need to be tethered to a fixed object, such as a tree or rock. This way, if you fall, your belayer will not meet you halfway up the route, giving you more of a dynamic belay than you expected.

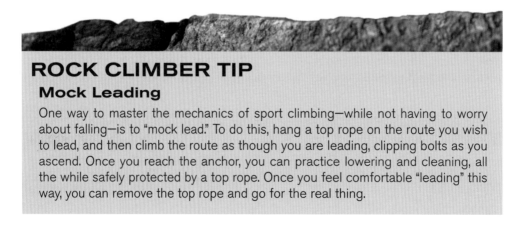

ROCK CLIMBER TIP
Mock Leading

One way to master the mechanics of sport climbing—while not having to worry about falling—is to "mock lead." To do this, hang a top rope on the route you wish to lead, and then climb the route as though you are leading, clipping bolts as you ascend. Once you reach the anchor, you can practice lowering and cleaning, all the while safely protected by a top rope. Once you feel comfortable "leading" this way, you can remove the top rope and go for the real thing.

Before the Climb

To sport climb safely and successfully, you must pay attention to a few critically important considerations. Safety begins before you even set off on a route. In this section, we discuss some of these issues.

Routine

To minimize the likelihood of errors, you should develop a preclimb routine that is inviolable. Because sport climbing involves performing the same tasks many times during a day (e.g., tying your rope into your harness, belaying, and so on), you must check and double-check that you are safely prepared to climb. In your routine, you need to ensure that your harness is on correctly (your belt must be "doubled back" through the buckle). Also make sure that your knot is properly connected to your harness (the knot should encircle both the leg loops and the belt on your harness) and that you have an adequate number of draws to complete the route (don't forget about taking extra for the anchors). You also need to ensure that your rope is organized correctly on the ground ("flaked"), verifying that it is free of knots or kinks that might bind up in a belay device. To prevent the rope from running out through the belay device, "close the system" by tying a figure eight knot in the end of the rope. Finally, check to make sure you are on belay correctly—even experienced belayers occasionally thread the rope through the Grigri incorrectly.

The atmosphere at many sport crags is quite festive. Do not let the noise distract you from your preclimb routine. As with top-roping, you must be sure to communicate with your partner before you start climbing as well as during the climb. For example, my climbing partner—who also happens to be my wife—alerts me when she has me on belay by saying, "You're on." Before every climb, we double-check each other's harnesses; we make sure our belts are doubled back through the buckle and that we are connected correctly to each other (from the leader's knot to the Grigri). When I know that I am on belay and I am ready to climb, I say "climbing" to signify that I am setting off. Your routine may differ from ours. Regardless of the specific order of your safety checks, you should ensure that you and your partner are correctly connected to the rope (the leader should tie in with a figure eight knot or a double bowline with a hitch), that the belay is on, and that you have an adequate number of draws. (Refer to chapter 6 for more detail regarding specific knots.)

Racking Your Gear

When you place your quickdraws on your harness, make sure they are easily accessible. As previously noted, you should have an equal number on both sides of your harness. Panic can set in quickly when you have to clip a bolt on your left side but you discover that all your draws are on the right side of your harness. Based on personal preference, the gates of the top carabiners (the ones attached to your gear loops) can be facing away

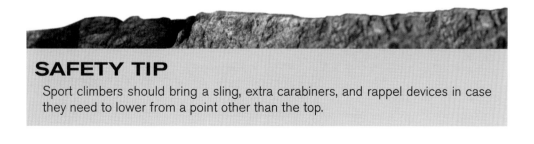

SAFETY TIP

Sport climbers should bring a sling, extra carabiners, and rappel devices in case they need to lower from a point other than the top.

or toward your body; however, you must make sure you can remove them easily. Fiddling around trying to remove a draw from a loop is a frustrating experience, especially when you're "pumped" (when your forearms become engorged with blood making it difficult to hold onto the rock).

When counting the number of draws you need on a route, be sure to include draws for the anchors. If there is a two-bolt anchor at the top of the climb, you will need to take two additional draws. If you will be cleaning the route—that is, removing the draws on the way down—you need to take additional draws, or a sling, so you can connect yourself to the draws attached to the anchor before untying from the rope (which is something you will have to do before lowering off). If you need to rappel off the route, make sure to bring along a rappel device.

Leading Sport Routes

Regardless of the style of lead—whether you hang the draws or clip prehung ones, climb on-sight, or redpoint a route—the goal of sport climbing is to ascend (or simply, "send") a route. This means that you climb the route, top to bottom, without falling or weighting your gear or rope. Climbing a route on lead requires not only technical expertise, but also a great deal of awareness, finesse, and strength. Leading is as much about moving smoothly and efficiently as it is about power. Having the technical aspects down (e.g., how to clip the rope, lower, and fall) frees you up to focus on the actual act of climbing, which you will learn from experience and practice. In this section, we discuss how to clip the rope into a quickdraw, how to fall, how to belay, and how to lower off and clean a route. We also discuss a few strategies that will help you maximize your performance as a sport climber, including how and when to "hangdog" and how to bail from a climb. Finally, we distinguish between different styles that can be used to ascend routes, including on-sight climbing, flashing, and redpointing.

Figure 11.3 Ensure that the gate of the lower carabiner, the one clipped onto the rope, is facing away from the climber's direction of travel.

Direction of Carabiners

The position of the quickdraws on your harness—whether the gates face the same direction or opposite directions—is a matter of preference. However, you must pay close attention to the direction of the gate on the lower carabiner, the carabiner that is clipped onto the rope, in relation to the direction you are traveling (see figure 11.3). The gate on the lower carabiner should face away from the direction you are traveling. For instance, if you arrive at a bolt and the route seems to trend left, the gate on the lower carabiner should face right. Having the gate situated this way limits the likelihood that the lower carabiner will come unclipped from the rope during a fall.

Another important point related to rope placement is that you must avoid getting the rope wrapped around your leg while leading. The rope should run directly down between your legs or over your thigh if you are traversing. A rope wrapped around your leg will cause you to flip upside down during a fall, increasing the likelihood that you will hit your head or otherwise injure yourself.

How to Clip

Clipping the rope into the lower carabiner on a quickdraw can be very frustrating for the beginning lead climber. Because of improper technique, many climbers expend a great deal of energy fumbling with the rope and trying to get it clipped into the carabiner. You may be relieved to know that you only need to master two methods for getting the rope into the carabiner. If you execute the technique correctly, you will never again botch a clip. The direction of the gate on the lower carabiner, as well as the hand you must use to clip, determines which of the two methods you should use. Imagine that you have to clip a bolt on your right side. First, hang a draw on the bolt. When you are ready to clip, pull up some slack from your belayer with your right hand (see figure 11.4, *a-b*). Next, if the gate is also facing right, away from your body, simply use your thumb to pinch the rope against the gate of the carabiner, making the rope drop into the carabiner (see figure 11.4*c*). To check that you clipped correctly, make sure the lead end of the rope (the one attached to your harness) emerges from the front of the carabiner (see figure 11.4*d*).

Figure 11.4 Clipping a rope into a carabiner from your right side.

On the other hand, if the gate is facing to the left (toward the midline of your body) and you are still clipping with your right hand, you should do the following: Pinch the rope between your right forefinger and thumb, placing your middle finger on the bottom inside edge of the carabiner (see figure 11.5a). Once you stabilize the carabiner (by pulling down with your middle finger), "flip" the rope through the gate with a quick, rotating movement of your thumb outward (see figure 11.5, b-c).

Before your first lead, you should practice clipping. One way to do this is to hang a quickdraw off a fixed object, such as from a rope hung from the rafters in a garage or on a low-level bolt in a climbing gym. Clip the carabiner as though it were on a route, working on getting the rope efficiently through the gate. Be sure to practice using both hands.

When pumped or facing a long fall, many climbers have a tendency to "rush the clip." This means that they clip the quickdraw from well below the bolt, typically using poor holds. At times, you might be tempted to think that clipping low is a safer option than climbing a few more feet to the proper clipping hold (usually a better hold). Do not give in to this temptation. Clipping in this manner takes more energy than clipping off bigger holds higher up, and it increases the distance you will fall. When you clip below the quickdraw, you have to pull up much more rope than if you clipped nearer to the bolt; this increases the distance of your fall if the fall occurs before the rope makes it into the carabiner. When clipping, you need to relax. Do not hold your breath; rather, inhale slowly through your nose, exhaling out your mouth. If possible, place three points of contact on the rock when clipping—one arm and both feet—placing your weight as much on your feet as possible. This provides stability and helps reduce forearm pump. You can further reduce your pump by hanging straight-arm while clipping.

Finally, if you are unsure whether you are close enough to the bolt (or the draw if it is already hanging) to clip before pulling up rope, you should try to touch the bolt with your clipping hand. If you are able to span the distance, you will be able to make the clip easily.

Figure 11.5 Clipping a rope into a carabiner if the gate is facing to the left.

CLIPPING DOS AND DON'TS

As noted earlier, sport routes have fixed protection, typically bolts, but they might also include fixed pitons, nuts, or threads (a knotted piece of rope threaded through a natural hole in the rock, typically on limestone). As you move up the route, you need to clip the rope either into a quickdraw that you clip to the bolt or into one that is already hanging (common on difficult routes). You *must* make sure you clip the rope into the lower carabiner correctly. You must clip the rope into the carabiner so the rope going to the belayer is behind the carabiner (the part of the carabiner facing the rock), while the rope connected to the climber comes out the front (the part of the carabiner facing away from the rock).

The opposite of this—called "back clipping"—is an error that many climbers make. Back clipping occurs when the rope behind the carabiner goes to the leader and the rope in the front goes to the belayer. The danger of this configuration is that, in the event of a fall, the rope will bend over the gate of the carabiner, unclipping it. This allows the rope to disengage from the carabiner, increasing the distance the climber falls. If the back-clipped draw is low on the route, the climber could deck. Obviously, falling to the ground is something best avoided.

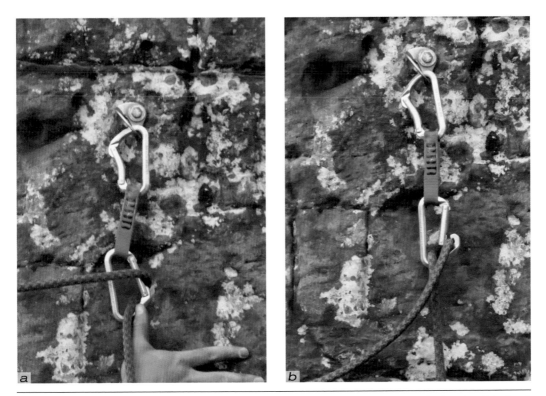

Avoid "back clipping" by clipping the rope-end carabiner on the quick draw correctly: from back to front: (a) back clipping and (b) how the rope can become unclipped.

STICK CLIPPING

A stick clip is a pole that allows you to clip the first bolt on a route from the ground. Stick clips are commonly used by climbers who do not feel comfortable climbing the first section of the route unprotected (this section is often very difficult). You can construct a stick clip yourself out of an extendable painter's pole and a strong spring clamp that you affix to the end of the pole. Alternatively, you can purchase one at your local climbing shop.

Falling

Inevitably, you are going to fall while sport climbing. On a difficult route, you will likely fall many times before ascending the route. All falls are potentially dangerous; therefore, when starting out, you should select climbs well below your maximum level. Nevertheless, when faced with the possibility of falling, you need to consider certain things.

First, when you fall while leading, the total distance you travel is double the distance you are above your last bolt. In other words, when falling, you fall the distance to the bolt and then an equal distance below the bolt. When you factor in rope stretch and a dynamic belay, you can fall quite a bit farther. When faced with a long run-out section or the possibility of falling onto a ledge, you should factor these considerations into your decision on whether to proceed or bail.

On severely overhung sport routes, a long fall doesn't ordinarily hurt (if you are given an adequate dynamic belay), but it can leave you dangling far away from the rock. When this occurs, you must either lower to the ground or "boink" back to the highest clipped bolt on the route. Boinking involves both the belayer and the climber. First, the belayer jumps up in the air, locking the belay device at the apex of the jump. This leaves the belayer dangling in the air. Using the belayer as a counterweight, the climber grabs the rope above his head and pulls his body upward. At the end of the hoist, he lets go of the rope quickly. The weight of the belayer falling toward the ground pulls the climber up. The climber and belayer repeat this process until the climber has reached his high point.

On most sport routes, especially overhung ones, falling is often a better option than downclimbing. On difficult routes, reversing a difficult sequence may be impossible or may have the potential to cause injury. For instance, reversing a dynamic move is simply not possible. On the other hand, although you might be able to lower yourself back through a series of small edges or monos (pockets that only accept a single digit), doing so can result in finger injury. Simply falling is the best thing to do if it can be done safely. Here is one exception: On a moderate route, or if you have only moved through part of a difficult sequence, you may want to downclimb, especially if doing so will help you preserve an on-sight or flash of the route (climbing the route the first time with no falls).

When falling, you should not grab the rope, the draws, or the hangers. Keep your hands in front of you, and if possible, try to face the rock. Grabbing the rope will start you spinning—similar to what happens when a figure skater brings her arms in close to her body—and flailing your arms will result in injury. Grabbing the quickdraw will only give you a nasty rope burn as the draw rips through your palm. If you hook your finger in a hanger while falling, you will likely arrive at the end of the rope with one less digit.

Hangdogging

If you rest on the rope after having fallen, you are "hangdogging." While often derided by traditional climbers as being in poor style, hangdogging is de rigueur among sport climbers, making it possible to work the moves on a difficult route. Many sport routes contain puzzling crux sequences that might take a sustained effort over many days to solve, even for elite climbers. Hangdogging allows you to figure out challenging sequences without having to climb the entire route each time.

When starting out, however, you will benefit more from moving consistently and smoothly over stone than you will from trying moves beyond your skill and strength level. In the first years of your climbing career, select routes that you are able to ascend relatively quickly. This helps you build up a solid base of skill and confidence. Save the hangdogging for later—when you are more experienced.

Lowering and Cleaning Sport Routes

Once you complete a route, you will need to lower off and retrieve your draws—climbers call this "cleaning a route." This is where errors occur; each year, some climbers fall to their death, or experience injury, because they botch the rigging used to lower off a route. If you follow the routine outlined in this section, you will be able to safely and efficiently lower off and clean a route.

Many newer sport climbs have fixed anchors that accept ropes directly, such as Metolius Super Shuts or, less common now, open cold shuts.

These types of anchors either have an open gap at the top (open cold shuts) or gates (Super Shuts) that will accept a rope. (The gates on Super Shuts are similar to those on carabiners.) These anchors make lowering off and cleaning the route straightforward: When you arrive at the anchors, simply clip your rope into them and tell your belayer to "take." This signifies that you are no longer climbing and that you would like the belayer to hold you on the rope.

When you are done basking in your successful ascent and you are ready to lower, you should tell your belayer "down." As you are being lowered, ask your belayer to "take" when you arrive at the highest bolt, giving you time to retrieve your draw. Place the

TECHNIQUE TIP

If the route you are cleaning is steep, "tramming" is an effective technique for removing your draws. Simply clip a quickdraw from your waist to the rope and lower down to the top bolt. (The rope keeps you close to the rock.) Pull into the draw and remove it. Repeat the same process for each draw. One word of caution: It is often safer to clean the bottom bolt on the route while leaving the rope clipped into a higher draw. In other words, you should stay clipped into a higher bolt as you unclip the last bolt. This will prevent you from swinging out from the rock face and hitting the ground. Once you remove the last draw, pull up to the higher clipped draw, retrieve it, and lower to the ground.

draw back onto a gear loop on your harness and say "OK" or "lower," continuing the process until you have removed all the draws.

Other routes, however, have double (or triple) bolts with closed lowering hangers as the anchors. This means that you must first thread the rope through the hangers before lowering. Most hangers are too narrow in diameter to accept a bight of the rope. As a result, you need to untie from your harness before you are able to thread the rope. To accomplish this task, do the following:

1. When you arrive at the top bolts, clip in using a couple of draws or a sling. Be sure to clip into at least two bolts. Tell your belayer that you are "off belay."
2. Pull up a length of rope from below, and tie a figure eight on a bight. Clip the knot into the belay loop of your harness. This prevents you from dropping the rope—a terrifying situation—and backs you up on the highest clipped bolt on the route.
3. Untie your climbing knot from your harness, and thread the end of the rope through the bolts.
4. Retie your climbing knot into your harness, untie the figure eight on the bight, and go back on belay.
5. Remove the quickdraws you used to clip to the anchor.
6. Communicate with your belayer to ensure that you are ready to be lowered.
7. Begin lowering.
8. Clean the route.

Bailing

For a variety of reasons—the weather is poor, the route is too difficult, or because of an injury sustained while climbing—a climber may need to retreat from a route, or "bail." If the length of the route you are on is half a rope length or less, the process is straightforward. If you are willing to leave a carabiner behind—this becomes expensive, so don't make bailing a habit—simply replace the draw with the carabiner; after clipping your rope into the carabiner, you can lower off, retrieving the lower draws on the way down. If you do not want to leave a piece of gear, you can thread a piece of webbing through the bolt hanger, connect the ends with a water knot, and rappel off. Under no circumstances should you ever be lowered by your belayer through a piece of webbing or the bolt hanger directly. Doing so can cut your rope, getting you to the ground faster than expected. Also, rope through nylon webbing can melt the webbing because of the heat caused by friction. If the route is longer than half a rope length, you should tie off to the bolt, pull up your rope, and drop the free end to the ground. Have your belayer tie another rope onto yours. Then pull it up. Connect the ropes together using a fisherman's knot (if this was not done by your belayer). Thread the rope through the bolt hanger, carabiner, or sling until the knot is next to the anchor; rappel down.

Belaying

The techniques used to belay a sport climber differ from those used on top-rope climbs, and even some trad climbs. The commands remain the same, but the mechanics of the belay differ. First, as with trad climbing, when belaying a sport route, you pay out the rope as the climber moves up the route. On a difficult sport route (one where there is a high likelihood that the leader will fall), you must give the climber enough slack so she can move upward—but not too much, in case she falls. This is especially important when the leader is ready to clip a quickdraw—you should provide an armful of rope so the leader can clip, taking in excess slack once you hear the gate of the carabiner snap shut.

Second, for the first few bolts, the belayer should stand close to the rock face. If you don't do this, you will be violently yanked forward if the climber falls. More important, failing to do this will increase the distance the climber falls.

Third, giving your climber a dynamic belay is often preferable, especially on steep routes. A dynamic belay minimizes the shock experienced by the climber when hitting the end of the rope, making for a more comfortable fall. Executing a perfect dynamic belay is a combination of technique and timing—as the climber is falling, you anticipate when she is going to hit the end of the rope. Just before you feel her weight on the rope, you take a little hop into the air, slowing her descent. Acting as a counterbalance, you slow her descent gradually (although it happens very quickly), lessening the shock transmitted to the climber's body when she hits the end of the rope.

During the process of catching the fall, the belayer should have the belay device in the locked position; the only thing that moves is you, not the rope through the device. When done correctly, a dynamic belay is a thing of beauty.

Those who contemplate the beauty of the earth find reserves of strength that will endure as long as life lasts.

Rachel Carson

You must be aware that a dynamic belay increases the distance the leader will fall. If there is a ledge below the leader, or if the leader is close to the ground, you should adjust your belay accordingly. It's better to give a hard belay than to let the climber hit an object or the ground. In addition, you should not use dynamic belays on slabs. Extending the distance of a fall on subvertical rock only results in the leader receiving abrasions and cuts—the sorts of injuries most climbers like to avoid.

Style

The goal of sport climbing is to ascend the route clean—to leverage your athletic, mental, and emotional abilities into climbing success. Three styles can be used to ascend a route: on-sight, flash, and redpoint. Climbing a route on-sight is the premier style of ascent. To climb on-sight means you climb the route to the anchors without falling or weighting the rope, all the while placing your own quickdraws. The distinguishing feature of on-sighting a route is that you climb the route without possessing any prior information about the climb—you have not seen anyone on the route, nor have you been given any hints (called "beta") on how to climb it. On-sight climbing is a one-shot deal: You only have one chance to complete a route in this style. Before trying an on-sight, you should mentally prepare yourself—remain calm and visualize success (i.e., clipping the anchors). From the ground, inspect the route; try to identify possible sequences, as well as places to rest.

Flashing a route is similar to on-sighting in that you climb without falling or weighting the rope. Flashing differs from on-sighting, however, in one very important way: When you are going for a flash, you possess information about the route, either because you watched another climber lead the route or because you have beta.

Finally, redpointing means that you ascend a route after taking a fall or weighting the rope on previous attempts. When you redpoint a route, this typically means that you have selected a route that you had no hope to on-sight or flash. In other words, the demands of the route exceed your current climbing abilities. Initial failure is not a setback, but rather a means for refining your technique, learning the proper sequences to get through the crux, and so forth. Depending on the difficulty of the route, it may take you a day or weeks to complete. For an especially difficult route—one that has become your "project"—you can divide it into pieces, perfecting the moves within each section. To gain confidence on the route before your redpoint burn, try linking several sections together. When you are finally able to link several sections and have memorized every crux sequence, you can go for the ascent.

Summary

Climbing is a discipline that includes many different genres, such as top-roping, bouldering, traditional climbing, and sport climbing. Excelling at climbing requires commitment, technique, flexibility, and an ability to learn from mistakes. As the late Wolfgang Gullich (Wald, 1987, p. 70) observed, "In climbing you are always faced with new problems in which you must perform using intuitive movements, and then later analyze them to figure out why they work, and then learn from them." To climb well and with good style, you must have creativity and an infectious verve—an enthusiasm for the activity.

To ensure a safe and enjoyable experience, be sure to receive training from a certified guide before leading your first climb.

Climbing on the sharp end allows you to experience the thrill and freedom of setting out into the unknown. At the same time, it forces you to face your weaknesses and fears. As a result, climbing can serve as an important catalyst for growth. The author William Arthur Ward (1969) suggested that the ". . . greatest hazard in life is to risk nothing . . . [one] may avoid suffering and sorrow, but . . . cannot learn, feel, change, grow or live." Lead climbing is an inherently risky endeavor, yet through the process of ascending upward, you discover new things about yourself, others, and nature.

Climbing is also about the pure joy of the climbing experience. The simple satisfaction of moving over stone, the texture of the rock, the numbing sense of exposure, and the camaraderie of good friends—all taking place while you are ensconced in the beautiful outdoors—is a sublime experience unmatched by most other pursuits. The love of the climbing moves us, impels us, to continue moving upward. We hope that in these few pages you have glimpsed the essence of what it means to climb—to lead onward toward the sky.

Web Resources

U.S. Organizations

Access Fund

www.accessfund.org

This advocacy organization was founded in 1991. The organization strives to keep climbing areas open and aids in conserving the climbing environment. The Web site is a great resource for getting involved on a local and national level.

Action Committee for Eldorado

www.aceeldo.org

A nonprofit organization composed of volunteers to help conserve and maintain the climbing opportunities in Eldorado State Park, Colorado.

American Alpine Club

www.americanalpineclub.org

Club aids in protecting climbing areas, history of climbing, and accomplishments of the climbers. Events, involvement opportunities, AA journal, and grant information are available through the Web site.

Association for Experiential Education

www.aee.org

A nonprofit, professional membership association dedicated to experiential education and the students, educators, and practitioners who embody its philosophy. The association publishes and provides access to relevant research and resources and raises the quality and performance of experiential programs through its accreditation program. Their Web site provides a list of universities and outdoor programs that have earned accreditation.

The Explorers Club

www.explorers.org

The Explorers Club has unified explorers and researchers since 1904. Site provides membership information, current projects, research, and publications.

Leave No Trace

www.LNT.org

Nonprofit organization that focuses on education, partnerships, and grants related to principles of minimal impact. The seven principles can be applied to front- and backcountry settings as well as specific recreational activities such as climbing. The site provides information on the seven principles and minimal impact in a variety of surroundings.

Continuing Education Opportunities and Trainings

American Alpine Institute (AAI)

www.aai.cc

Founded in 1975, AAI is longest-accredited climbing guide service in the United States. Institute specializes in advanced training and expeditions in rock, snow, ice, glacier, and high-altitude climbing. Courses are conducted year-round worldwide.

American Mountain Guides Association

www.amga.com

This association trains and certifies guides, sets standards of safety for the climbing industry, and aids in protecting the natural environment. View current listing of certified guides and companies or enroll in a training course.

Christian Adventure Association

www.caainfo.org

This organization seeks to advance wilderness and adventure programming through educating and equipping wilderness and adventure leaders. Outdoor leadership labs are offered regionally by members who are trained professionals in the outdoor education field.

Lord Stirling School Outdoor Education Center

www.lordstirling.org/outdoors/index.html

While maintaining safety and a concern for the environment, this organization provides instruction on backcountry travel and designs and constructs ropes courses, climbing walls, and experiential education programs. View ropes course and climbing wall construction portfolio and courses on the Web site.

Montana Mountaineering Association

www.montanamountaineering.org

This association, based in Bozeman, offers a variety of instructional programs. Individual or group instruction is offered year-round in the mountains of Montana as well as the Andes Mountains in South America.

Mountain Rescue Association

www.mra.org

This organization responds to remote emergency situations, trains rescuers, and provides education to promote safe travel in the backcountry.

National Outdoor Leadership School

www.nols.edu

This organization provides educational and leadership training in a variety of recreational activities in settings worldwide. Courses vary in length from 7 days to more than 69 days. Course descriptions, course calendar, and online registration are available.

Outward Bound

www.outwardbound.org

This organization provides at-risk youth expeditions, custom programs, expedition learning school, and wilderness training. The courses are held in a variety of settings worldwide. Courses vary in length from 7 days to more than 69 days. Course descriptions, course calendar, and online registration are available.

Professional Climbing Guides Institute

www.climbingguidesinstitute.org

This organization seeks to further develop and define the safety standards of guided rock climbing in grade III and lower terrain. They provide and maintain logical, factual, and practical guided rock-climbing safety standards through educating, training, assessing, certifying, and empowering current professionals and aspiring rock-climbing guides.

Solid Rock Outdoor Ministries

www.srom.org

SROM is a premier Christian outdoor leadership education and wilderness adventure program in the heart of the Rocky Mountains. Their programming activities include backpacking, rock climbing, mountaineering, backcountry cooking, alpine and backcountry living, orienteering, and community building. SROM is one of nine wilderness adventure programs accredited with the Association for Experiential Education.

Wilderness Education Association

www.weainfo.org

This organization promotes professionalism of outdoor leadership and safety. Web site contains membership information, publications, WEA course offerings, and LNT course offerings.

International Organizations

The Alpine Club (UK)

www.alpine-club.org.uk

Site provides membership information, places to climb, discussion forums, and publications.

Alpine Club of Canada

www.alpineclubofcanada.ca

This club offers adventures in Canada and worldwide. Club also publishes books and journals, supports access and environmental issues, and provides opportunities for climbing-related projects.

British Mountaineering Council

www.thebmc.co.uk

Site provides membership information, access and conservation efforts in Wales and England, places to climb, safety and skills, equipment forum, and publications.

Chockstone (Australia)

www.chockstone.org

This resource is a sponsored but nonprofit and noncommercial Web site that features Victorian climbing areas, a photo gallery, videos, gear resources, useful knots, and technique tips.

International Mountaineering and Climbing Federation (UIAA)

www.theuiaa.org

Often recognized for their safety labels on climbing equipment, the associations of the UIAA also lobby for access, encourage global friendships through climbing, and assist in preserving mountainous areas.

Italian Alpine Club

www.cai.it

Site provides membership information, places to climb in Italy, discussion forums, and publications.

New Zealand Alpine Club

http://alpineclub.org.nz

Site provides membership information, places to climb, mountain huts, calendar of events, discussion forums, and publications.

Scottish Mountaineering Club

www.smc.org.uk

Web site caters to its members as a private club. Site provides information on guidebooks and mountain huts.

Victorian Climbing Club (Australia)

www.vicclimb.org.au

Site provides membership information, places to climb, discussion forums, and publications.

Fitness

ActiveLog

www.activelog.com

This Web site enables you to keep track of your exercise routine online. The site includes rock climbing as an activity in addition to entries for aerobic and muscular fitness. As you log each workout, the site offers a way to summarize weeks, months, and years of activity, including duration and types of activity. Also, because your log is online, others can view it (if you allow them), or you can share it with friends to motivate them or yourself to keep training!

Exercise Prescription Guidelines

www.exrx.net

This Web site is endorsed by major exercise and sport science organizations in the fields of sports medicine and strength training (American College of Sports Medicine and National Strength and Conditioning Association, respectively). This site illustrates the various techniques related to building muscle from head to toe. Peruse the site and learn information about exercise prescription for aerobic and strength routines.

MountainZone

www.mountainzone.com

This is a site for athletes of all kinds, including rock climbers. At this site, you can read blogs by climbers and be inspired to chase your climbing aspirations. You'll also find advice from various climbers on performance and training.

MyPyramid (U.S. Department of Agriculture)

www.mypyramid.gov

This site helps you assess the amount of calories you need per day based on your sex, height, weight, age, and activity level. You can choose your current fitness level and then view the appropriate number of servings required per day related to grains, vegetables, fruits, milk, and meat and beans. You can even track what you eat each day by keeping an online (and ongoing) record.

National Strength and Conditioning Association (NSCA)

www.nsca-lift.org

This is a great site to explore in order to get acquainted with strength and conditioning conferences nationwide. You can learn about how to enhance sport performance through optimal training and nutrition. This site also contains information about NSCA certifications for those who want to gain more practical knowledge in the field.

Indoor Climbing

Asana Climbing

www.asanaclimbing.com

Based in Boise, Idaho, Asana Climbing is the definitive source for custom climbing flooring surfaces, bouldering crash pads, handholds, and route-setting equipment and supplies. Asana works directly with clients to design and develop solutions for their climbing gym needs.

Climbing Wall Association

www.climbingwallindustry.org

The Climbing Wall Association (CWA) is a nonprofit trade association that addresses the needs and interests of the climbing wall industry and climbing wall operators. The CWA provides its members with access to insurance programs, operations standards, engineering standards, training programs, and an annual conference.

Eldorado Wall Company

www.eldowalls.com

Based in Boulder, Colorado, Eldorado Wall Company serves the recreation industry as a source for wall construction, modular handholds, consultation, and training of climbing gym operators.

Entreprises

www.epusa.com

Based in Bend, Oregon, Entreprises Climbing Walls is a worldwide source for wall construction, modular handholds, consultation, and training of climbing gym operators. Entreprises has built over 4,000 walls in the United States alone.

Nicros Incorporated

www.nicros.com

Based in St. Paul, Minnesota, Nicros is a source for large project wall construction, modular handholds, consultation, belay systems, flooring systems, and training of climbing gym operators. Nicros has built over a million square feet of wall space for climbing enjoyment.

Rockwerx

www.rockwerxclimbing.com

Based in Barre, Massachusetts, Rockwerx does school and home wall construction, design and engineering, and consultation. Rockwerx has built over 1,000 walls to date.

Trip Planning and Guidebooks

Amazon

www.amazon.com

Amazon has an extensive selection of guidebooks on local climbing areas.

Mountain Project

www.mountainproject.com

This site enables you to research notable rock-climbing ascents and destinations in an extensive collection of routes, ranging from easy (5.5) to expert (5.14). You can search for rock-climbing destinations all over the United States.

Rock Climbing

www.rockclimbing.com/routes

The Routes section of this Web site is an invaluable source for climbers who want to learn about the types of climbing available at specific locations.

SuperTopo

http://supertopo.com

SuperTopo is an online retailer that specializes in rock-climbing guidebooks for very popular areas.

Gear

Beal

http://bealplanet.com

This is a French company that produces over eight million meters of rope annually. Products include an assortment of ropes for various specialties. The Web site includes detailed information on ropes, standards, and technicality.

Black Diamond

www.bdel.com

This is an employee-owned climbing company that evolved from Chouinard Equipment. The company's specialty is climbing gear, but they carry many other products.

Five Ten

www.fiveten.com

This family-owned company introduced Stealth rubber for approach and climbing shoes in 1986. Products include a variety of shoes for outdoor athletes, including paddlers, hikers, and trail runners.

Metolius

www.metoliusclimbing.com

Founded in 1983 by Doug Phillips, this company introduced the first flexible-stem camming device and the slider nut. Products include climbing gear, clothing, and training equipment.

Mountain Gear

www.mountaingear.com

Mountain Gear is one of the largest online retailers that specialize in rock-climbing gear and apparel. Climbing guidebooks can also be purchased on this Web site.

Petzl

http://en.petzl.com

Originally focused on underground equipment for caving, this company is now a leader in rock climbing, mountaineering, and rescue work at heights. Products include a variety of climbing gear, helmets, and headlamps.

Knots

Animated Knots by Grog

www.animatedknots.com

This is a great site for visual learners. The site includes short moving slide shows of a variety of knots being tied. You can watch an entire video or stop on tricky sections.

Montreat College

www.backcountry.montreat.edu/techtips

This site has written directions as well as short instructional videos on tying the knots described in this book. The site also provides technical information on which knots work best in specific situations.

Anchors

American Safe Climbing Association

www.safeclimbing.org/education/bomberbolts.htm

The association focuses on replacing deteriorating anchors in the United States and educating people about the importance of maintaining anchors. The Web site lists areas that have been inspected, maintained, and replaced.

Periodicals

Climbing Magazine

www.climbing.com

This site is operated by *Climbing* magazine and contains articles and information on bouldering and sport and traditional climbing. The site contains information regarding an initiative by the magazine and two climbing-related companies: The North Face and Petzl. The initiative is the Anchor Replacement Initiative (ARI) and aims at replacing old, damaged, or misplaced artificial pieces of protection. Check the magazine Web site (under the community section) to find more information about ARI. The site provides updates on the climbing areas that have seen their climbing anchors improved.

Rock and Ice

www.rockandice.com

This site offers articles on climbing areas, gear, and rock and ice climbing.

Books

Ajango, Deb. *Lessons Learned: A Guide to Accident Prevention and Crisis Response.* Boulder, CO: Association for Experiential Education, 2000.

Allen, George B. *Ultrasafe: A Guide to Safer Rock Climbing.* Highlands Ranch, CO: Preventive Press, 2002.

Brown, Terry. Adventure Risk Management. In *Adventure Programming,* edited by John C. Miles, Simon Priest. State College, PA: Venture, 1999.

Cox, S., and Fulsaas, K. (Eds.). *Mountaineering: The Freedom of the Hills.* (7th ed.). Seattle: Mountaineers Books, 2003.

Fasulo, David J. *How to Climb: Self-Sescue.* Helena, MT: Falcon, 1997.

Goddard, Dale, and Neumann, Udo. *Performance rock climbing.* Mechanicsburg, PA: Stackpole, 1994.

Graham, John. *Outdoor Leadership: Technique, Common Sense & Self-Confidence.* Seattle: Mountaineers Books, 1997.

Harvey, Mark. *The National Outdoor Leadership School Wilderness Guide: The Classic Handbook.* New York: Simon & Schuster, 1999.

Hattingh, Garth. *Rock & Wall Climbing.* Mechanicsburg, PA: Stackpole, 2000.

Horst, Eric J. *How to Climb 5.12.* (2nd ed.). Helena, MT: Falcon, 2003.

Hurni, Michelle. *Coaching Climbing.* Helena, MT: Falcon, 2002.

Long, John. *How to Rock Climb.* Helena, MT: Falcon, 2004.

Long, John. *More Climbing Anchors.* Helena, MT: Falcon, 1998.

Long, John, and Gaines, Bob. *Climbing Anchors.* (2nd ed.). Helena, MT: Falcon, 2006.

Long, John, and Luebben, Craig. *How to Climb: Advanced Rock Climbing.* Helena, MT: Falcon, 2006.

Long, John, and Raleigh, Duane. *How to climb: Clip and go!* Helena, MT: Falcon, 2004.

Luebben, Craig. *Rock Climbing: Mastering Basic Skills.* Seattle: Mountaineers, 2004.

Mellor, Don, and Hildebrand, Rod. *Trailside Guide: Rock Climbing.* New York: Norton, 1997.

Richardson, Alun. *Rock Climbing for Instructors.* Marlborough, Wiltshire: Crowood Press, 2001.

Success Checks

Chapter 1

1. What style of rock climbing presented in chapter 1 is most appealing to you?
2. How is protection for the climber accomplished in bouldering?
3. Identify the two forms of lead climbing and explain the primary difference between the two.
4. What are some reasons you might choose to go top-rope rock climbing?
5. Select one of the Leave No Trace principles and explain how following this principle when rock climbing can help to protect the natural environment.
6. What are four sources that you can consult to locate various styles of rock climbing in your area?
7. Name a benefit of rock climbing that is important to you.
8. Why is personal instruction from a qualified climbing instructor or guide so critical in rock climbing?

Chapter 2

1. As a rock climber, it is NOT important for you to maintain cardiorespiratory conditioning.
   a. true
   b. false
2. Muscle mass contributes more to rock-climbing ability than other tissues do.
   a. true
   b. false
3. To improve as a climber, you should develop climbing-specific muscular fitness (endurance and strength).
   a. true
   b. false
4. One of the best ways to increase your overall climbing strength is through climbing itself.
   a. true
   b. false

5. It "pays" to invest in a structured fitness class, such as Pilates or yoga, in order to gain flexibility in climbing muscles.

   a. true

   b. false

6. Climbing tends to be 100 percent mental and 100 percent physical.

   a. true

   b. false

7. Climbers do not need to develop an aerobic base of fitness.

   a. true

   b. false

8. Rock climbers routinely use which of the following energy systems throughout a climbing session?

   a. aerobic

   b. ATP-PCr

   c. glycolytic

   d. all of the above

9. Overall climbing fitness is defined as

   a. flexibility

   b. muscular fitness

   c. cardiorespiratory endurance

   d. all of the above

10. During long-duration climbing sessions, you should focus on eating

   a. carbohydrate

   b. fat

   c. protein

   d. all three of the above equally

Chapter 3

1. What is the most important safety step when using an auto belay system?

   a. Climb slowly so that the belay mechanism remains engaged and operating.

   b. Keep hands and clothing clear from the cable so that they do not become caught in the system.

   c. Examine the cable and connecting hardware for visible wear or damage before climbing.

   d. Make sure that your belay partner is ready for you to climb.

2. What is the most important safety consideration when climbing at a gym that uses Super Shuts?

   a. Always clip into one Super Shut before lowering.

   b. Never put your fingers on the spring mechanism of the Super Shut.

   c. Never climb above the Super Shuts.

   d. Always tie into a Super Shut with a figure eight knot.

3. What types of floor anchors are used in a climbing gym?

   a. fixed

   b. mobile

   c. human

   d. all of the above

4. What is the best terrain for a beginner climber?

   a. vertical

   b. overhanging

   c. slab

   d. horizontal

5. What is the most common material used for the framing of a climbing wall?

   a. wood

   b. concrete

   c. steel

   d. fiberglass

6. What other services are commonly offered at climbing gyms?

   a. special events

   b. climbing instruction

   c. fitness classes

   d. all of the above

Chapter 4

1. As a beginner climber, you should _____when deciding on a location to go rock climbing.

   a. find a climb that will challenge you both physically and psychologically

   b. define your style, know your abilities, then confer with a trusted source about which location would best suit your style and abilities

   c. do research online about each possible climbing site within a one-day drive from your house

   d. trust your heart

2. The "10 essentials" are only important on multiple-day climbing trips.

   a. true

   b. false

3. Bringing equipment for every possible danger on a climb is always the safest thing to do.

   a. true

   b. false

4. Fear is an important aspect of personal climbing safety.

   a. true

   b. false

5. Confirmation bias is the psychological phenomenon that

   a. tells your brain when you have exceeded your abilities

   b. positively influences your current decisions based on prior assumptions

   c. negatively influences your current decisions based on prior assumptions

   d. causes dogs' mouths to water when they hear a bell

6. When climbing with a large group, it is a good idea to

   a. cordon off an area for your group for safety and liability purposes

   b. climb on other parties' ropes to disperse your impact

   c. climb during the week to avoid crowds

   d. disperse your impact by spreading out along the crag

Chapter 5

1. The _____ measures the amount that a rope stretches when weighted with a standard load.

   a. tension

   b. elongation

   c. elasticity

2. _____ connect the rope system to natural or artificial protection.

   a. Webbing and accessory cord

   b. Harnesses

   c. Quickdraws

3. What are three things that can be done to properly take care of climbing ropes?

   a. Check the rope regularly.

   b. Use the rope only for what it is designed to do.

   c. Make sure that the rope is always clean.

   d. Do not step on the rope.

   e. Keep the rope out of direct sunlight.

4. A cordelette, which is primarily used for equalization of anchor systems and for rescue techniques, is constructed from

   a. runners

   b. accessory cord

   c. quickdraws

5. You really want to get into rock climbing. You read up on it, and you spend time surfing the Internet trying to find good deals on equipment (your budget as a college student is very limited). You find a bunch of used gear for sale on the Internet. Someone is getting out of climbing and wants to sell all his used equipment.

You look at the pictures, and the equipment appears to be in pretty good condition. What should you do?

    a. Buy the gear—it's a great deal.

    b. Buy the gear and only use what looks like it has not been used very much.

    c. Don't buy the gear because you do not know the history of this equipment.

6. Oval, D, asymmetrical D, and pear refer to what type of hardware?

    a. figure eight

    b. carabiner

    c. Grigri

7. This active protection device can be purchased with either flexible or rigid stems.

    a. tri-cam

    b. spring-loaded tube chock

    c. spring-loaded camming device

8. This type of harness is most appropriate for children or adults with narrow waists, and it helps reduce the chance of flipping over backward.

    a. full body

    b. diaper

    c. leg loop and waist belt

9. Dry treatment for ropes provides all the following except

    a. increased abrasion resistance

    b. waterproofing

    c. decreased effects of ultraviolet rays

10. Which belay device is commonly used in rescues?

    a. ATC

    b. figure eight

    c. Grigri

Chapter 6

1. You are climbing with a large group and want to have the ability to change quickly between climbers. Which of the following is a good knot to use to attach a climber to the rope with carabiners, rather than retying every climber?

    a. bowline

    b. bowline on a bight

    c. figure eight follow-through

    d. overhand on a bight

2. Which of the following harness tie-in knots absolutely must be backed up because the knot alone is not considered safe to hang your life on (choose all that apply)?

    a. figure eight follow-through

    b. bowline

    c. bowline on a bight

3. What is a good rule for determining if the tail (the amount of rope coming out of the knot) is acceptable?
    a. The tail should be the length of your forearm.
    b. The tail should be 2 inches (5.1 cm) long.
    c. The tail should be the distance between your extended thumb and pinky.

4. Incorrect tail lengths cause which of the following (choose all that apply)?
    a. If the tail is too short, the knot may be unsafe because it could untie unexpectedly.
    b. Tails less than 4 inches (10.2 cm) make the knot more compact, therefore reducing the potential of the knot to distract the climber.
    c. Extra long tails increase the strength of the knot.
    d. Long tails become a hindrance because they can cause distractions and get in the way.

5. Which of the following friction hitches is usually considered strongest when pulled in only one direction?
    a. Prusik
    b. klemheist

6. If you need to tie a friction hitch and you only have a sewn runner, the smoothest operating option is:
    a. klemheist
    b. munter mule
    c. Prusik

7. If you need a friction hitch and all you have to tie it with is a Spectra or Dyneema runner, you need to be careful because
    a. Spectra is more slippery than nylon and won't grab as tightly to the main rope.
    b. Spectra has a lower melting point than nylon so it might burn through if it moves quickly over the main rope.
    c. Spectra is much stronger than nylon so there is nothing to worry about.

8. If you need to attach yourself to the anchor, which of the following provides the greatest ease of adjustment?
    a. figure eight on a bight
    b. overhand on a bight
    c. clove hitch

9. If you need a loop that is strong no matter what direction you pull it in, the best choice is the
    a. figure eight on a bight
    b. overhand on a bight
    c. butterfly

10. When you are joining two rappel ropes together, a flat figure eight bend is safer than a flat overhand.
    a. true
    b. false

Chapter 7

1. Before you attempt to lead belay, you should have a complete understanding of the _____ belay system.
   a. top
   b. slingshot
   c. mechanical blocking
   d. auto-locking

2. The _____ hitch is an essential tool that can be used for belaying, rappelling, and releasable systems.
   a. clove
   b. girth
   c. half
   d. Munter

3. Lead belaying is more challenging because if the climber falls, increased _____ can make arresting the fall more difficult.
   a. distance
   b. bolts
   c. forces
   d. stemming

4. Auto-locking devices are very easy to release if a climber cannot get to the top of the climb and must be lowered to the ground.
   a. true
   b. false

5. The belayer is responsible for _____ friction by ensuring good communication with the climber; the belayer is also responsible for _____ friction within the belay system in the event of a fall.
   a. resisting; creating
   b. maximizing; minimizing
   c. minimizing; maximizing
   d. sustaining; coordinating

6. Top belaying directly off the body (without a redirect) using a tube device, an auto-locking device, or a mechanical blocking device is highly recommended.
   a. true
   b. false

7. Bends in the rope between the belay device and carabiners create _____, which is essential to holding the falling climber.
   a. difficulty
   b. friction
   c. heat
   d. twists

8. Mechanical belay devices can be set up incorrectly, and this can cause catastrophic failure in the belay system.

    a. true

    b. false

Chapter 8

1. An anchor system is composed of three essential components. These components are

    a. trees, knots, and master points

    b. anchor points, a rigging system, and a master point

    c. an anchor point, a rigging system, and master points

    d. an anchor point, knots, and a master point

2. Natural anchor points can include all of the following except

    a. trees

    b. boulders

    c. shrubs

    d. rock features

3. A very large tree that is well rooted and healthy can be used as a single anchor point if the rig connecting the tree to the master point is redundant.

    a. true

    b. false

4. Which of the following angles at the master point will place the least stress on the anchor point in an anchor system?

    a. 120-degree angle

    b. 90-degree angle

    c. 80-degree angle

    d. 30-degree angle

5. ADDRESS is an acronym summarizing the essential principles of an effective anchor system. The acronym stands for

    a. angle, distance, direction, redundancy, equalization, shock load, strong

    b. angle, diverse, direction, redundancy, equalization, shock load, slick

    c. angle, distance, direction, redundancy, environmental, shock load, slick

    d. angle, diverse, direction, redundancy, equalization, shock load, strong

6. The master point is a critical point, so it should always

    a. be accessible to the climber

    b. include more than two carabiners

    c. be multidirectional

    d. be redundant

7. A passive piece of protection is well placed when it has all of the following characteristics except this one.
   a. It is placed in a reliable rock fracture or formation.
   b. It is placed appropriately for its direction of pull.
   c. It is placed parallel to the line of fall.
   d. It has a large surface of contact with the rock.
8. What types of rope or webbing can be used to rig a safe anchor system?
   a. 5.5-millimeter nylon cordelette
   b. 1/4-inch nylon webbing
   c. 7-millimeter nylon cordelette
   d. 4-millimeter polyethylene cord
9. What is the most significant difference between a slingshot anchor system and a multipitch belay anchor?
   a. The belay anchor is redundant.
   b. The belay anchor is multidirectional.
   c. The belay anchor has anchor points that can sustain an upward pull.
   d. The belay anchor has a master point that includes two carabiners.
10. To be safely used, a "sliding X" rig must have which of the following characteristics?
    a. It must have a 180-degree twist in one of its strands.
    b. It must be made using a 5.5-millimeter nylon cordelette.
    c. It must have strands of equal length.
    d. It must have a 180-degree twist in both of its strands.

Chapter 9

1. Describe three ways to check the quality of a hold. What steps can be taken to use the hold safely if no better option exists?
2. List several ways to maintain proper balance. What is one indicator of a climber being off balance?
3. Describe three different crack widths and the techniques used for climbing each.
4. Differentiate between smearing and edging.
5. Describe proper body orientation when falling.
6. What does the phrase "Climb like a hawk" refer to and why is it important?

Chapter 10

1. Scenario: You and your partner are climbing a four-pitch trad route at Tahquitz in southern California during spring break. At the top of the third pitch, your friend slips and hurts his wrist. He can't climb. It is 3:00 p.m. You have two 60-meter ropes. Which of the following is the best solution, and how would you set it up?

   a. Lead the last pitch and set up a haul system for your partner. Then you can walk off the top on a trail.

   b. Lower your partner, and then rappel down to him. Continue until you reach the ground.

   c. Help your partner get on rappel with a backup. Take turns rappelling back to the ground.

   d. Create an anchor, secure your partner to it, and rappel down alone to go for help.

2. When you are planning your climb, you should take all of the following into consideration except

   a. the equipment needed to climb the route

   b. the weather conditions and forecast for that day

   c. the ability of all climbers in your party

   d. the descent route from the climb

   e. the climb's proximity to your favorite restaurant

3. Which bend would you use to join two ropes for a long rappel down a low-angle climb with lots of rock features? Why would you choose this bend?

4. You are the first in your party to rappel to the next station. When you arrive, you find an overhanging station with two bolts; the bolts are connected by a sling. You see no rappel ring on the sling. How do you proceed?

Chapter 11

1. Learning scenario: Analysis of recent climbing accidents indicates that it is not merely the dangerous environment or the hazardous activity that causes injuries. Behind the weather or the rock fall, certain aspects of the climbers' attitude were often what led to suffering in the backcountry. Review the following list, and then ask yourself these questions (or discuss them with another outdoor enthusiast): "Have I witnessed or heard of accidents that may have been caused by any of these human attitudes?" "Am I honest enough to acknowledge that I have at times held some of these attitudes?" "What am I going to do about it?"

   ○ An unwillingness to change plans—even in the face of overwhelming evidence that one should do so—and its accompanying behavior; an unfounded need to keep to a predetermined schedule

   ○ A desire to impress; overweening arrogance or ego and its accompanying competitiveness

   ○ A lack of awareness of or failure to acknowledge some critical change in conditions (e.g., group strength, weather)—or its near cousin, a reliance on wishful thinking instead of dispassionate acceptance of objective data

   ○ A blind trust in personal invincibility and the benevolence of the universe; a belief that nature cares about me

2. When falling during a lead climb, you should not

   a. face the rock

   b. grab the rope

   c. keep your hands in front of you

   d. none of the above

3. When belaying a lead climber, you should
    a. stand far away from the route in order to avoid falling rocks
    b. keep the rope taut between you and the climber
    c. always keep at least one hand on the brake strand
    d. keep at least three arm's lengths of slack in the rope

4. Traditional lead climbing tends to emphasize _____, while sport leading provides _____.
    a. climbing for middle-aged and older individuals; a climbing experience for the younger generation
    b. alpine-style mountaineering; Yosemite-style techniques
    c. ascending while minimizing permanent alteration of the environment; solid lead anchors from which to practice difficult free-climbing moves
    d. anchoring to preset bolts and hangers; the opportunity to place and then retrieve one's own removable protection

5. In multi-pitch climbing and leading, the concept of "overlapping your safety systems" would suggest
    a. not unclipping from an anchor until you are on a live human belay
    b. using a Prusik or autoblock backup when rappelling
    c. not saying "off belay" until you are clipped to another solid anchor
    d. all of the above

6. When constructing a traditional protection system, which of the following is NOT true of extending nut placements with slings?
    a. It creates unnecessary rope drag.
    b. It increases the shock absorption capability of the overall protection system.
    c. It reduces rope drag on the lead climber and during the subsequent rope pull-up.

7. When a climber gets "pumped" on a sport route, he should
    a. clip the next bolt on the route as soon as possible
    b. breathe slowly and hang straight on the arms
    c. skip the next bolt and climb to the anchors
    d. tell your belayer to "take"

8. "Hangdogging" on a route is an effective way for a novice climber to increase his ability.
    a. true
    b. false

9. Using quick draws on a sport route
    a. reduces rope drag
    b. reduces the length of a lead fall
    c. is ill-advised on a steep route
    d. none of the above

10. When arriving at the top of a sport climb the leader should first
    a. tell the belayer to take
    b. pull up a length of rope from below and tie a figure eight
    c. clip into the anchors
    d. untie and thread the rope through the anchors

Answers

Chapter 1: 1. answers will vary; 2. crash pad; 3. traditional and sport. In trad, the climber places artificial anchoring devices. In sport, the climber clips into already placed hangers; 4. answers will vary; 5. answers will vary; 6. Web sites, guidebooks, local organizations, and climbing periodicals; 7. answers will vary; 8. incorrectly practicing safety procedures could be serious or fatal

Chapter 2: 1. false; 2. true; 3. true; 4. true; 5. true; 6. true; 7. false; 8. d; 9. d; 10. a

Chapter 3: 1. a; 2. c; 3. d; 4. c; 5. c; 6. d

Chapter 4: 1. b; 2. false; 3. false; 4. true; 5. c; 6. c and d

Chapter 5: 1. b; 2. a; 3. all are correct; 4. b; 5. c; 6. b; 7. c; 8. a; 9. b; 10. b

Chapter 6: 1. b (The figure eight on a bight may also be used, but it is much more difficult to untie after being repeatedly weighted.); 2. b and c; 3. c; 4. a and d; 5. b; 6. a; 7. a and b; 8. c; 9. c; 10. false (The flat figure eight has been shown to be very dangerous.)

Chapter 7: 1. b; 2. d; 3. c; 4. false; 5. c; 6. false; 7. b; 8. true

Chapter 8: 1. b; 2. c; 3. true; 4. d; 5. a; 6. d; 7. c; 8. c; 9. c; 10. a

Chapter 9:

1. Look, listen, and feel. Pull down not out, and minimize force on the hold.
2. Keep feet underneath your body mass.

   Counter balance appropriately using techniques such as flagging or body tension.

   Indicators of being off balance: falling, tiring quickly, and "barn door effect."
3. 1 inch—finger locks and jams

   2.5 inch—hand crack. Hand jams and fist jams

   4 inches plus—off width. Chicken wing, hand/fist stack.
4. Smearing utilizes overall friction of the shoe on the rock, whereas edging involves balancing on a protruding edge on the rock.
5. "Like a cat"—hands out, legs out, legs and arms slightly bent to absorb impact.
6. Look where you are going. Constantly reassess route and plan ahead. This will keep you from going off route and adjust more easily to upcoming moves.

Chapter 10:

1. The second option (b) is the best answer, assuming the route can be rappelled without having to traverse. If that is not the case, then the first option (a) is the best answer. The third option (c) could work if your partner is able to control a

rappel with one hand (and is able to clip in to the next anchor while hanging from the backup); however, this option is more risky. The fourth option (d) is probably the worst choice unless the party is unable to self-rescue.

2. e

3. The flat overhand is a good choice because it rides the best over uneven rock surfaces when pulling the ropes down.

4. First, you will need to engage your backup or tie off your rappel so you may go hands free. Now you are free to inspect the anchor more closely. Because the station has no rappel ring, you may assume that the last party pulled their ropes through the webbing directly during retrieval. This may have damaged the webbing. If you have webbing with you, you should cut the existing webbing off and replace it with yours in such a way that the load is shared equally between the two bolts (pre-equalized or self-equalizing system). You should add a rappel ring if you have one. If you don't have webbing or a rappel ring, be sure to inspect the existing webbing thoroughly before trusting it. If you see any evidence of damage, you need to back up the system. You may have to use a sewn runner or cordelette from your rack. Regardless of whether you add your own webbing, or leave the existing webbing, be sure the two anchors are equalized so they each take half the load.

Chapter 11:

1. Answers will vary; 2. b; 3. c; 4. c; 5. d; 6. a; 7. b; 8. false; 9. a; 10. c

Photo Credits

Age Fotostock
© Greg Epperson / age fotostock — Page 9, 10, 89, 177
© Adventurephoto / age fotostock — Page 15
Himsl Leo / Prisma / age footstock — Page 45
Greg Epperson / Index Stock / age fotostock — Page 257

Aurora Photos
Corey Rich / Aurora Photos — Page 48
Greg Epperson/Aurora Photos — Page 81
Bernardo Gimenez / Aurora Photos — Page 125
Corey Rich / Aurora Photos — Page 159
© Paul Souders — Page 229
Kennan Harvey / Aurora Photos — Page 272

© Keith A. Barker — Page 98, 105 (top middle and bottom right), 106 (all photos), 108 (all photos), 109 (bottom right), 110 (both photos), 111 (both photos)

© Christian Bisson — Page 189 (both photos), 190 (both photos), 191 (top right)

Brand X Pictures
Bill Crump / Brand X Pictures — Page 32 (bottom)

© Scott Drum — Page 28

© Mat Erpelding — Page 161, 162 (all photos), 166 (all photos), 167 (both photos), 169 (both photos), 170 (both photos), 171 (all photos), 172 (both photos)

Getty Images
ERIK ISAKSON / Tetra Images / Getty Images — Page 3
Mike Powell / Getty Images — Page 6
Bernhard Limberger / Getty Images — Page 8
Zigy Kaluzny / Getty Images — Page 21
Glowimages / Getty Images — Page 23
Matthias Tunger/Photonica/Getty Images — Page 61

Geoff Harrison

Page 49 (right),
50, 51 (both photos),
52 (all photos),
53, 56, 57 (bottom right), 58

© Jennifer Hazelrigs

Page 26 (both photos),
35, 55, 102, 218 (all photos)

© Jennifer Hopper

Page 231 (top right and bottom
photos), 235, 236 (all photos),
237, 238, 239, 240 (both photos),
241 (both photos), 242, 243 (top right),
246 (both photos), 247, 248 (all photos),
249, 250, 253, 254, 259

© Human Kinetics

Page 38

Icon SMI
STL / Icon SMI
Christian Tatin / DPPI / Icon SMI

Page 267
Page 285

© International Wilderness

Page 208 (all photos), 209 (all photos),
210 (both photos), 211 (all photos),
212, 213 (both photos), 214 (both
photos), 215 (all photos), 216 (both
photos), 217 (top right), 219 (all
photos), 220 (both photos),
221 (both photos), 222 (both photos),
223 (all photos), 224, 225,
226 (both photos), 227

Leave No Trace

Page 17, 19

© NICROS, Inc.

Page 47, 49 (left),
54, 57 (top left and right)

© Frank Niles

Page 278, 279 (all photos),
280 (all photos), 281 (both photos)

© David Sperry

Page 137 (top photo), 141 (both
photos), 143 (middle and bottom
photos), 144 (top photo)

U.S. Fish and Wildlife Service
Steve Hillebrand / U.S. Fish and Wildlife Service

Page 18

References

Chapter 1

Ament, P. (2002). *A history of free climbing in America: Wizards of rock.* Berkeley, CA: Wilderness Press.

Hankinson, A. (1972). *The first tigers: An early history of rock climbing in the Lake District.* London: Dent & Sons.

Outdoor Industry Association. (2005). Via Ferrata European Rock Climbing System is Introduced in North America. www.outdoorindustry.org/media.outdoor.php?news_id=1180&sort_year=2005.

Roberts, D. (1997). *In search of the old ones: Exploring the Anasazi world of the Southwest.* New York: Simon & Schuster.

Thorington, J.M. (1964). Oliver Perry-Smith: Profile of a mountaineer. *Journal of the American Alpine Club.* www.128.pair.com/r3d4k7/HistoricalClimbingImages1.html.

Chapter 2

American College of Sports Medicine (ACSM). (2006). ACSM's guidelines for exercise testing and prescription. Baltimore: Lipponcott Williams & Wilkins.

American College of Sports Medicine, American Dietetic Association, and Dieticians of Canada Joint Position Stand. 2000. Nutrition and athletic performance. *Medicine and Science in Sports and Exercise*, 32 (12), 2130-2145.

American College of Sports Medicine Position Stand. (1998). The recommended quantity and quality of exercise for developing and maintaining cardiorespiratory and muscular fitness, and flexibility in healthy adults. *Medicine and Science in Sports and Exercise*, 30 (6), 975-991.

Baechle, T.R., and Earle, R.W. (eds). (2000). *Essentials of strength training and conditioning.* 2nd ed. Champaign, IL: Human Kinetics.

Bompa, T. (1999). *Periodization: Theory and methodology of training.* Champaign, IL: Human Kinetics.

Bonci, L. (2007, March). Sports nutrition: Nutrition for optimal performance. Special Selections: Training Room. http://espn.go.com/trainingroom/s/2000/0324/444124.html.

Giles, L.V., Rhodes, E.C., and Taunton, J.E. (2006). The physiology of rock climbing. *Sports Medicine*, 36, 529-545.

Grant, S., Hasler, T., Davies, C., Aitchison, T.C., Wilson, J., and Whittaker, A. (2001). A comparison of the anthropometric, strength, endurance, and flexibility characteristics of female elite and recreational climbers and non-climbers. *Journal of Sports Sciences,* 19, 499-505.

Grant, S., Hynes, A., Whittaker, A., and Aitchison, T. (1996). Anthropometric, strength, endurance, and flexibility characteristics of elite and recreational climbers. *Journal of Sport Sciences,* 14, 301-309.

Heyward, V.H. (2002). *Advanced fitness assessment and exercise prescription.* 4th ed. Champaign, IL: Human Kinetics.

Jeukendrup, A., and Gleeson, M. (2004). *Sport nutrition: An introduction to energy production and performance.* Champaign, IL: Human Kinetics.

Jones, P., and Hill, E. (2007). Resistance training for distance running: A brief update. *Strength and Conditioning Journal,* 29, 28-35.

Kraemer, W.J., et al. (2002). American College of Sports Medicine position stand. Progression models in resistance training for healthy adults. *Medicine and Science in Sports and Exercise,* 34 (2), 364-380.

McArdle, W.D., Katch, F.I., and Katch, V.L. (1999). *Sports and exercise nutrition.* Baltimore: Lippincott Williams & Wilkins.

Mermier, C.M., Janot, J.M., Parker, D.L., and Swan, J.G. (2000). Physiological and anthropometric determinants of sport climbing performance. *British Journal of Sports Medicine,* 34, 359-366.

Mermier, C.M., Robergs, R.A., McMinn, S.M., Heyward, V.H. (1997). Energy expenditure and physiological responses during indoor rock climbing. *British Journal of Sports Medicine,* 31, 224-228.

Sharkey, B.J., and Gaskill, S.E. (2006). *Sport physiology for coaches.* Champaign, IL: Human Kinetics.

Sheel, A. W. (2004). Physiology of sport rock climbing. *British Journal of Sports Medicine,* 38, 355-359.

Watts, P.B. (2004). Physiology of rock climbing. *European Journal of Applied Physiology,* 91, 361-372.

Watts, P.B., and Drobish, K.M. (1998). Physiological responses to simulated rock climbing at different angles. *Medicine and Science in Sports and Exercise,* 30, 1118-1122.

Wildman, R., and Miller, B. (2004). *Sport and fitness nutrition.* Belmont, CA: Thompson and Wadsworth.

Chapter 4

Atkins, D. (2003). The role of perception and risk in avalanche accidents. *Wilder News: Newsletter of Wilderness Medical Associates,* 7(1).

Cox, S., & Fulsaas, K. (Eds.). (2003). *Mountaineering: The freedom of the hills* (7th ed.). Seattle, WA: Mountaineers Books.

Ford, P., & Blanchard, J. (1993). *Leadership and administration of outdoor pursuits.* State College, PA: Venture Publishing.

Terray, L. (1963). Conquistadors of the useless : from the Alps to Annapurna. Seattle, WA: Mountaineers Books.

Chapter 5

Cox, S., & Fulsaas, K. (Eds.). (2003). *Mountaineering: The freedom of the hills* (7th ed.). Seattle, WA: Mountaineers Books.

Drury, J., & Bonney, B. (1992). *The backcountry classroom.* Guildford, CT: Globe Pequot.

Fyffe, A., & Peter, I. (1990). *The handbook of climbing.* London, England: Penguin Books.

Long, J. (1993). *Climbing anchors.* Helena, MT: Falcon Publishing.

Long, J. (2004). *How to rock climb* (4th ed.). Helena, MT: Falcon Publishing.

Loughman, M. (1981). *Learning to rock climb.* San Francisco, CA: Sierra Club.

Powers, P. (1993). *NOLS wilderness mountaineering.* Mechanicsburg, PA: Stackpole Books.

Chapter 7

Long, J. (1989). *How to rock climb.* Evergreen, CO: Chockstone Press.

Luebben, C. (2004). *Rock climbing: Mastering basic skills.* Seattle, WA: The Mountaineers Books.

Chapter 8

Cox, S.M., & Fulsaas, K. (2003). *Mountaineering: The freedom of the hills.* Seattle, WA: Mountaineers Books.

Lewis, S.P. (1998). *Top roping.* Helena, MT: Chockstone Press.

Long, J. (1993). *Climbing anchors.* Guilford, CT: Falcon.

Long, J., & Gaines, B. (1996). *More climbing anchors.* Guilford, CT: Falcon.

Luebben, C. (2004). *Rock climbing: Mastering the basic skills.* Seattle, WA: Mountaineers Books.

Luebben, C. (2007). *Rock climbing anchors: A comprehensive guide.* Seattle, WA: Mountaineers Books.

Powers, P. (2000). *NOLS wilderness mountaineering.* Mechanicsburg, PA: Stackpole Books.

Powers, P., & Cheek, M. (2000). *NOLS climbing instructor notebook.* Lander, WY. NOLS.

Chapter 10

Cox, S., & Fulsaas, K. (Eds.). (2003). *Mountaineering: The freedom of the hills* (7th ed.). Seattle, WA: Mountaineers Books.

Luebben, C. (2000). *How to rappel.* Guildford, CT: Globe Pequot/Falcon.

Chapter 11

Achey, J. (1999, June 15). Path of the elders. *Climbing Magazine, 186,* 108-119.

Burnett, J. (2005). *Hey ranger: True tales of humor and misadventure from America's national parks.* Lanham, MD: Taylor Trade Publishing.

Hepp, T. (1995). *Wolfgang Gullich.* Birmingham, AL: Menasha Ridge Press.

Long, J., & Luebben, C. (1997). *Advanced rock climbing*. Helena, MT: Chockstone.

Wald, Beth. (1987). Wolfgang Gullich Interview. *Climbing.* June 1987, 64-70.

Ward, W. (1969). *For this hour*. Anderson, SC: Droke House.

Williamson, J. (Ed.). (1995). *Accidents in North American mountaineering*. Golden, CO: American Alpine Club.

Williamson, J. (Ed.). (2000). *Accidents in North American mountaineering*. Golden, CO: American Alpine Club.

Williamson, J. (Ed.). (2003). *Accidents in North American mountaineering*. Golden, CO: American Alpine Club.

About the Editors

Timothy W. Kidd, PhD, associate professor in outdoor leadership ministries at John Brown University, coauthored chapter 1. Tim also coauthored a chapter in *Hiking and Backpacking,* another book in the Outdoor Adventure series. He received his master of science degree in recreation administration with a concentration in outdoor pursuits administration from George Williams College of Aurora University. He received his doctorate degree in educational studies from Trinity International University. He has led rock climbing, caving, and backpacking experiences for his students throughout the southeastern United States, including Arkansas, Kentucky, North Carolina, Tennessee, Virginia, and West Virginia. He is a WEA National Standard Program instructor and a Leave No Trace master educator, completed the AMGA top-rope site management course, and serves on the Christian Adventure Association board as vice president. Tim and his wife, Sandy, enjoy spending time with their three kids and two dogs in the outdoors.

Jennifer Hazelrigs, MEd, is an assistant director in the intramural/recreational sports department at the University of Arkansas, where she oversees the outdoor education program. She manages two climbing facilities and administers national and international trips, instructional clinics, an equipment rental program, student staff development, and an outdoor outreach program that serves the northwest Arkansas area. Jennifer supplements the academic curriculum of the health science, kinesiology, recreation, and dance department by guest lecturing, leading trips, and facilitating workshops. She is an LNT master educator and serves as the state advocate for Arkansas. Prior recreation management experiences include ropes course facilitation, inner-city youth adventure programs, parks and recreation, outdoor adventure camps, and guiding. Jennifer received her master of education degree in recreation management from the University of Arkansas.

About the Contributors

Christian Bisson, EdD, is an associate professor of adventure education. He designed, tested, and published a new nomenclature and a new scoring scheme for teaching anchor building systems. He also wrote a chapter based on his doctoral dissertation about sequencing in *Adventure Programming* by Miles and Priest. Bisson holds a top rope instructor certification from the American Mountain Guide Association (AMGA) and has taught top-rope rock climbing at the National Outdoor Leadership School since 1990. He is a member of the AMGA. Bisson has received many awards, including the 1999-2000 Outstanding Teaching Award, the 1999-2002 William B. Mark Memorial Professorships, and the 1998 Momentum Award presented by Northland College. He received his EdD in physical education (pedagogy) from the University of Northern Colorado.

Scott Drum, PhD, is an assistant professor of exercise and sport science at Western State College of Colorado. He is also the director of the Western State College of Colorado High Altitude Performance Lab (HAPLab). He works with students on a variety of research topics, including strength and endurance of rock climbers. He was a trip leader in climbing Denali in Alaska with a group of recreation students. He also belongs to the American College of Sports Medicine and the National Strength and Conditioning Association. Drum received his PhD in exercise physiology from the University of Northern Colorado.

Craig Elder, PhD, is an associate professor at Southeast Missouri State University and the director of the athletic training education program. He is certified as a BOC athletic trainer, strength and conditioning specialist, and wilderness first responder. He leads many outdoor adventure trips and has been a facilitator for outdoor adventure programs since 2002. He also facilitated rock climbing for summer camp instructors at Hell's Gate National Park in Kenya and assisted in leading a group of over 100 employees from Chick-fil-A on a summit of Pikes Peak. Elder has summitted Mount Kenya, Mount Elbert, Mount Katahdin, Mount Washington, and Pikes Peak. He did a technical summit of the Shark's Tooth in Rocky Mountain National Park.

Mat Erpelding, MA, is an experienced outdoor educator and professional guide. He earned his MA in adult education from the University of Idaho and has worked internationally as a program consultant, educator, and trainer. He is working toward his IFMGA certification. Mat is a member of the Association of Outdoor Recreation and Education and has served as president of the board of directors. He teaches for the Wilderness Medicine Training Center, American Alpine Institute, and Boise State University. He co-owns a leadership consulting company called Experiential Adventures LLC, which specializes in corporate, educational, and outdoor leadership development programs. Mat lives in Boise, Idaho, where he enjoys immediate access to the best trails in the country.

Geoff Harrison, MS, is an outdoor program director at Boise State University. He designed, financed, built, and manages a 7,200-square-foot collegiate climbing gym. He has worked in climbing and mountaineering environments in the United States and abroad. He is the co-owner of Experiential Adventures LLC, a private consulting business that provides outdoor program design and development, risk assessment and management, and staff training. Harrison has also been a mountaineering guide and an outdoor climbing instructor. He is a member of the Association of Outdoor Recreation and Education and has served as national office director and as a member of the board of directors. Harrison received his MS in sport and recreational management from the University of Idaho.

Nathan Helweg, PhD, is the owner and president of Altus Adventures, Inc. He has worked with youth in an institutional rock-climbing environment since 2001. He is researching how outdoor adventure affects leadership. Helweg belongs to the Christian Adventure Association and the Wilderness Education Association. He received his PhD in leadership studies from Gonzaga University.

Tom Holman, PhD, is an assistant professor of recreation at Southeast Missouri State University in Cape Girardeau. Tom has been teaching and leading outdoor adventure since 1979 and has 5 years teaching experience in the public classroom. He has an MA in experiential education from Minnesota State University at Mankato and a PhD in outdoor education and recreation from the University of Minnesota. He lives in Cape Girardeau, Missouri, with his wife and two kids and teaches outdoor recreation classes and leads students on outdoor adventure courses.

Jennifer Hopper, MS, is a manager of outdoor excursions at the University of California at Riverside. She became certified as an AMGA top-rope site manager in 2003. She was involved in the creation of three rock-climbing safety videos that are sold through Guide Tricks for Climbers. She has climbed in California, Nevada, Utah, Washington, Arizona, Alaska, Africa, and Bolivia. Hopper served on the board of directors of the California Mountaineering Club. She also served as staff advisor to the climbing club at the University of California at Riverside and is a member of the San Bernardino County Technical Rescue Team. She wrote the university's climbing leader manual. She is a wilderness first responder and a part-time guide for Sierra Mountaineering International. Hopper was invited to instruct a Leave No Trace master educator course in 2006. She has taught many other classes, including guided climbs of Mountaineer's Route on Whitney, introduction to kayaking, introduction to snowboarding, introduction to backpacking, and introduction to canyoneering.

International Wilderness Leadership School (IWLS) is one of the premiere leadership and guide training programs in the country. Fully accredited by the Association of Experiential Education, IWLS leads the industry in quality of technical instruction, safety standards, and outdoor leadership training. IWLS staff and instructors are experts in the field of professional outdoor education. The school hosts 12- and 24-day rock-climbing guide training courses in Alaska, Washington, Utah, and Mexico. Learn more about the International Wilderness Leadership School at www.iwls.com, or call 800-985-IWLS (4957). IWLS contributing authors include Brian Gillespie, Ted Roxbury, and Eli Fierer.

Brian is the assistant program coordinator at Ohio University. He brings over 4 years of experience working with IWLS as a rock and high-altitude mountain instructor around the world to his new position in Ohio. Ted, an experienced rock climber, moonlights as a professional photographer and has worked since 2005 for the International Wilderness Leadership School in Alaska, Utah, Mexico, and South America. Eli, the director of operations for IWLS, has worked as a guide and instructor since 2001.

Kelli K. McMahan, MS, is an assistant director of campus recreation and outdoor adventure. She coordinated the outdoor adventure program at Baylor University for seven years; before that, she developed an outdoor adventure program for city parks and recreation. She taught climbing and rappelling for many years for the Christian Adventure Association's Outdoor Leadership Lab. She is also a top-rope site manager with the AMGA. McMahan belongs to the American Mountain Guide Association, the Association for Outdoor Recreation and Education, and the Christian Adventure Association. She received her master of science degree at Oklahoma State University.

Frank Niles, PhD, associate professor of political science at John Brown University, coauthored chapter 11. He is an accomplished rock climber who, for over 25 years, has ascended difficult routes in the United States and abroad. He has been at the forefront of the new wave of route development in the Ozark Mountains of Arkansas, having helped pioneer some of the area's most difficult routes and boulder problems and logging many first ascents. He has appeared in numerous climbing-related media, including *Climbing* magazine and the *Climb On* video series, and speaks on peak performance to college and corporate audiences, using climbing as a metaphor. Despite arthritic fingers and a recent shoulder surgery, he somehow manages to climb 8a+, just enough to keep up with the youngsters. Niles received his doctorate in political science from the University of Houston.

R. Jared Skaggs is a youth minister using experiential education methods in Stillwater, Oklahoma. He has led participants into the outdoors and managed the climbing programs at Oklahoma State University and Texas Tech University. Jared is finishing his master's degree in outdoor education from Oklahoma State University. He has been fortunate enough to continue leading private adventure trips throughout lower North America.

David Sperry, MS, is an assistant professor of outdoor education. He is certified as a top-rope manager through the American Mountain Guide Association (AMGA). He has worked with Outward Bound and various summer camps. He is a frequent presenter on rock rescue at professional conferences. Sperry developed three new rock-climbing classes at Montreat College in Montreat, North Carolina. He is a member of the AMGA and Wilderness Education Association. He is also an instructor trainer in whitewater canoeing and swiftwater rescue with the American Canoe Association. He is a certified wilderness first responder. Sperry received his master of science degree in education from Alfred University.

Lester R. Zook, EdD, a professor in the outdoor ministries and adventure leadership program at Eastern Mennonite University in Harrisonburg, Virginia, coauthored chapter 11. In addition, he owns WILD GUYde Adventures, providing climbing, caving, and paddling adventures in the Shenandoah Valley, along Virginia's Blue Ridge, and in the Allegheny Front of West Virginia. His master's degree is from Temple University, and his doctorate in higher education administration is from the University of Virginia. His recent research and presentation efforts have involved exploring human attitudes that lead to suffering in the backcountry. He is a certified member of the American Mountain Guides Association, the National Speleological Society, and the Christian Adventure Association. He is also the happy husband of one (Robin) and father of four.

Need more adventure?

Want to go canoeing, kayaking, hiking, rock climbing, or Nordic walking? Start today with the Outdoor Adventures series. This practical series provides you with the essential information to get ready and go. The Outdoor Adventures series is designed to prepare you with instruction in the basic techniques and skills so you can be on your way to an adventure in no time.

Hiking and Backpacking
by the Wilderness Education Association

Canoeing
by the American Canoe Association

Kayaking
by the American Canoe Association

Rock Climbing
by the Wilderness Education Association

Nordic Walking
by Malin Svensson

To learn more about the books in this series, visit the Outdoor Adventures series Web site at **www.HumanKinetics.com/OutdoorAdventures**.

For a complete description or to order
Call **1-800-747-4457**
In Canada, call **1-800-465-7301**
In Europe, call **44 (0) 113-255-5665**
In Australia, call **08-8372-0999**
In New Zealand, call **09-448-1207**

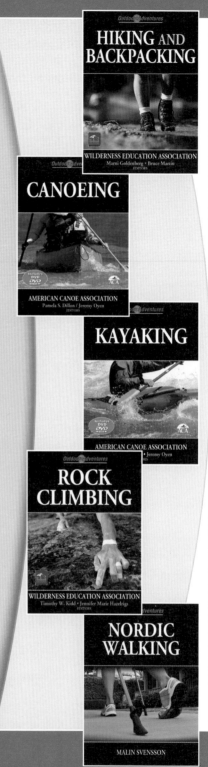

 HUMAN KINETICS
The Information Leader in Physical Activity